Never
Too
Old

The Aged in
Community Life

Esther E. Twente

FOREWORD by Robert Morris

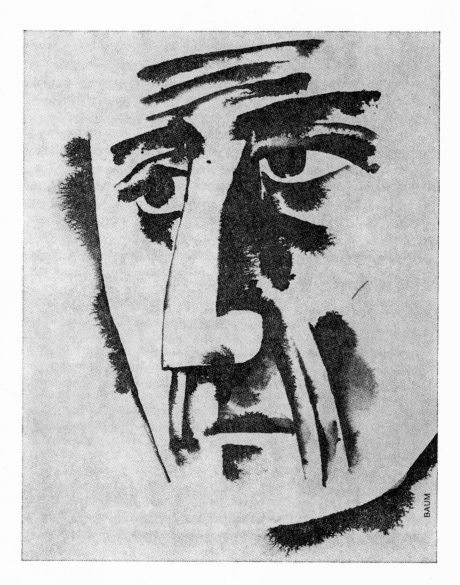

NEVER
TOO
OLD

Jossey-Bass Inc., Publishers
615 Montgomery Street · San Francisco · 1970

NEVER TOO OLD
The Aged in Community Life
Esther E. Twente

Jossey-Bass, Inc., Publishers
615 Montgomery Street
San Francisco, California 94111

Library of Congress Catalog Card Number 74-128697

International Standard Book Number ISBN 0-87589-076-8

Manufactured in the United States of America
    Composed and printed by York Composition Company, Inc.
    Bound by Chas. H. Bohn & Co., Inc.

JACKET DESIGN BY WILLI BAUM, SAN FRANCISCO

FIRST EDITION

Code 7032

The Jossey-Bass
Behavioral Science Series

General Editors

WILLIAM E. HENRY
University of Chicago

NEVITT SANFORD
Wright Institute, Berkeley

Special Adviser in Social Welfare

MARTIN B. LOEB
University of Wisconsin

Foreword

Western, industrial urban society has created a distinctive environment in which men live, but it has not resolved century old contradictions and conflicts between the individual, as an achieving and self-analyzing person, and other persons who set many of the boundaries for the human experience. The elderly are a special case in the more general search for identity, for satisfying relationships with others, and for self-realization. Welfare institutions, of which social work is one, have emerged because men have sought formal ways to help each other in this search as society became complex, impersonal, and unpredictable. Unfortunately, the tendency of such institutions has been toward specialization; the effort to see man whole, in relation to his society, has been frustrated by the specialized views of physician, psychologist, behavioral scientist, economist, and social worker.

Esther Twente brings a lifetime of experience and thought to these twin issues: the realization of individual potential and the replacement of narrow specialization in human service institutions by a more general capability. What makes *Never Too Old* especially valuable is the author's ability to communicate the sense, feel, touch, and emotion of living human beings, each with his own history and make-up. They are not helpless objects of charity or of pity; they have dignity, a contribution which they have made and can still make, and a meaning in their lives which overcomes the leveling sameness which the modern world attributes to old people. These elders have value and significance in their own right, not as objects of study.

Wide experience is buttressed in *Never Too Old* by a synthesis of systematic studies and empirical research, all of which attest to the persistent vigor of the living impulse. Recent study has begun to explain human growth and development beyond the childhood stage through the entire life span. It may be an accident of industrial history that human development in the terminal years has begun to receive more attention than has development in the middle years. Only in this century have the elderly, as a group, been forced to confront a last change in role and status for which society has had no precedent. The urban, industrial world neither requires the labor of older persons nor relies upon their store of wisdom, given the rapid technological changes of the twentieth century. However, it has become impossible to ignore the developmental impulses of some 10 to 12 per cent of the population who may survive fifteen or twenty years beyond the age of sixty. Miss Twente presents with eloquence the capacity of the elderly to see themselves and their world clearly; their capacity to behave creatively; their interest in their world as well as in themselves. Their vigor is affected by the views which others hold about aged persons, views which are complex and varied. Studying the ways in which these views—of self and others—interact is an adventure in discovery, both moving and creative.

But *Never Too Old* is much more than a human interest recital. The chain is seldom forged between the individual, in all his unique richness, and the institutions he has created to make a society possible and bearable. This gap is bridged here by illuminating the interaction among older persons, between the young and the old, and among the aged, their youthful counterparts, and the surrounding community, which they both help create and must sustain. This gap is troublesome in urban areas as well as in rural communities. In one, there are too few specialists; in the other, there may be more. And, whether those in the helping professions are over- or under-trained, they are troubled about using their talents inappropriately to help the individual or the community confronting them. What knowledge and skill are required to cope with social needs which involve equally the individual, the family, the informal association of friends, and the community? Can a professional be expert in all directions; and if he is not so expert, must he ignore conditions, lacking enough specialized resources?

A solution to this dilemma is found in information which can be used by professional and by informed amateur, by specialist and by generalist. In social work this solution has involved identifying which of the casework, group work, or community skills (each specialized in its own way) can be applied by a worker who is not a specialist in all three. What elements can a skilled worker functioning in a thinly populated area, with limited resources, bring to bear to effectively help an individual, group, or community to cope with the problems of aging? This resynthesizing effort is a significant contribution to the attempt to define a general social work practice sufficient in its richness and competence to replace the specialized efforts of the past twenty years. This turnabout has been characterized by a philosophical commitment to a holistic approach to human existence, but the technical capacity to carry out this commitment has not yet been much developed. This wedding of technical information to a philosophical viewpoint characterizes the present effort. Although presented around the problems and the needs of older persons in rural areas or in thinly populated areas, the analysis here is not limited, parochial, or superficial. If it is not always necessary to have all work specialized in rural areas, then perhaps we can also create a new relationship between the specialist and the generalist in urban areas.

This development *within* a human service profession comes at a time when the relationship between profession and citizen-consumer is also undergoing change. The recent movements in community mental health, community health, community control of education and welfare services, and the use of indigenous workers with limited training as health and mental health aides, all point to a reordering of professional-clientele relationships. If the present forces tend to alter the balance of professional influence in community affairs, wisdom, experience, and also logic point to the practical ways a new relationship can be established among the citizen, the consumer, the expert, and the agency.

Much of this new relationship comes from a mutual recognition of the creative potential derived from each person's experience. The professional helper not only cures or treats or takes care of another but also succeeds most when he recognizes that creative expression continues and grows and changes throughout a lifetime. This resource within the individual, amplified among the usually retired elderly, is as valuable a social and community resource as the public budget or the professional manpower pool. The strength of this work lies in the wedding of this humanist viewpoint to the practical requirements which individuals have in a complex world.

Brandeis University   Robert Morris
September 1970   *Levinson Gerontological Policy Institute*
        The Florence Heller School for
        Advanced Study in Social Welfare

Preface

The ideas and philosophies reflected in *Never Too Old* have developed over many years of practice and teaching. These ideas have proved professionally and personally useful and for that reason they are being shared. Many persons have contributed to them: authors, teachers, colleagues, friends, students, and others. To list their names is impossible. Not only would such a list be long, but also it is difficult to trace how one's ideas come into being. In looking back, I think that the stimulation derived from student discussion in class contributed most. The many in-service training sessions through the years with local social work personnel also added much. In my reminiscences about these discussions, one student and one local social worker after another stand out clearly. Many should be given personal credit. Directly related to the writing and content of this book is the help of three students who deserve special recognition: Shirley Patterson, Bradford Sheafor, and Mary L. Wylie. Thanks to them and to all the others.

The experience gained in two research projects, in Marion County and Holton, Kansas, is reflected directly throughout *Never Too Old*, but my other professional activities have contributed to the book, such as almost twenty years of social work practice, most of it in small communities, thirty years of teaching sociology and social work in universities, and a nine-month teaching and community-development assignment while a Fulbright lecturer at the University of Adelaide, Australia.

The vignettes and illustrations have many sources and are by no means taken only from professional experience. The characters have been disguised to assure anonymity. They should not be attributed to any one community unless specifically indicated. Unless another author's name is attached, the vignettes are mine.

Throughout the preparation of the manuscript a number of persons read parts of it; others read the volume in its entirety. All made valuable suggestions. Those who read the whole manuscript in its final stages were Shirley L. Patterson, School of Social Welfare, University of Kansas; Mary L. Wylie, Experimental City Project, University of Minnesota; Marcial Burroughs and Dorothy Bradley, Kansas Department of Social Welfare; Carrol Clark, professor emeritus of sociology, University of Kansas; Douglas Hink, Brandeis University; and Ollie Randall, The Ford Foundation. I am deeply grateful to all. Very particularly am I indebted to Dr. Hink and to Dr. Randall for their many contributions.

Two former colleagues at the University of Kansas, Eleanor Loeb and Aase George, gave much appreciated assistance in the last days of preparation for publication. The former helped with revisions of the introduction and of Chapter One; the latter undertook the laborious task of editing the total volume.

Alice Kirchhoff typed the manuscript in its final form and organized the footnotes and bibliography. As in the case of all the others, her help was invaluable.

The completion of this work was made possible by a grant from the Ford Foundation, made through Brandeis University as part of a study of obstacles to effective community planning for the elderly in seven communities. This assistance is greatly appreciated. The encouragement, support, criticism, and, above all, patience of Robert Morris and Robert Binstock of Brandeis University, of Ollie A. Randall of the Ford Foundation, of the National Council on Aging and of many other organizations for the elderly contributed not only to starting this book but also to completing it. My sincere thanks to all three.

This book is dedicated to my friend Annie and to other retired small-community social workers like her, who never forget to look for potential resources in all people.

Lawrence, Kansas   ESTHER E. TWENTE
September 1970

Contents

Never
Too
Old

The Aged in
Community Life

Never Too Old

Introduction

Never Too Old concerns the aging person in small communities and the clusters of persons with whom he is, has been, would like to be, or could be affiliated. This is a large concern and calls for elaboration. As every casual observer knows, a sixty-fifth birthday does not automatically mark the beginning of old age any more than does the sixty-fourth or sixty-sixth or even the sixtieth or sixty-second. Neither does it describe the degree to which characteristics of old age manifest themselves after a man or woman has lived six and one-half decades. Some people at fifty have many of the traits commonly attributed to old people; others are young at seventy. Yet for classification, a common denominator must be applied. Prevailing retirement policies and Social Security benefits are two major administrative arrangements that have made it convenient to place those sixty-five-and-over (and, more recently, those sixty-two-and-over) in the elderly and old category.

This group in the United States, as of July 1, 1967, was estimated to consist of 18,796,000 persons, an increase of 11.8 percent since 1960 (U.S., Bureau of the Census, 1968). A much pub-

1

licized finding of the Bureau of the Census in 1960 was the heavy concentration of older persons in states with large rural populations. By 1967, the highest percentage of men and women sixty-five and over was estimated to reside in Florida, Iowa, Nebraska, and Missouri. South Dakota and Kansas ranked almost as high (Brotman, 1968b). Data for 1966 show 39.8 percent, nearly 7½ million people, living in rural areas (Brotman, 1967).

The number and proportion of aging persons in small communities in America[1] are greater now than earlier for three major reasons: Young people move from their rural and small town homes to work in larger centers, leaving behind parents and possibly grandparents. Some retired persons, for a variety of reasons, move back from large cities to a former place of residence or to one that resembles it. Their move may enable them to live with a widowed brother or sister, with a parent or parents, or in a place with a lower cost of living than the metropolis. Possibly, too, some may move to a small town hoping to find the satisfactions, real or imagined, that they experienced in their childhood homes in small communities. An increasing number of people residing in small communities live beyond sixty-five, as they do in metropolitan areas. In both the Marion County and Holton communities, evidence of all these reasons for the increase of aging people in small communities was found.

Whatever his reason for living in a small village or town, each elderly person residing there is not primarily a statistic but a

---

[1] Studies of others to which references in this book are made often refer to populations of 2,500 or fewer. However, in most of the discussion in this book the term *small community* may refer to centers with as many as 10,000 people. The number 10,000 is justified for several reasons. Communities including up to that number are small enough to enable residents to have face-to-face contacts and to be able to know one another personally. This does not apply to all residents but to a large number of them. Also, the limited existence of organized resources, characteristic of small communities, is likely to be found. Moreover, residents of such centers tend to regard their communities as small and rural. This was true, for example, of physicians residing in towns of 10,000 people in Missouri (Hasinger, 1963). Of the many kinds of small communities in the United States, agricultural communities, farms, towns, and small cities are the focus of this book. The discussion centers primarily, but not exclusively, on small centers in the Midwest.

human being with his own strengths and loss of strength, with his own realized and thwarted goals, and with his own moments of exhilaration and frustration. He has his family or memories of his family, with whom relationships are, or were, positive or negative or somewhere in between. He has his friends, some old, some young, with whom he associates, has associated, or wishes he could associate. He has his affiliations, strong or weak, with groups and institutions in the community. Some affiliations serve him well, some not at all. He finds other societal forces impinging upon his way of life and upon him as a person. Some enhance his well-being; others restrict it.

Many people of advanced years in small communities live, at least for a number of years, in a reasonably comfortable and independent fashion. Their situations make most easily possible the use of abilities or what remains of them. Although opportunities do not always exist for mobilizing these abilities, their use promotes satisfaction and movement toward self-other realization.[2] This potential for satisfaction also applies to persons less comfortable or independent, whose remaining potentials are not easily harnessed.

Often persons who have the best opportunities to continue to use abilities and skills are prominent men and women. Their social status may be derived from sizable financial investments or political influence. Because of their influence, they can continue to work. Others may have positions which continue regardless of ad-

[2] The term *self-other realization* is used rather than the more common designations—self-realization, self-fulfillment, and self-actualization—in order to stress the fact that both self-interests and the interests of others are involved in the development toward optimum well-being. This development occurs in persons individually and also in a family and in other groups. Self-other realization involves a high degree of harmony between what a person or group wishes the self were and what it really is. It also connotes satisfaction with the progress made toward achieving the major goals in life. The term is used as interpreted by Lowenthal, Berkman, and associates (1967, p. 269): "It is applied to both the personal and social systems, in the Parsonian sense, and in particular, to the interaction between the two systems during the aging process." The state of self-other realization is not static. The effort to achieve it is viewed as a movement on a continuum which at times is toward and then away from its goal. It is visualized loosely as a horizontal line with zigzags. Some of the elements of this continuum are developed in detail as a part of a hypothesis described by Linden and Courtney (1953, pp. 906–915).

vancing age, such as those of a housewife or a self-employed busi-
nessman or an independent farmer. As disabilities increase, these
persons may be able to shift to part-time work in line with their
declining energies. Some older men and women find other activities
that prove satisfying. However, all small communities also have
elderly and old people who are not so fortunate. They have to cope
with illness, widowhood, low incomes, unsatisfactory housing arrangements, and other difficult conditions. Lack of motivation or of
opportunity to use their remaining strength optimally, or perhaps
only nominally, may lead to their having little purpose in living. In
such cases, limited well-being or discomfort, unhappiness, and loneliness may occur and may call for a response from a helping person.
Others who experience some satisfactions but have unmet needs,
undeveloped interests, and untapped resources need opportunities
to release these potentials.

Since rural areas and small cities contain a high proportion
of older people, possibilities for improving their condition pose a
challenge to all helping persons—including agricultural extension
personnel, public health nurses, social workers, neighbors, and
friends. This volume may have value for any one of these groups.
However, the experiences on which the content is based were those
of a social worker, and thus the book is addressed primarily to
members of the social work profession. In small communities county
welfare workers largely represent social work and so they especially
have been kept in mind during the preparation of these pages.

Two demonstration and research projects provided part of
the experiences on which this book is based. From 1961 to 1963
the author directed a Ford Foundation project, *Community Organization for the Elderly,* in Marion County, Kansas, a rural county
of fifteen thousand persons, of whom over 14 percent were sixty-five
years old and over. Marion County had ten little towns and villages,
each with its own attitudes and ways of life. The project was one
of seven in the United States. Robert Morris, of the Florence Heller
School of Advanced Studies in Social Welfare, Brandeis University,
was chief investigator for all seven. The County Welfare Department provided physical facilities and clerical help, contributed funds
for travel, and, with the Division of Services for the Aging, State

Department of Social Welfare, assumed major responsibility for the beginnings of the program. A group of local citizens known as Golden Years, Inc., was organized to administer the program.

From 1964 to 1967 the author was codirector and, later, director of a National Institute of Health project, *Mobilization of Aging Resources for Community Service* (Patterson, Wylie, and Twente, 1968), in a small town of three thousand persons, of whom more than 25 percent were sixty-five and over. The investigation, conducted under the auspices of the University of Kansas, was supported by Public Health Service Research Grant No. MH 01472 (later known as No. MH 14888) from the Mental Health Project Grants Section of the National Institute of Health.

The Ford project in Marion County highlighted a number of facts about elderly persons in small communities: the rapidly increasing proportion of older people in small towns and villages; the large proportion of economically unproductive citizens in small communities because of current retirement policies, declining health, and other factors; the great variety of talents, many unused, of older people; the prevalence of feelings of loss of status and worth. These conditions seem to call for an attempt to make use, in the service of the community as a whole, of the wasted talents of aging persons. A pilot study in Marion County attested to the feasibility of such an attempt (Wylie, 1963).

The following agencies are particularly useful sources of information on this topic: American Public Welfare Association, 1313 East 60th Street, Chicago, Ill. 60637; National Council on Aging, 1818 L St., N.W., Washington, D.C. 20036; United States, Department of Health, Education, and Welfare, Federal, regional and state offices.

Frame of Reference

1

The possibilities for encouraging and helping older people in small communities to mobilize and use their potential capacities are many. The challenge will reward both the older man and woman and the person who tries to help. Social workers, especially county welfare workers, are in a position to be of genuine service, but social workers generally are not well prepared to meet the challenge.

Organized social work developed in large cities and its methods have become highly specialized. In small communities such specialization does not exist nor is it possible. Yet, in small communities too, old people need programs that nurture their capacities. There should be opportunities for releasing potentialities, or what remains of them, and when illness or other obstacles interfere, older people should be helped to eliminate, reduce, relieve or, at times, accept the obstacles. The rural social worker, although unable to share responsibilities with highly skilled professional colleagues or with persons of other disciplines, must be able to work with the strengths and limitations of older people and with the community groups in which such persons participate. As well as serving old people individually, a small-community social worker must be competent to deal with at least three other aspects of the community: family units, which Burgess (1926, p. 3) years ago called a "unity of interacting personalities," peer and nonpeer interest groups and associations, and community-service organizations and facilities. He or she must also be able to mobilize neighbors, employers, dispensers of information, voters, financial or personal contributors to causes, and policy makers in various areas of community life. Small-community workers even more than urban workers ought to be able to use all three traditional social work approaches: casework, group work, and social community work. (The term social community work is used to describe social work with a community, and it may involve community organization, community planning, and community development.)

To equip social workers for the varied roles demanded by practice in small communities, practice courses are taught as social work, or social welfare, not as traditional social casework, group work, or community organization and planning. Such courses are taught at the California State College at San Diego, the University of Wisconsin, Madison, the University of Kansas, St. Louis University, and others. Some educators subscribe to the idea that a broad approach has value also for practitioners in certain metropolitan programs. However, up to now very little has been published which definitively presents a clear version of such an approach. No comprehensive, systematically developed frame of reference to guide the educator and practitioner has been offered. This book is not intended to fill that void. Instead, it recounts some concepts and principles which have proved useful; they constitute a guiding frame of reference, and may also be considered as theoretical biases or even working philosophies. Perhaps they will serve as suggestions for some small-community social workers and others serving older people. They may help clarify and give greater meaning to the many-faceted responsibilities that those in a variety of fields who help others will encounter in small communities.

CONCEPT OF THE SELF-IMAGE

Most of the principles and concepts represent applications of some aspects of the symbolic interactional theory, of which the central tenets are the ideas of the self and the self-image. The idea of the self relates to a recognition that every person, through social interaction with others, evolves a relatively consistent, unique personal identity. Self-image refers to the inference that each person also develops a consciousness of what he himself is like. He can have, according to Mead (1934, p. 137), "an experience with, an experience of, one's self." He makes of himself an object of his own perception and feeling.[1] He evolves a mental picture of what he thinks other people think of him and part of the self-image will be the actual opinions that others hold of him (Cooley, 1902).

The self-image of an aging person may include everything from his opinion of his own grooming, his physical appearance, his behavior, and how all of this appears to others, to his concept of who he is, his purpose in life, and how much worth he feels he has and others accord him or are thought to accord him. If his image of himself is consonant with his values,[2] and his appraisal is shared by others who are important to him, his self-identity will be clear and his self-esteem high.

The self-image of a person, including the concepts of his identity and self-esteem, may or may not coincide with the image others hold of him. For example, an old man may see himself as still physically strong and mentally alert, and may think that others share this assessment. In reality, however, members of his family,

---

[1] As used in symbolic interaction conceptualizations, the idea of the self of the individual is often dated back to James (1890). Cooley's concept (1900) of the "looking-glass self" made a significant contribution by emphasizing the reflexive character of the self. Mead (1934, pp. 178, 260–262) elaborated further James's idea of the I and the Me, with both the I and the Me evolving when the child begins to perceive himself and has thoughts and feelings about himself. Mead related the evolving self to his conception of the organized process of which he is a part: the Me is to the self what social institutions are to society. Strauss (1956), who both gathered and edited much of Mead's work, has also written on the theory of symbolic interaction. Allport (1955; 1961) has creatively and sensitively developed the concept of self. Others writing recently on the subject include Rose (1962), in which see especially Stone (Ch. 5, pp. 86–118), and Yinger (1965). Erikson (1968) develops the idea of self from a psychoanalytic point of view; Goffman (1965) pays special attention to deviancy and deformity in relation to the self-image. Elkin (1960) on the subject is eminently brief and readable.

[2] Williams' (1951) analysis of values and value systems seems particularly pertinent.

his friends, and fellow employees see his strength declining and his mental ability deteriorating, and they treat the old man in terms of their image of him. His behavior is in response to his own appraisal. Others may hold a lesser image of the aging person than he himself does, and yet regard him more highly than he thinks they do. This was very clearly illustrated by the pilot study (Wylie, 1963) in Marion County referred to earlier.

An individual of advanced years, or of any age group, may also have a lower opinion of himself than relatives, friends, neighbors, and people in the community generally have of him. That is, he underrates his potential and worth, perhaps in all, perhaps only in some, important aspects of his life. When this occurs, reassurance, through word and deed, from trusted others, and the use of potential capacities with some success may remedy or alleviate the situation. Reassurance, no matter how realistic or positive, will restore a shattered self-image or improve one that has always been low only if the relationship between the reassuring and the reassured is based on mutual trust and confidence. The communication, which is greatly influenced by the self-image and the image held by others of such a relationship, consists of written or verbal language, facial expressions, physical movements and actions, touch, and any other means of conveying attitudes, feelings and degrees of understanding. The interaction of such a relationship is spiral in nature, that is, an act or statement of one person elicits a response from another and each subsequent response is affected by the accumulation of preceding ones.

If enough satisfaction with his identity and sufficient self-confidence exists or is restored to enable the person with a low self-image to mobilize his resources, and if there are opportunities to use the resources successfully, even when success is small, improvement in the self-image is likely to follow.

Symbolic interactionists apply the concepts of self and self-image to persons individually, not to persons in groups, to the extent that the concepts are not entirely relevant to clusters of persons. However, a partial application of the concepts is useful. Strictly, self-image is a psychological, subjective concept. Its literal application to groups of people is, therefore, questionable. By analogy, however, it may be extended beyond individuals. There is some precedent for doing so. Durkheim (1933) refers to the phenomenon as "collective consciousness." Etzioni (1968) uses the phrase "societal consciousness" which, he writes, can be viewed as "generalized awareness [p. 226]."

The members of a family collectively have a notion about the group as a whole. This applies only when the parents and their immediate offspring are the focus of attention, and when a larger kinship group is taken into account. The family image may be one of pride or of shame. It may provide satisfaction or disappointment. It may reflect a better opinion of itself than that which the community holds, or it may consider the group inferior to the appraisal made by others. A poor family living in a dilapidated house and flouting some accepted customs may not be held in high esteem within the community. As a group, however, its members may have strong affectional ties, much fun together, and consider themselves fortunate. From their point of view, the family is exactly right. Conversely, an affluent family may be highly regarded, its charitable activities many, its political contributions obvious, and it would seem that the family is all and has all that could be desired. But the husband and wife have disagreements which are carefully hidden from the public; the children feel the lack of understanding; and even the high economic status is on shaky grounds. The family's outward behavior merits the high opinion of the community; its private behavior does not.

Other groups and associations, including service agencies, have self-images and images held by others. Conscious efforts are sometimes made by groups of all kinds to improve their public image. Sizable portions of the yearly budget of an organization may be devoted to achieving this purpose. Members of small groups and staffs of service agencies tend to behave in terms of their own image of their group or organization and the image the public has or is thought to have.

In the group, as in the individual, self-esteem and self-identity (or, when applied to clusters of persons, group pride and group identification) can be potent motivating forces in harnessing and using family and group potentialities. The esprit de corps which accompanies group pride and group identification aids in the kind of positive interaction that assures achievement.

SIMILARITIES IN GROUPS AND INDIVIDUALS

In addition to a concept of the individual or group self, older persons, family units, and other small groups have other characteristics in common, all of which affect and are affected by the self-image. Among the most significant are uniqueness, change, social status, and potential.

Every older man and woman, every family unit, and every other cluster of persons is unique. Similarities exist but so do differences, and realistic images must account for them. Stereotyping is based primarily on similarities, such as chronological age, marital status, a particular kind of group goal. The exceptional characteristics of each person or group are overlooked. Uniqueness is what gives each aging person, family, or group, his or its peculiar worth. Likenesses may make for important values but not for special values.

Individuals, families, and clusters of persons undergo many changes, such as changes from babyhood to childhood, adolescence, young parenthood, middle age and old age. Similar changes are evident in family and other groups. The family as a group is very different when the parents are young and children are toddlers and teenagers from when the parents are old, the toddlers middle-aged, and their children have children of their own. Always needs and behavior are affected by the physical, intellectual, and emotional condition at a given time. Even communities of people reach different stages of growth, as was dramatically demonstrated by three community development projects in South Australia in 1956. The author was responsible for the three projects while holding a nine-month Fulbright Lectureship at the University of Adelaide.

One community was just being born. Ninety "soldier families" living in government barracks on Kangaroo Island were selecting a site for a town to be built on the island by the residents. The Australian Commonwealth Government gave its veterans of World War II opportunities to clear and homestead land. The families were living in temporary barracks for the two to three years that it took the men to clear twelve hundred acres of land apiece for sheep grazing and homes. A town with the essential community facilities was needed for the families after they moved onto their land.

The second community, a one-hundred-year-old small town, had achieved much recognition for its many cooperative ventures.

Through "working bees" the people of the town had built, among other facilities, a community center, hotel, library, children's clinic, park, arboretum, and swimming pool. The town was having some temporary problems of professional leadership but had much community pride, vision, clearly established goals, and a desire to attain them. It was a strong, virile town.

The third community was a small village which, like many villages in the United States, had a declining population. Community activities were at low ebb and the few buildings in a state of bad repair. Even though some rural leaders living nearby expressed an interest in reviving it, and despite the efforts made to rehabilitate a community building and to stage a community picnic, the village seemed to be in its last struggle with death.

These three communities were affected by the images their inhabitants held of them. The strong group identification and group pride which existed on Kangaroo Island and in the one-hundred-year-old town contributed greatly to the achievement of goals.

Closely related to the different stages of development of the aging person and of the groups that are important in his life is the fact that each phenomenon is continuously changing on a variety of fronts and for a variety of reasons. The situation may be societal in origin and may affect all older people, or it may originate in the life of one particular person who will most keenly feel the effects. In the family, the changes may occur within the group itself or within the social institution as a whole, for example, an economic change which involves one particular family, or a change which influences all families and the accepted ways of doing things. Similarly, groups and associations change. A complicating factor of change is that the rates of change may vary with the individual, the group, or other forces in life. Ogburn (1922) introduced the idea that a lag occurs in different parts of a culture in times of social change. Changes in the family as a social institution call for changes in filial responsibility. Problems may arise when the need for shifts in responsibility precedes the family's ability to accept them. The long, steep steps leading to church sanctuaries may not serve the increasing number of members who, because of advanced age, are more likely to be crippled than are younger church members.

In the process of change certain characteristics of the older person, his family, and other clusters of persons abide. However, each person and each group is also continuously changing into somebody or something else. Allport (1955), Coutu (1949), and Maslow (1962) apply the idea of "becoming" to an individual. It seems to have equal relevance to groups of people. The aging man and woman and each group with which he is affiliated continues in the process of being and becoming. Integral aspects of being and becoming are the self-image or the group concept and the images held or thought to be held by others. Change may evoke uncertainties about identification, pride, and even about the purposes and goals which form the reason for continued existence. The doubts may be temporary, but help may be needed to reestablish a positive self-concept or a better group image.

Each older person, his family, and other significant groups have a social status and role structure, that is, assigned or assumed positions and tasks and accompanying responsibilities (Elkin, 1960; Yinger, 1965). Each position and task, when acceptable to the self-image, contributes to the self-esteem and self-identity of an older man or woman or to the group pride and group identification of a family or other cluster of persons. The status of old people on farms and in villages and small towns is low when contrasted with that of aged men and women in an earlier agricultural era. The tasks expected of them are few and of limited use; they are no longer regarded as conveyors of knowledge of farming, cattle-breeding, or weaving; they are no longer needed to perform useful chores. The family may have as high a status as formerly and may perform as important, though different, functions. The elderly or aged member, however, is likely to have a lower status in the family group and his role or tasks, in general, seem to be less important to the welfare of the whole "unity of interacting personalities."

As the older person moves out of the family circle into apartments and into care and nursing homes, or as the young person moves out of the family home, leaving the parents living alone in the old home or in a new house designed to serve them better, interest groups and service organizations tend to assume some of the functions that the older person himself used to perform. With such increased activity and responsibility there seems to follow increased importance and a consequent rise in public esteem for the interest groups and service organizations. Currently it seems that society tends to hold a lower image of older persons as they come to have fewer positions and perform fewer tasks. Families, however, seem to maintain the image they held previously, and compared with attitudes held when persons now sixty-five and older were young, the attitude of the public is positive toward interest groups and associations.

Almost all older persons, families, small groups, and associations of people have some capacity, actual or potential, which can be used to promote greater self-respect and, hence, improvement in well-being. Perhaps because of stereotyped notions about the deteriorated capacities of older people, their potential tends to be overlooked by themselves and by others. Older persons in particular, because of their low status, family units, and other groups important to old people, should have encouragement and opportunities for discovering and revealing used and unused capacities. The current press on many different fronts for a more equitable distribution of influence and authority in the decision-making process strongly suggests that old people, individually and in groups, should have the opportunity to assess their own capacities, needs, and interests and make the decisions that affect their well-being. Families, groups of all kinds, institutions, and organizations consist of human beings, so similar consideration and respect are due to them.

Older persons and clusters of persons have potential for creative and empathic experience. Creative expression by older persons or by groups, especially if they consider it excellent, fosters self-confidence and strengthens self-identity. Such creative efforts can result in something new and different from anything that has been done before and that, at least in variety of detail, can far surpass whatever others would be able to do for the older individual or group. Empathy—the capacity for putting oneself into the position of others and being interested in them and concerned for them— lessens self-centeredness and nurtures in others feelings of worth and self-esteem. For many older men and women in small communities, empathy provides a purpose in living.

SOCIAL WORK IN SMALL COMMUNITIES

The overriding objective of a small-community social worker and others who would serve older persons is to facilitate the discovery, mobilization, and use of potential abilities, or what remains of them, in individuals, families, and other groups, and also in the person or group of people who has lost much—in the spry, healthy, active, alert old man who performs one useful task after another and in the listless, apathetic, crippled old woman who gazes endlessly into space. The potential and actual strengths of family units and of peer and other interest groups cover a like range of possibilities and deserve similar interest and attention.

The self-image and its components, self-identity and self-esteem, and group identification and group pride, play an important role in the mobilization of potential abilities. Previous experiences when revealed may lead to the discovery of capacities and, if the experiences were successful in the past, may give impetus to reviving the use of latent or manifest abilities, thus enhancing the self-image and engendering greater well-being. To help strengthen the self-image, the generalist in small communities is predominantly increment-geared. Increments are the capacities in an individual which may constructively aid growth and development; decrements are the deficiencies and potentially declining activities. Work with the elderly and old and with any of the groups that are involved stresses primarily the strengths. When, because of illness, capacities cannot be used, the emphasis is first on eliminating or relieving some of the difficulty so that increments can be mobilized. In such situations the older person, family, or group may be able to participate to a limited degree. There are times when the aged individual takes little responsibility for action, for example, when need for protective service is indicated. The situation is similar in the case of a family when its members become immobilized, perhaps because of a serious family tragedy, or if members of a group are unable to function when they lose their leader.

Any activity of the social worker, even that of enabling the elderly individual, family, or group to take complete responsibility for charting a course and for finding ways to implement goals, is considered intervention. Successful intervention requires varying assessments of the needs of the individual or of the group. Briefly, the frame of reference for procedural models is based on the concept of differences in the capacities of individuals, families, and groups to be self-directing. There are two kinds of differences: those between individuals and those between groups, and they are within the same person or group at different times. No two older persons, no two families, no two clusters of people are equally capable of self-direction; neither is the same individual, the same family nor the same group equally able at all times to mobilize potentials for making decisions and for implementing them. The self-image and the image of oneself held, or thought to be held, by others always plays a vital part in the capacity to use potentials and to be self-directing.

Subjective and
Objective Images

2

The old in small communities are represented by many different attitudes to life, ranging from one of satisfaction in and zest for living to one of hopelessness, spent sitting in long gray lines in hallways painted a dark brown. Between is the whole gamut of reaction from the pursuit of new interests and an excited use of capacities developed over the years to the relinquishment of the struggle. The ways of life extend from their sharing the fruits of their efforts and standing by with wisdom, courage, and support to their having "no one to love, nothing to hope for . . . except death." Some have a purpose in life which they energetically and productively pursue, and as a result they continue to grow. Others are without aim or goal and deteriorate so that when death comes there is little left of their personalities.

It was at a meeting of a group of elderly and old people. Some three dozen paintings were hanging on the walls.

They depicted scenes of farm life in the late nineties and in
the early twentieth century and portrayed the colors of the
landscape of the nearby countryside. The audience listened
attentively. Faces reflected the happy memories of childhood days. Enthusiastically and with humor Mr. Osborn
explained that he had "taken to painting from memory"
three years before. His eyes, his voice, his posture, all reflected his complete pleasure in what he was describing.

He spends most of his time in his "studio" in the basement of his home. "He doesn't even dry dishes any more,"
Mrs. Osborn later remarked, teasing him. When not painting he and "the missus" get into the car and drive "out into
the country." There he sketches the rolling hills, cotton-
wood trees, and flowers in the spring. Sometimes he includes
a meadowlark. In perspective the bird on the canvas is too
big but the painter loves meadowlarks and for him the size
is right. He delights in sketching the hills during the different seasons of the year. When he transfers his drawings to
canvas, he does so in the appropriate colors of spring or
autumn, summer or winter. He makes gifts of his paintings
to friends and hopes to leave a collection to a small museum
located in the county seat near the place of his birth. A professor of art has adjudged his work as "excellent primitive
art."

He was eighty-one, he said, and his wife would soon be
eighty-one. After the meeting, she chuckled delightedly, "He
could have talked a long time without telling everybody my
age." He grinned.

Mrs. Osborn, too, has interests. Her display of needlework and handicrafts in the home shows originality and
much skill. Both like to "putter" in the garden. There are
many flowers and early in the season there are "roasting
ears" ready for the table. They share them with neighbors
and friends.

Mr. and Mrs. Osborn also "stand by" their widowed
daughter and grandson. "She works and needs us to help
out occasionally," they explain.

A dull red, three–story brick building that served its purpose as a hospital earlier in the century. Now it is the Home.
Hallways painted a dark brown; small cramped rooms
brightened only by a photograph, a brilliantly colored afghan, a bit of crochet or embroidery, a well–loved Bible.
Women and men, labeled "aged," inhabit the Home. The
blankness of their lives is reflected in their faces. Long, gray

faces appear in long gray lines. Nothing to do. Nothing to say. No one to love. Nothing to hope for . . . except death.

"I want to die and go to heaven," cried a 95–year–old lady in her native Swedish tongue. She shielded her eyes with a veined, knotty hand and wept.

For the tenth time a small, perky 84–year–old asked, "Did I tell you about my son Eric? He's a teacher and a very intelligent boy. When he was a youngster the preacher always said, 'That Eric, he's going to make his mark in the world'!"

An old lady with bowed head and hunched shoulders, painstakingly spelling out the Swedish words in the ancient family Bible . . . never looking to the right nor to the left, but always reading, day in and day out.

Erect of bearing and militant in manner, the woman in her late seventies flatly stated, "I can't and I won't be like those old ladies . . . sitting in the hall all day long, staring at nothing. Not that I think I'm superior, but I must have something to do or life has no meaning."

"Where did you come from? Where did you come from?" asked a sweet old lady in a monotonous singsong voice. Her face held no lines of pain or sorrow and her eyes reflected the innocence of a child. She had found her escape.

Persons with long gray faces seated in long gray lines. Nothing to do, nothing to say. No one to love. Nothing to hope for . . . except death.   *Shirley Patterson*

The illustrations are not designed to show that remaining in one's home is necessarily satisfactory or that one's losing all purpose in living is peculiar to an institution. Certainly the physical surroundings may, on the one hand, aid and abet a buoyancy of spirit, and, on the other, nurture despair and apathy, or, if the person is struggling against his fate, irascibility. The illustrations show how great the range between happiness and unhappiness may be. Sometimes the urge to grow wins out; sometimes there seems to be little reason for existence and rapid decline follows. One thing is clear: the individual's personality is not static, even in old age. Growth may come at eighty-five or ninety; decay may become the dominant pattern at sixty or earlier; the two may occur simultaneously. For example, the eighty-one-year-olds of the vignette do not have as much physical stamina as they had when they were thirty or forty, but they have developed strengths of mind and spirit. The reverse may be true of the apathetic, listless patients in the Home: there may be those whose heartbeat is stronger and more regular than it was in the past but, as living, loving, interested, and interesting, human beings, they will have lost ground.

On farms and in small towns, older men and women may have lost all reason for living or may find satisfactions in pursuing objectives and goals in life. Some become passive and resigned; others struggle valiantly to make life worthwhile. Some have physical disabilities and succumb to them; others take note of what is left and use the remnants of health and energy in amazingly effective ways. Some retain excellent health and remain mentally alert until they die; others become permanently disabled.

Among the major causes of such variations are the state of the person's self concept and the concepts that others have or are thought to have of him.

CONCEPT OF SELF

Adios

Now that I'm old, and fear the cold,
    I will confide in you
That people say, most every day,
    There's nothing I can do.

But you must know if I should go
    To some nice warmer place,
I could enjoy, like some big boy,
    To work like all the race.

I've lived my life through lots of strife
    I don't think I'm worn out,
I still could do a thing or two
    And know what I'm about.

But office men think now and then
    I might get tired or sick
And farmers think—though I don't drink—
    I might fall in the "crick."

Where things are made in tempered shade
    Of factory and shop

> Employers say, in their nice way,
> "At fourscore you should stop."
>
> So I suppose an old man goes
> Out to his garden rows,
> And fights the weeds like evil deeds,
> 'Til Gabriel's trumpet blows.
>
> *H. D. Hostetter*

So writes an octogenarian living in a small town in Kansas. He clearly has an image of himself and he realizes that others have one of him. However, there is a discrepancy between how he views himself and how, judging from his experiences, he thinks he is viewed by others. He is sure he can still "enjoy, like some big boy, to work like all the race." Not so sure are those who might be able to employ him. Very kindly, but nevertheless quite firmly, they relegate him to his "garden rows" where he may "fight" the weeds like evil deeds, 'til Gabriel's trumpet blows." Human beings at any age assess their own capacities, that is, they have notions, perhaps vague, perhaps definite, of what they are and can do, and what for them is impossible, views which others may or may not share. The judgment of others may be either less or more favorable than those of oneself. When the verdicts of oneself and of others are favorable, a sense of well-being ensues; when unfavorable, disappointment, discouragement, or even shame may result.

When there is a discrepancy between how a person pictures himself, or thinks others picture him, and the picture that others actually do have of him, the difference must be resolved, at least partially, or it will cause frustration and conflict. The individual may try to meet the situation either by attempting to prove to others that his view of himself is correct or by modifying his views and accompanying behavior to conform more closely to the expectations he believes others have of him. If he tries to prove the validity of his image and is unsuccessful because his assessment is inaccurate or because he does not have sufficient opportunity to prove that it is accurate, he becomes frustrated and will probably be irritable and difficult to live with. Through his behavior he may flaunt his image, perhaps to annoy those who do not share his own assessment. If he conforms without finding a satisfying outlet for his interests and energies, he is likely to become apathetic and withdrawn; he adopts the attitude, "What's the use?" Sometimes others modify their judgments of him. For example, if the potential employers who consider that Mr. Hostetter is unable to "work like all the race" were to follow him about for a day, they would no doubt change their opinion of him and perhaps convey to the old man some glimpse of the change.

People everywhere have self images. Old people living in small towns, villages, and farms have self concepts and attach meanings to them that are, to some extent, peculiar to small communities.

TO SEE ONESELF

The vignettes have their source in many communities and in a variety of experiences, as is true of the other material of this book. However, this volume is based largely on two research and demonstration projects conducted in small communities. *Mobilization of Aging Resources for Community Health,* funded by the National Institute of Mental Health, was conducted in Holton, Kansas, where slightly more than a quarter of the population of three thousand persons was over the age of sixty-five. *Community Organization for the Elderly,* funded by the Ford Foundation, was conducted in Marion County, Kansas, where more than 14 percent of the population of fifteen thousand persons were over the age of sixty-five.

Although the Holton project did not include a study of self-images as such, images are reflected in what one hundred respondents said in tape-recorded interviews. These interviews, each about an hour and a half long, were an integral part of the research. In Marion County about half of the 2,200 persons sixty-five and over were interviewed, but, because of the variety of approaches used by the one hundred volunteer interviewers, the tabulated data were not completely reliable. The Marion County respondents were more representative of the total elderly population of the community than the one hundred Holton respondents, who were only those able and willing to answer the preproject LSI-Z (Life Satisfaction Index-Z) questionnaire, a modified version of the Life Satisfaction Index-A (LSI-A) developed on the Kansas City Study of Adult Life (Neugarten, Havighurst, and Tobin, 1961, pp. 134–143).

The image of an independent person or one who desires to regain independence was clearly mirrored in the statements of most of the respondents. The image came in the form of expressions of satisfaction that, in spite of their age, they could still get around and take care of themselves, or dissatisfaction if this were no longer so. Many seemed to fear that already they were a burden or would become one. The great emphasis upon the importance of good health seemed motivated much more by a desire to remain independent or regain independence than by a fear of pain or even death. Said one eighty-five-year-old man, "I just want to live and when I get more decrepit than I am now, pass on."

Like the writer of *Adios,* both men and women put a high value on work, and it was clear that when they were still gainfully employed they were pleased with themselves; when not, they emphasized gardening and housework and "something useful to do." When the question in the Holton interview was asked, "Some people say that a person's success in life depends mostly on getting good breaks; others say it depends mostly on personal effort and hard work. Which do you agree with most?" the reply was almost unanimously, "Work and effort." One respondent elaborated his statement with stress on the fact that he did not believe in the "gimme-gimme" attitude. "To most older Americans, a high degree of independence is almost as valuable as life itself. It is their touchstone for self-respect and dignity. It is the measure they use to decide their importance to others. And it is their source of strength for helping those around them" (*The Older American,* 1963, p. 7). When persons were not working, many expressed feelings of uselessness. (This seemed especially true in the Marion County community.) In such cases, much stress was often placed on declining health, perhaps to justify the idleness. For some, particularly in certain parts of the county, work seemed almost to take on religious significance (Nosow and Form, 1962, Ch. 2).[1]

---

[1] Ethnically, the Holton community was homogeneous: most of the older residents had either farmed land nearby and upon retirement had moved to town, or they had always, or for much of their lives, lived in the town. Marion County was represented by a number of ethnic groups: Mennonites, most of whom now in their later years, from Russia or Germany who came when they were children or young people, or whose parents had come to the United States before they were born, sizable groups of "Missouri"

Many men and women in both communities viewed themselves, or perhaps at times they wanted others to think of them in
this way, as having been good parents with a continuing close relationship with their children. In answer to a question in the Holton
interview, the majority of parents thought that their children were
doing well. Not all claimed credit for the success of the children but
quite a number frankly stated that they thought that the home they
had provided influenced the outcome. Their interest in and concern
for their children was repeatedly expressed. One great-grandmother
of eighty exclaimed almost vehemently, "My children, my children.
That is the most important thing in my life."

In both communities most of the older residents seemed to
take pride in their church affiliations, as long as they were active
participants. When no longer able to attend services, some were
rather bitter about their church experiences. Generally speaking,
most older people considered it right and proper to belong to
church. The regularity of attendance seemed to be an index of the
measure of the man. In their self-images most persons of advanced
years either were, or thought they should be, loyal church members.

Both project settings reflected other self-concepts. Some men
and women were always meticulously groomed. One neatly dressed
widow confined to her wheelchair never failed to wear matching
jewelry and invariably her white hair was carefully combed. Others
emphasized good adjustment to tragedies and difficulties in life.
One recently widowed woman said, "What is important right now
is to adjust myself to being left . . . if other people can do it, I
can too." Another quite old lady thought that it was important for
her to try to "be agreeable." A high proportion of persons considered themselves to be old and no longer able to do things. A statement heard frequently was, "You know, I am over sixty-five (or
seventy-five, or eighty-five) and I can no longer get around like I
used to." This was said even by individuals apparently in quite
good health. Yet some persons with obvious disabilities were proud
that they were able to carry on as usual. Some persons seemed to

---

Lutherans, "Bohemian" Catholics, and French and Swiss residents. A large
proportion of the older residents were descendants from families coming from
states "farther East."

have a self-image of youth, or at least of middle age. Types of clothing, hair styles, mannerisms, and conversation all attested to this. Some thought of themselves as adventurous; others were "through with all those new things that come along."

Significantly, a large number of older people held images of competent selves in relation to service activities of all kinds in both project communities. To test the feasibility of the program that became the Holton study, a pilot study (Wylie, 1963) was made in a small town in Marion County. Only a few respondents were interviewed, so the evidence was not conclusive, but the number of older men and women who reacted positively to discussions about their ability and availability for contributions to community betterment activities was so marked that the Holton study was conducted.

AS OTHERS SEE ONE

Some younger people in Marion County thought that their elders could assume a community participant role. However, the proportion of younger persons holding this concept was smaller than that of the members in the older age group and they had fewer concrete suggestions of what the older people could do. Nevertheless, the number of younger respondents who answered in the affirmative was greater than the older respondents thought it would be. These results differ slightly from those reported by Katzenbaum and Durkee (1964, pp. 237–239) who found that young people held a negative image of the elderly. However, the mean age of their young subjects was considerably lower than that of the subjects in Marion County, who consisted of community leaders aged from about thirty to fifty-five. Katzenbaum and Durkee included some subjects up to the age of fifty-five but most were junior and senior high, college, and graduate school students. The higher age level may or may not have made the attitudes of the Marion County group somewhat more positive.

Katzenbaum and Durkee (1964, pp. 250–260) also summarized a variety of studies of how older people view themselves and think others view them. The studies tended to show that older persons attributed to others a less favorable attitude toward themselves than they held of themselves. The authors suggest that the elderly person "is aware that he is the target of a volley of negative

stereotypes." The more favorable attitude of the aging toward themselves might stem from the older person's trying to compensate or
overcompensate for the low appraisal he knows or senses is made
by younger people so that he may "look more like the aggressor
than the victim," or from his being "in a transitional psychological
state characterized by an attempt to develop the new coping techniques seemingly required for successful adaptation, but techniques
which cannot easily be integrated with their long-term habits and
viewpoints."

The authors emphasize that it is important to remember,
when one applies a concept of life adjustment, that the dynamic
rather than only the static qualities of older people be considered.
Even in old age people change, and so perhaps will their images of
themselves.

In small communities, particularly those with a fairly stable
population of people well acquainted with one another, the notions
that relatives, friends, and neighbors have of an older person will
have a powerful effect upon their behavior toward him as well as his
toward them. If their actions show that they think well of him and
what he is and does, his self-esteem is bolstered and he is likely to
find courage to use his remaining capacities to good advantage.
When their image of him is low, he may revise his self-image and
lose confidence in his abilities. The judgment of some neighbors
and friends in small communities can be pretty harsh. Hink (1966)
found that the differences between an older person's self-assessment
and the opinions held of him by what Hink called "significant others" were more marked in circumstances where there was frequent,
regular and varied contact between the older person and others.
He speculates that frequent, close contact with an older person is
likely to reveal more clearly than will occasional contact any declining capacities. Since, in many small communities, interaction
tends to be frequent and intimate, it may possibly follow that the
images held by significant others of elderly people tend to be lower
than such images might be in urban centers.

TO BE OLD IN AMERICA

Not all younger people on farms and in small communities
depreciate the contributions of older persons. The pilot study in

Marion County seemed to attest, although not strongly, to this. Yet it remains true in small as in large communities that the image held by our society and the dominant values of the present are not conducive to a positive self-concept in the elderly. According to Linden (1954) "our culture is a juggernaut of ideals . . . and . . . our values are the values of youth, vigor, physical beauty, motion, quantitative productivity and, to some degree, arrogance [p. 30]." Such values do not take into account some of the positive characteristics and possible contributions of older people. Thus, sooner or later the older person tends to fashion his self-concept after the rather lowly assessment of him made by his community. The assessment will vary in different settings, but some lowly opinions seem to persist everywhere. Even though "a precise American cultural attitude towards the aged is not easily discerned . . . our elders seem neither devotedly revered nor yet unceremoniously excluded. Perhaps our attitude may be described as an amused tolerance and a legally imposed and grudging acceptance" (Linden and Courtney, 1953, p. 912). Some may think this description unkind. In small communities numerous examples of situations where it does not apply can be cited. Yet, considering some of the overt attitudes toward aging persons—attitudes reflected in our retirement policies, in many of our community service programs, in the place of the older person in most small-community activities—the low appraisal seems justified. It is fairly clear that there is more condescending benevolence than genuine respect for the contribution, real and potential, of old persons. Instead of honestly facing issues with him, some are likely to be evasive, protective, dilatory, and patronizingly reassuring when he loses composure. Even when the performance of the older individual is acknowledged to be good, the acknowledgment seems to be accompanied by surprise and depreciation. In small communities it would seem that to be old is to be regarded as physically weak, mentally slow, and emotionally insensible—an assessment shared frequently by the older person himself and one which often becomes increasingly a part of his own self-image as he gets older. When, as may happen, his own children, neighbors and friends make this assessment, the effect on his own more positive self-concept is marked.

Old people do change physically and physiologically. The

rate of change varies greatly among individuals, but does tend to limit the abilities of elderly persons in a rapidly changing world. When speed and sensory acuity are required, old people cannot compete with youth. Educationally the younger generation has the better opportunities. The current labor market does not absorb all those able and willing to work and it would seem just and fair that the young and middle-aged should have priority. It also is possible that the contributions of old people are depreciated both in their own minds and in the minds of younger persons to justify forced or voluntary retirement. The young and middle-aged have never been old, and cannot from personal experience fully comprehend the aging process. Every adult has been a child and may be able to place himself in the position of a child.

In any event, old age tends to be equated with a declining capacity for useful work. This development is more recent in rural than in urban areas and may therefore be more puzzling and frustrating. As others have recognized, our society has not yet managed to assign to the aged productive, not necessarily economic, tasks which are better suited to their potential capacities than they are to those of younger people (de Ropp, 1960). This is true of rural as well as of urban settings.

The self-image of most older men and women who come to the attention of the small-community social worker has either declined or long been low. The process of growing old will more than likely have aided and reinforced the low esteem. As well as the dominant values of society and the stereotyped image held of older people, not only by the general public but also quite often and quite specifically by younger neighbors and friends, other major factors will influence the self concept of older people in small communities. Such factors include changes in status and role, retirement from productive work, physical and physiological changes, reduced income, changes in housing arrangements, loss of spouse and friends, and changes in personality patterns.

TO BE OLD IN A SMALL TOWN

Studies of older people in villages and small towns seem to indicate that most of the subjects spent their early years on farms (Loomis and Beegle, 1950), and were oriented to the way of life of their rural parents and grandparents, who will have remained "in the saddle" or in positions of authority until they either became quite disabled or died—at a somewhat younger age for most people than now. As manager of the family farms, the father usually controlled the purse strings and the mother managed the house and often helped milk the cows and tend the chickens. As long as both parents were physically able, they could perform useful tasks.

Persons now old recall the past when advancing years were less of a reason for old people's being relegated to the back seat. Many may think that it would be right and proper for them to be regarded in the same way. Yet, with the emphasis upon retirement at sixty-five or earlier and with the tendency to equate retirement age with inability to be productive, the back seat seems to be the only place, distasteful as it might be. But to resent the role or "to fight the weeds like evil deeds, 'til Gabriel blows his horn" may seem to serve little purpose. It may be more to the point to conclude that, in fact, the judgment of others is correct and life really does hold very little anymore. A feeling of worthlessness and lack of purpose is often the result. All that seems to be left is the need to remain as self-directing as possible and thus retain a maximum degree of identity. Another outcome may be a life that is devoted primarily to the attainment of such satisfaction as may be derived from the next meal, an occasional visit from a neighbor or church member who, either from friendship or benevolence, "pops in," the next program on television which is sometimes stimulating, sometimes nap-inducing.

In rural communities changes in role and in status tend to be more difficult for men than for women. Most women living on farms, in villages and small towns have been mothers and housewives throughout their adult lives. Their positions declined and their tasks decreased in importance when their children left for school or to be married, events which usually occurred before the women had reached sixty-five or even sixty. Unless a woman had additional interests which kept her busy, such as active memberships in farm, church, or social groups, she may have had difficulty in adapting to the new situation. However, if her husband were still living, she would have continued to cook the meals and manage the home in the familiar pattern, and, as she grew older, to retain the responsibilities. If she were a widow, she might even have assumed her husband's duties. One woman of over seventy in Marion County continued to drive a truck and to feed cattle; another managed a small business after her husband died. In any event, by the time she reached sixty-five or seventy, the wife and mother would very likely have made some adjustment to changes in her former position and roles. Such familiar tasks as keeping the cookie jar filled, remembering birthdays, overseeing family dinners, baby-sitting for grandchildren, sewing, mending, and keeping house are activities to which she is likely to be accustomed. When relationships are healthy, all these activities have the effect of keeping members of the family in touch with one another, of enabling her to make them comfortable and mete out love and affection as needed. Hers is a useful role. If, as a resident of her community, she is responsible for tasks in her church, farm organization, or other group and if, as she becomes older, the responsibilities are no longer hers, she can always continue with her housework and in her role as grandmother or neighbor. It is not so difficult to give up a president's gavel or a place on a church committee if there are children's mittens to be knitted or a coffee cake to be baked for a sick neighbor.

Her husband tends to be less fortunate. When he retires from his job as farmer, business man, bank clerk, filling station operator, or whatever was his occupation, he may not have another role in which he can automatically find opportunities for using his potential abilities. Many older men on farms and in small towns devote little time during their younger years to recreation and so do not easily find a substitute in play. Relatively few men in small communities seem to have hobbies. "My work has always been my hobby" was an expression heard in both Holton and Marion County. Perhaps tasks around the home could well be performed, but for many men in rural areas, such tasks are not appealing. As a matter of fact, in earlier years their wives and children may have performed them and to fit into a role that members of the family have performed, and may continue to perform, may not be very enticing. The man surely cannot bask in the importance of such a new role. Anthropologist Clark (1967, pp. 55–64) of the Langley Porter Neuropsychiatric Institute, San Francisco, brings out clearly the fact that in a culture in which familial or occupational roles are related to age or sex, those roles may be the source of stress when they conflict with the dominant values of that culture.

Yet, as was particularly evident in Marion County, both men and women at times find something interesting to occupy their time. They painted, wrote poetry, made articles out of wood, metal and stone, rebuilt furniture, fed and watched birds, sewed, knitted, crocheted, and tatted. What they needed at times was some encouragement and recognition of their efforts and occasionally opportunities to obtain the necessary materials. Both studies showed that when made possible, community participation, like creative effort, is conducive to an increase in morale. This was specifically demonstrated in Holton.[2] Contributions of older people to the total community or to some segment of the population other than primarily older persons met with the most positive response from the older residents themselves. Of the ten projects selected by the local group sponsoring the Holton program, the three that were considered failures were specifically designed to serve older people. The most popular of all was a long-term community beautification project.

To recapitulate: role and status patterns of the elderly in small communities tend to decline in importance with advancing years and to contribute little to self-esteem. Older women find more opportunities than do men to continue their former way of life. Both men and women may discover some substitutes for their former economic-productive roles by forming new and maintaining old social relationships in creative activities of all kinds, and in community services. All old people have a past and death is sure to come, perhaps soon, perhaps not for twenty or thirty years, but many of those living in small communities do not have a meaningful present—as may be seen in the following vignette:

> Mr. Rohrmann, a short, gnome-like old man, is a retired farmer. All his life he liked to sing. So I visited him to ask

[2] "Participation in the demonstration program was associated with an increase in morale as well as a 'more' socially oriented post-program participation style. The morale increase was significant at the 1.8 E-06 level of probability with 20.4 per cent of the variance explaining participant and nonparticipant status. The control group of nonparticipants incurred a significant loss in both morale and social participation during the two-and-one-half year study period." (Patterson, Wylie and Twente, 1968.)

if he would get together a group of old people to sing two songs at a coming event. He hesitated, and then said a bit doubtfully, "Do you think we can sing good enough? You know our voices are not what they once were."

"Your voices are no longer as clear as they used to be, but you can still sing, and people will like it," I replied.

He remained thoughtful. Then he asked, "What would you want us to sing?"

"What would you like to sing?"

Again he hesitated. Then he said, "You know we old people like to sing of the past, but I guess you would like for us to sing of the future."

"I would like to have you sing of both the past and the future."

"We like to sing *Sunshine Today,*" he said. "We sang that when we were children." And then his face lit up. "Just last winter I discovered the music for it. We can sing a religious song to remind us of the future."

"I think the audience would like *Sunshine Today* and a religious song."

There was a pause. Then, "Would you plan to have them both together?"

"What would you like?"

"Well," he replied, "it may be just a notion of mine, but I would like something in between. If the two songs follow each other, the message of neither the past nor the future can be appreciated."

"I feel like you do," I said.

Again he was quiet, and when he spoke, he said, "I believe my time here on earth is almost up. My life has been lived, but if I can still do a little good—"

"You can, Mr. Rohrmann. I think about four hundred people will enjoy your songs."

"How much time have we?" he asked.

"Six weeks."

"We'll practice," he said.

As birthdays come and go, meaningful roles vanish and those that remain take on less importance and more uncertainty. Grandchildren need pretty mittens, but often they want some like the ones worn by their playmates and bought at Penney's and Sears, Roebuck. Mr. Rohrmann and his friends are asked to entertain a group on one occasion but most of the time their talents go unrecognized.

"Doing a little good" is satisfying, yet the chorus of men and women cannot feed indefinitely on the self-esteem that that one occasion stimulated. Rolelessness or an uncertain role and reduced status take the glow out of a self-image.

RETIREMENT AND WITHDRAWAL

Retirement from productive work has a tremendous impact upon small-community older people, particularly as it affects role and status and, in turn, the self-image. The effects may be positive or negative. In small communities they seem more often to be on the debit than on the credit side. This at least seems true of the immediate impact. For persons in small communities in which a high value has been attached to work, the adjustment to retirement is likely to be difficult. Inherent in retirement, wherever it occurs, is what Lindesmith and Strauss (1956, p. 417) describe as "old patterns breaking up under the impact of disjunctive experiences." This for many seems to bring with it feelings of being unsafe, unsure, unrecognized, and unneeded, and almost always means a reduced income. Status and prestige, which the job brought, diminish. Regular hours and a place to go to work are no longer a necessary part of the day's schedule. As far as the person's previous employer or fellow-employees are concerned, few people seem to know or care how and when the retired employee comes and goes or whether he continues to exist. The associations with a circle of younger friends who were also co-workers decrease in number. When contacts are made, the conversation is no longer around topics of common interest in the job. The other employees are busy with their duties; a visit with them while they are at work is out of order. One sixty-eight-year-old described his experience: "I looked forward to retirement. I wanted to remodel my house and work in my yard. I did all of that. I also bought the organ which I always wanted to learn to play. But I got lonesome. I wanted to talk to people. I went back to the shop, but my old buddies were all busy with their jobs. I never returned." Physical withdrawal from past friends seemed to him to be the only course left. What may appear to be a rebuff may cause both physical and emotional disengagement from activities and from interests that may or may not be related to the former job. There is evidence that, when people in small communities advance in years, and particularly after they retire, a large number do withdraw from life's activities, some gradually, some precipitately. Retirement certainly gives them a powerful shove in the direction of withdrawal, particularly when it is accompanied by declining health and loss of role and status. Cumming and Henry (1961) were the first to postulate a hypothesis on withdrawal by the aging: "Disengagement is inherent in the aging process and is evident in the mutual withdrawal or 'disengagement' between the aging person and others in the social system to which he belongs—a withdrawal initiated by the individual himself, or by others in the social system" (Cumming, 1964, p. 3).

The normal aging process, if it has progressed far enough in bringing about disengagement, should mitigate the upsetting effects of retirement from gainful employment. What is difficult to ascertain, however, is just how much of the withdrawal is due to a natural aging process and how much results from expectations dictated by the culture of society and accepted as inevitable by the elderly. Certainly physical disabilities, such as loss of vision and hearing, or curtailed locomotion, are conducive to withdrawal, as are declining energy and days of "feeling poorly." Yet some people grow old without losing their hearing and vision, without losing much energy and still seem to withdraw; others with many disabilities continue to interact with others. Older persons in Holton, both those in very good health and those with varying degrees of disability demonstrated that many older persons will not withdraw when given opportunities for meaningful involvement with others. But some did not respond. Apparently aging persons differ in their need for interaction. Some may be able to remain engaged with life with very minimal interaction. Perhaps neither a disengagement theory nor an activity theory (Maddox, 1964, pp. 195–204) which postulates that people are best served by being encouraged to become involved explains the behavior of all old people.

Frequently, discussions of successful retirement stress the virtues of new interests and activities, regardless of whether or not such interests and activities will use to good advantage the potentials of retirants and are in harmony with their needs. The "impact of disjunctive experiences" is not easily erased and new patterns to replace old ones which have been "broken up" are not automatically accepted. If a person's productive work has had much meaning, if much of himself has been invested in the job at the shop, in the store, classroom, or field, or in the role of a mother whose children have left home, new interests are not easily or immediately acquired, former avocational activities are not readily extended. Thus, two steps rather than one are necessary before a retirant can become reengaged: he has to retire *from* the old pattern of life before he can retire *to* the new one. This is true even if eventually the new pattern is "what he has always wanted to do but did not have time for." It has to be lived through; it involves struggles and takes time. For some it is easier than for others. A person facing retirement, no doubt, can make some conscious preparation for the event, including adjustments in his way of life and in his attitudes toward the changes that await him. It may be difficult to anticipate fully just what is actually involved in those changes and the preparation for them may not necessarily prove relevant. Specific plans for retirement may turn out to be disappointing. Physical disabilities, of vision, hearing, or locomotion, may play havoc with plans that involved reading, concerts, travel and so forth. The death or invalidism of a spouse, relative, or close friend who had been included in the plans may interfere.

In Marion County and in Holton gardening, without doubt, topped the list of new and continuing interests. For some it was part-time work to furnish food for the table and produce for the market. The same was true when chickens or a cow was kept. Often the activity became a hobby. For the gardener, his being able to grow an exceptionally big turnip or cabbage head, or being able to point to a particularly large sunflower or a perfect rose or iris blossom, or being able to display the results of his labors at a county fair or at a hobby show, gave much satisfaction. In winter the men who live in small towns often may be seen on the courthouse steps, if there should be enough warmth from the sun, or in the lobby of the rarely-patronized hotel. They smoke and swap yarns and life is not too bad. Others have a work bench in a garage or basement and repair and build furniture which, for example, in one instance was turned into profit by the auctioneer son of an eighty-year-old. Others resort to needlework and boast of being better at it than their wives. Some find the study of birds or some other object of nature an absorbing pastime. One retired farmer in Marion County not only knows all the many species of birds that come to his farm during the year and their habits, but also can imitate their song so realistically that the birds respond. He says, "I talk with the birds, and they talk to me."

In the two project communities the pattern of life for women, most of whom are housewives and mothers and have become grandmothers or great-grandmothers, remains strikingly unchanged. If, after retiring from her duties as a mother, she remains able-bodied, she will still feel that the washing must be done on Mondays and the ironing on Tuesdays, that special housekeeping and baking chores will still be reserved for Saturdays, and on Sundays there will still be church attendance and visiting. However, except for relatives and children, the visiting will be more limited than it used to be: it will no longer take up the whole Sunday afternoon with Sunday dinner and often "lunch" or supper served in the evening, but may be restricted to home calls lasting for an hour or two. Children and grandchildren will still come and go unless they have moved to other parts of the country, as happens frequently. Keeping in touch with them is still of paramount importance. Wednesday afternoons are still reserved for club meetings, such as the Sew and Chatter of STE (Stitch, Talk and Eat) clubs and for church meetings. In some communities Thursday instead of Wednesday is set aside as the principal day for getting out of the home and the sequence of the household duties may vary. There are, of course, also older women in any community whose patterns of life do not fall in such orderly routines. Though the specific cultural heritage of the women, and their individual differences, make for variations in what they do in their spare time, many older women in rural areas and small towns engage in needlework and handicrafts of all kinds. Though not designed primarily to serve older women, Agricultural Home Demonstration Units have tended to encourage such activities. Both men and women in the older age groups may engage in a variety of group activities, ranging from participating in the work of the church to that of a political party. However, these activities tend to decrease in the later years. Perhaps it should be stressed that in rural areas quite a number of older people feel that the community institutions have withdrawn from them and so they withdraw from the institutions. Informal and formal groups and associational activities are further discussed in Chapters IV and V. Reengagement activities, as described above, represent new or continuing interests. A good many men and previously-employed women sidestep some of the upsetting effects of retirement by continuing to work either full or part-time. Montgomery (1965, p. 15) reports that of 505 respondents sixty-five-years-old and over of the Pennsylvania Small Community Study, about 18 percent of the men and 6 percent of the women were employed when interviewed.

A Kentucky study (Youmans, 1963, pp. 9–10) which included rural and urban men aged sixty and older, found that 48 percent of the total number were in the labor force. Fifty-two percent of the men were classified as rural, 42 percent as urban. Of the total sample of those who reported themselves in the labor force, 26 percent of the men considered themselves to be partly retired. About 75 percent of the rural men, who were mainly engaged in farm work, and 70 percent of the total were fully or partly retired. Rural men reported themselves to be partially retired at an earlier age than did the urban respondents. Fuller, Wakeley, Luden, Swanson, and Willis (1963) made a similar study, in Linn County, Iowa, in which they included men and women aged sixty and over. However, no women were interviewed unless at some time in their lives they had been gainfully employed. The percentage of such women decreased steadily with increasing age, particularly after the age of sixty-five. Nevertheless, about 25 percent continued to work past the age of seventy-five, and two-fifths of the persons eighty and over who lived on farms remained at work. Part-time employment increased with increasing age. Retirement, unless health interfered, occurred at an older age for farm dwellers than for those in villages, towns and cities. Most of the respondents indicated that they planned to continue to work as long as they were in good health; they said they enjoyed working. Financial reasons for working were cited by only 20 percent.

Information on retirement as gleaned from the studies of communities situated in different parts of the United States—Pennsylvania, Kentucky and Iowa—varies greatly. Some variations are the results of including persons sixty years and over in two studies and excluding them from the third; of including in one study women who had worked; of including differing numbers of farm dwellers as compared with village, small town and urban dwellers; and of including differing proportions of persons self-employed and employed by others. In summarizing findings of recent studies, Bertrand (1964, p. 16) concludes that limited changes have taken place in the traditional attitudes of small-community older persons toward work. They tend to continue to feel that work should be terminated for reasons of health only. Thus, whenever opportunities are available, as in the case of a self-employed farmer, work, full-time or part-time, continues as long as enough physical strength can be mustered. Havighurst and Albrecht (1953, pp. 105–106) in one small community found mixed attitudes toward retirement. Most of the respondents were against arbitrary retirement policies, but some liked the experience of being relieved from the responsibilities of work.

Whether retirement from economic activity is more or less disruptive on farms, in villages, and small towns than in cities was not specifically ascertained by any known research conducted to date. Variations in communities and among individuals are so many that definitive conclusions from any one study or a series of studies that apply generally, even when designed to answer the question, may be impossible. Yet people continue to hold the notion that retirement and growing old are likely to be more successful in small than in large communities. Care homes, retirement villages, and individual retirement residences continue to be built in rural surroundings. Hall (1922) pointed out in the early twenties that advocacy of the advantages of a rural environment for the aging dates all the way back to Cato. Hall himself seemed inclined to concur. He wrote: "Love also tends to broaden into the higher and more sublimated form of interest in the subhuman world, in animals, plants, trees, gardening and country life generally. The charm of the rustic contrasted with the urban environment increases" (p. 415). This may be true of the old who have found earlier rural or small town experience satisfying. Others, no doubt, would prefer the hubbub of the city, considering it much more stimulating. For them the rustic life might well be downright dull.

To be retired, or to reach the age when economic production

as an important part of a person's way of life is ruled out is likely
to be upsetting to a person regardless of the size of the community
in which he resides. In any circumstances, retirement has in it
elements that may be especially demoralizing for the current generation of older people who live on farms and in small towns. For them,
especially for men, their not working and the realization that society
considers them unnecessary to economic production can affect their
self-image. Most of them will have grown up on farms or been
close to farm life, and they, with their parents, were obliged to work
hard to eke out a living. The experience, and values inherited
from previous generations, made it not only necessary but also
right to work. A man's self-respect was bolstered or weakened by
the amount of energy expended on getting the job done. These
values were thoroughly internalized and lasted even when the man
or woman moved to town although, in larger centers, the emphasis
by unions on shorter hours and on the needs of the worker rather
than of the job to be done may have helped to modify some attitudes
toward work. The older generation of city dwellers, as children and
young people, had many more opportunities than had rural youth
for commercial and noncommercial recreation, and may therefore
be more geared to thinking in terms of leisure-time values. In another generation the values of small communities no doubt will have
changed. The middle-aged of today, even from the open country,
work and play quite differently from their parents. Retirement,
therefore, may become a less devastating event in life.

For today's retirants, their self-image, when strongly supported by employment that they consider significant, started to be
challenged in their fifties, or at least in their sixties. They began
to become aware that sooner or later they would have to quit
work either voluntarily or forcibly. Increasingly they sensed that
their abilities to produce might be questioned. Perhaps declining
health, employment policies, or possibly the promotion of younger
men or women to jobs to which they themselves had aspired,
served to remind them. When retirement did come, for whatever
reason and regardless of prior preparation, life patterns had to
change. In the process self-concepts suffered and it was necessary
to find a way out. Some persons withdrew completely and apparently permanently. Others found or are finding a satisfactory new

way of life and a new purpose in living. Some just struggle along meeting day-by-day requirements as best they can. Yet, despite a low position in life and insignificant tasks to perform, a good many people in small communities grow old with positive, apparently unscathed, self-concepts, something especially evident in eighty- and ninety-year-olds. They may have had doubts about their usefulness earlier when recently retired, or when the children had just left home, but by the time they are known (in their advanced years), they seem to have found a genuine purpose in living and a place in the scheme of things. In Marion County and in Holton many old men and women, like Mr. and Mrs. Osborn, were filling their lives with creative activities. Some continued to be active in church or other community affairs.

Influences on Images

3

An elderly person's positive self-concept may be enhanced or undermined by his earlier adaptations throughout life to his many experiences, by the image held, or thought to be held of him as a person, by his children, other relatives and friends and by the way in which all older people are viewed generally in the culture of which he is a part. The role and status that he has or achieves in his family and community as he advances in age have a major impact upon his view of himself and his ability to use his potential capacity in accustomed or new ways. The impact becomes particularly significant after he retires. His self-concept will also be affected by his mental and physical health, the adequacy and certainty of his finances, his housing arrangements, the number of persons in his age group and by other demographic characteristics.

HEALTH AND OLD AGE

His state of physical health is a potent factor in an older person's life. His attitude toward health, in addition to the actual condition of his health, also affects him and those with whom he has relationships. Gerontological research currently focuses on both the physically healthy and the physically sick in the upper age groups. A survey of social work literature, however, shows a preponderance of references to declining health and capacities. Since sick persons come to the attention of social workers more often than those who are well, the preoccupation with poor health and limitations of the aged can well be understood. Yet with a decrement-geared emphasis it is possible to overlook the capacities that remain. In fact, with the public generally sharing the focus upon decrements of the aged, one may be warranted in concluding that the most serious handicap in reaching the later years of life is the lack of recognition that potential capacities may be substantially the same as always. Viewing the situation from the vantage point of the older person, one sees that it takes a hearty self-concept to remain in good or fair health when people all around seem to say "he is no longer able to do much." A number of persons in Marion County spoke of the shock when suddenly they became aware that younger persons, who had always regarded them as able-bodied and physically capable of pulling their own weight, suddenly seemed to become protective, to assert their own superior strength, and in many other ways assume what appeared to the older man or woman a condescending attitude. Some spoke of observing changes in the attitudes of their own children and the toll resulting from their devaluation; "I surely do not feel as 'good' as I used to," they would conclude. This does not mean that old people do not have disabilities: partial or total loss of eyesight or hearing, or both, may occur and will affect communication, and in time, memory. Indistinct sounds and blurred pictures of persons and things cannot be filed away as memories to be recalled clearly later. However, such deficiencies do not necessarily limit the intellectual and emotional capacities of the individual or his ability to continue a variety of activities. Strokes, hypertension, and diabetes may prove limiting but not completely disabling. In Marion County a group of men severely crippled by strokes, were still able to sandpaper blocks of wood for toys. Poorly healed broken hips or arthritis may confine a man or woman to a wheel chair but did not keep one such disabled woman from producing afghans that excelled in beauty and workmanship and won the highest award at a county-wide hobby display. Disorders of the kidneys or bladder and incontinence may occur, but the disabling effects vary and many men and women suffering from these chronic ailments continue to function quite normally. Malignant growths and heart attacks are frequent, yet older persons with malignancies have been known to continue to live active lives for some years and numerous heart patients, with proper medical supervision and appropriate self-discipline, remained busy and productive. Whatever the disease, the degree to which it crippled ranged from slight to extensive. The same degree of physical disability affects different people differently. As McFarland (1956) pointed out: "in appraising the capacities of older people, the important variable to consider is the person's functional age, i.e. the ability to perform required duties effectively and safely [p. 27]," and, one might add, to perform them in any degree, large or small. That is a matter not only of the kind and extent of the chronic illness or crippling condition, but also of the patient's self-confidence, the state of his self-concept, and the support and encouragement offered by others. For example, there is Jennie Rose, who is arthritic:

> Even though not quite seventy, she has been confined to a wheel chair for some years. Her husband is a stroke patient and completely bedfast. There are many things Jennie cannot do and many persons in her condition might have become helpless and quite unable to take care of themselves. But not Jennie. Even though she suffers severely and finds even small household tasks, such as preparing vegetables, difficult, she performs many duties which make it possible for her and her husband to stay in their own home. To be sure, two married children live in the same small town and stand by and help their parents as needed. They do so with patience and good humor. This would not be possible if it were not for the superb way in which Jennie herself functions. Her optimistic outlook, her great courage, her unfailing fortitude regardless of acute pain and one blow after another in her life, her continued interest in helping herself, her husband, and others, and her undemanding appreciation of the efforts of her children give them freedom and pleasure as they assume their heavy responsibilities.
>
> It is not so much what has been lost that counts, but how, and to what extent that which remains can be mobilized and used, and one should also emphasize how, when possible, further deterioration can be prevented.

A favorite way to assess the health of persons in a small community, but one that would seem to have many limitations, is through self-ratings. A number of studies of such assessments are available, but generalizations based on them are difficult to make. The age groups of the various studies do not coincide. The interpretation of the questions by the respondents varies, for example, in referring to health, cultural use of terms such as "good," "fair," and "poor" may differ: in some communities people customarily say "fair" when describing what, in other communities, would be "good." Some studies describe the health of older persons only; others compare the health of the aged with that of the community as a whole. Some self-rating studies include institutionalized patients; others do not. Some include urban and rural subjects. Some distinguish between open country and villages and towns of varying sizes, others do not. With so many variables, percentages of responses on the basis of "good" (sometimes "excellent" or "very good"), "fair," and "poor" cannot be expected to coincide. However, a few conclusions seem to be pretty clearly indicated.

Regardless of sunshine and fresh air and all the health advantages that are claimed for rural and small town life (Sorokin, Zimmerman and Galpin, 1932), older people in small communities do get sick. In fact, evidence seems to point to more illness among rural aged than among their urban counterparts. Youmans (1963, p. 10), in comparing the findings of rural respondents with those in an urban area, reported that "for example, 71 percent of the rural men aged sixty to sixty-four reported that they were bothered by one or more health ailments. In contrast, only 49 percent of urban men in this age category reported ailments" and he concluded that "not only did rural persons assess their physical health as poorer than that of urban persons, but for the rural man, ill health appeared at an earlier age." He attributed the relatively high number of reported disabilities among rural men aged sixty to sixty-four to the ". . . greater demands of the rural environment as compared with the urban. Agricultural work requires considerable strength and agility." A study in Linn County, Iowa, classified as a metropolitan statistical area, found that respondents in the urban zone consistently rated themselves in better health than "did all respondents considered together." The health assessments of those residing in villages and small towns ranked between the urban and rural country assessments (Fuller et al., 1963, p. 15). Loomis and Beegle (1950, p. 760) conclude that "despite the natural advantages of rural life, in many respects rural people in the United States are less healthy than urban." Fewer aged persons in small communities assess their health as "poor" than as either "fair" or "good." In Marion County, 78 percent rated their health as either "good" or "fair." Of the eleven hundred respondents, the 22 percent who considered their health to be "poor" included residents of three nursing homes which accepted patients from within and outside the county who had serious chronic conditions. Some were unable to respond personally and others in a position to know responded for them. A Wyoming survey (Ruthmeyer, 1964) included 108 persons, of whom 60 per cent were living in communities designated as urban, and showed that 58.3 percent of the respondents considered their health to be good, 31.5 percent fair, and 10.2 percent poor. In a recent Missouri study (Pihlblad and Rosencranz, 1967, p. 26) of 1,716 noninstitutionalized persons in small towns with populations ranging from 250 to five thousand persons, 34.6 percent rated their health as good, 41.3 percent as fair and nearly 24.1 percent as poor.

Pihlblad and Rosencranz also show the correlations between the self-ratings of respondents and a variety of variables. High self-ratings were significantly related to income. "As income goes up, health was viewed more favorably by both men and women." Old Age Assistance recipients, particularly women, rated their health lower than did "non-welfare respondents."[1] A consistently strong correlation existed between the level of education and the self-rating: the higher the education, the more favorable the assessment of health. Contrary to common belief, illnesses did not seem to increase significantly with age. A greater percentage of persons eighty-five years and older rated their own health as good than did younger

[1] Most studies find a high correlation between health and income, usually explained on the basis of more regular visits to physicians which those with comfortable incomes can afford. Persons with higher incomes tend to enter hospitals in earlier stages of illness and therefore stay for shorter periods of time.

respondents. More females rated their health poor than did males.[2]

Youmans (1963) lists the ailments reported by persons sixty years and older. Heart trouble headed the list for men in small communities; arthritis for women. Problems of blood pressure and urological, digestive, and respiratory ailments ranked high. Other disabilities mentioned were those of the skeletal structure, vision, hearing, and "nervousness." Foot and throat troubles also appeared on the list.

According to the Bureau of Vital Statistics, United States Department of Health, Education and Welfare (1967), in 1966 the five illnesses that most frequently caused death for persons sixty-five to seventy-four were diseases of the heart, cancer, cerebral hemorrhage and other vascular lesions, influenza and pneumonia, and diabetes mellitus. Peerboom (1968, p. 7) noted that relatively more women than men are afflicted with rheumatoid arthritis, heart disease, hypertension, and diabetes. Broad classifications and medical diagnoses of physical illnesses are important for medical treatment and care, and also to provide a focus for education and research. Such work, however, is the responsibility of physicians, researchers, and administrators. For small-community social workers a perception of what the illness means to the patient is of much greater value. Sometimes arrangements for long-term personal care are necessary. In small communities relatives are likely to assume this responsibility. It may prove to be a long and strenuous task. Steve Baran, a doctoral student at the Heller School, Brandeis University, in a recently completed study of care of patients in their own homes, identified two types of helping relatives: one who organizes family members and friends to help care for the disabled patient, and one who does the dirty work herself. Both are needed; both are extremely important resources.

Social workers in small cities and rural areas need to be aware that illness and disability in old persons tend to become

[2] Genetic factors seem to be important in the case of persons who reach "very old" age. By the time a man or woman is eighty or more, whatever resistance to being considered old that may have followed retirement and other societal indices of old age have abated. Worries over health that may well have accompanied the first awareness of approaching old age should have subsided.

chronic; in 1965 more than 9,600,000 persons aged sixty-five-and-over were disabled from chronic heart disease, arthritis, mental disorders, and orthopedic impairments. The first realization that he has to learn to live with chronic disability and the effort of making the necessary adjustment to what promises to last for the rest of his life may be quite difficult for an old person. The understanding of family and friends and expressions of interest and concern that stop short of taking over the responsibilities that the patient himself can carry, will be of great help. Without such interest and support, the adjustment may be a very lonely experience, for it may mean that certain pleasures of a lifetime can never again be enjoyed and that a cherished independence is gone forever. The understanding of his family and friends, even after the first shock of learning of a permanent disability has subsided, may also be reassuring. More important than mere understanding is an awareness that the disabilities of old age, although chronic, are not always irreversible. Defective eyesight may be corrected, even though often only partially, with properly fitted glasses, or made less frustrating with a magnifying glass. Glaucoma may be checked by medication, and cataracts removed by surgery. Hearing deficiencies may be improved through surgery or with well-fitting hearing aids. Dentures may correct difficulties in eating. Someone to hold onto, when necessary, may help one unsteady on his feet and thus make walking possible and perhaps stimulate sluggish circulation. Walkers, canes, wheel-chairs, and special supports in bathrooms may make the difference between a person's being helpless or his being able to move about somewhat independently. Corns and toenails, the cause of frequent discomfort, may be trimmed. But corns and toenails reappear, especially when, because of poor vision or tremors, the old person himself cannot take care of them. Glasses, hearing aids, dentures, and special equipment all cost money, and need to be supplied by competent professional personnel who, in small communities, frequently are not accessible. Aids have a way of getting broken or out of line, or are misplaced and in numerous ways lose their usefulness—all relatively minor problems if there is money for examinations, new appliances, or repairs, and if the facilities for necessary services are available to the patient. Many persons postpone changing glasses, buying a hearing aid, getting dentures, or having them repaired for the simple reason that

either there is no money for such expenditures or they hesitate to
make inroads into small savings. They tend not to tell their children, the county welfare department, or some other agency that
might help, of their needs. The ill-fitting dentures continue to aggravate canker sores until in desperation they are removed entirely;
the dead hearing aid gets lost and the broken glasses are finally discarded. Walkers, canes, wheel-chairs and so forth are difficult to
come by in many small communities, and often have to be purchased because a loan service, such as exists in larger centers, may
not be available.

Even in the predominantly rural counties where hospital and
medical services are, relatively speaking, adequate, they may not be
readily available. A twenty-mile drive to a doctor's office is simple
when the roads are good. But that requires a car and a driver. Often
old people are physically unable to drive and, despite the fact that
many elderly women in rural areas do drive—even twin sisters of
ninety in one rural community were driving their own car—a large
number of farm and small town housewives, who are now in their
later years, have never learned to drive. If a son or daughter or a
daughter-in-law lives nearby and can perform the service, the parent is lucky. This was often the case in Holton and Marion County.
However many young people work outside the small community
and frequently are not on hand to perform personal services for
their parents. That leaves public transportation and neighbors. Most
small communities, and certainly outlying farms, do not have easy
access to buses and trains. Frequently, in Marion County, we were
told that: "The bus runs on the highway and stops on the edge
(of the village). I have no way to get to the bus and the only service to town (where the doctor is located) is late in the afternoon
and I cannot possibly make the trip in one day." Small towns generally do not have any commercial taxi service, and distances to bus
stops may be too far to walk. So the only resource is a neighbor or
friend. Many people attest to the fact that they have good neighbors. Invariably they will say: "I have the best neighbors in the
world." But: "When Bill or John or May can take me, my doctor
can't see me"; or "the doctor is very busy and I usually have to
wait quite a while. I can't ask Bill to wait that long." These are

some of the practical day-by-day problems of health that older people face. They surely do not exist because doctors in small communities do not care. Small-community doctors seem to work day and night seven days a week. Many are also willing to donate their services. In many communities, public welfare departments have stood by even before the Kerr-Mills, Medicaid, or Medicare programs. Yet the problems remain, and their solution is of the utmost importance for the large numbers of elderly persons in small communities.

The same delay and failure to get proper medical attention may be found even in cases of serious illnesses. A widow of eighty-eight, who was living alone and managing to exist on less than sixty dollars a month rather than make her needs known, finally confided that she had frequent dizzy spells and was painfully bruised from a number of falls. She had not sought medical help because she did not want to trouble her neighbors and she did not want to deplete her small savings. So she was living in constant fear that she would fall, be unable to call for help and perhaps suffer severe pain for many hours without being discovered.

One problem which plagues some older persons is that of thinking that they are properly insured against all kinds of health emergencies and finding, when the test comes, that they have not understood the conditions of their insurance policy. The policy may state very clearly, albeit sometimes in quite small print which the older person may be unable to read, that certain illnesses are not covered, or are excluded in certain circumstances. One couple who, in their late seventies, had invested a sizable portion of their small savings in an insurance policy to take care of all emergencies, discovered, when the wife had to be hospitalized for a recurrent illness, that the particular illness was excluded from the coverage. In a short time what remained of their savings was exhausted. Hopefully, now that Medicare is a reality, older adults in small communities, especially those with low and marginal incomes, will be served with a greater degree of certainty, promptness, and adequacy. There is no doubt, however, that a good many elderly patients, both in and out of hospitals and nursing homes, will require assistance in taking full advantage of the service (and the ever-present problem of transport). If they have to pay their own bills or a major share of them at the current cost per patient per day, even large savings will shrink rapidly.

The illustrations thus far have described conditions observed in villages, small towns, and on the farms in the Middle West. The situation becomes more serious when other sections of the country are considered, particularly the rural areas of the United States heavily populated by Negroes. The National Urban League (1964, p. 15) has pointed out that: "Negroes in this age group (65 and over) visit their physician an average of 4.6 times a year, but white people this age see their physicians an average of 6.9 times a year . . . what happens to the aged Negro who is ill or infirm and has no one to care for him? State after state has indicated in reports and other documents that, because there is literally no other place for them to go, chronically ill Negroes have been condemned to live out their lives in custodial care mental hospitals [pp. 15, 16]." Many ill Negroes are aided by their children, neighbors, and friends in getting necessary medical services. When this aid is not available, the plight of the ill, elderly Negro, particularly if he lives in rural areas largely populated by Negroes, is more serious than that of most whites.

Yet many old persons in small communities retain much residual good health, even though their functioning is limited. Some keep their good health with few apparent disabilities until they are very old.

Grandma Matson, for example, in her ninety-first year, lived alone in a small town and took care of herself. She told with great animation about the coming visit of her grandchildren from New York State. Two years before, she reported, these same grandchildren had visited her and she returned with them for a month's stay in their home. She said, "If they ask me, I will go again." They did. It was reported that she accompanied them, traveling the long distance by car. She returned home and still apparently felt spry and well. Several weeks later she died after a very brief illness. She had never known hospital care and seldom had had need for the services of a physician.

If more preventive and restorative health services could be made available in rural areas and small towns, and if there were more encouragement from others able to visualize the potential strengths that the aged, even when disabled, possess and could use, the number of Grandma Matsons and Jennie Roses would increase. Moreover, their contributions would be sizable and of importance to family and community.

Among the old, the mentally healthy far outnumber the mentally sick. (The criteria for good mental health, relatively speaking, include the ability to function day-by-day in a pretty adequate way as far as physical strength and resources permit, a continuing interest in life and living, and some concern for others as well as for oneself. (Some of the preoccupation with the mentally sick aged persons that is reflected in social work publications and in other literature, may be due to the evidence of mental illness in old patients in hospitals and in nursing homes—sources of a good many subjects for study. The concentration in institutions, no doubt, indicates inadequate provisions for the care of older patients in their own communities. These inadequacies may include undesirable housing arrangements, insufficient or nonexistent home care services, insufficient social contacts and, above all, unsatisfactory family relationships. It may also point to a lack of clinics and other local services which would enable patients to receive treatment in their own communities.

The reasons for mental illness are many and complex. The high correlation between psychiatric impairment and physical illness in older people has been well documented. That social factors also play a part is clear (Lowenthal, Berkman and associates, 1967). For some older patients mental illness represents organic brain pathology; for others, it is psychogenic in character. It may also be a combination of the two as Trier (1966) points out. Bookover (1964, p. 222) has described six classifications of older patients with mental disorders. Helping persons in a small community may become involved with an older patient fitting into any one of the six categories. However, the friend, neighbor, or other helper who is not specifically trained to cope with psychiatric illness will probably be able to contribute most to "those (patients) whose senescence is not complicated with any well defined physical and mental disorder but who are demoralized by having no role in life and who become invalids due to sociogenic and iatrogenic forces [p. 222]."

Whatever the origin and classification of the psychiatric illness of the older person, the social worker, friend, or neighbor needs to take cues for the ways in which they can help from the patient's doctor. He has the knowledge and skill to diagnose and prescribe treatment or to refer the patient to a specialist. The county welfare worker can make a genuine professional contribution in recognizing and dealing with some of the psychosituational factors that may cause or aggravate mental and emotional disorders. He especially is in a position to find potentials that can be stimulated and mobilized.

In a nursing home in a small town a perceptive administrator discovered that a resident, who was almost completely withdrawn and who spent her time in bed staring at the walls and ceiling, had earlier in life found pleasure in playing a harmonica. At first she had said very little. After a while she said nothing at all. She scarcely bothered to answer questions. The administrator brought a harmonica to her bed with the request: "Maggie, will you play a tune for me?" At first she looked at the harmonica. Then she gently stroked it. Finally, she began to play. Her face became animated. Other patients came into her room to listen. Maggie started to talk again.

In small communities it is possible, not only to aid in the restoration or partial restoration of mental health, but also to work toward the goal of an improved mental health atmosphere. This, just as do all efforts in promoting community service, involves the cooperation and coordination of other professionals in the community—doctors, ministers, teachers and others—and also requires the concern and understanding of members of the family, neighbors, and the community at large. It assuredly demands the use of capacities, or what remains of them, of old persons, and requires that the need to have an acceptable self-image and to give and receive affection can be met. For many mentally and emotionally disturbed older persons, such conditions do not prevail, or are limited.

Partly because mental illness can go undiagnosed and unreported, the total number of older people with psychiatric disorders is unknown. However, statistics of persons actually diagnosed and receiving care in psychiatric facilities give some hint of the total.

In 1964, in the United States, approximately two hundred seventy-seven thousand persons sixty-five and over received care in psychiatric facilities: fifteen out of every one thousand persons in the older age group (Rosen, Anderson and Bahn, 1967). If one includes the many obviously mentally ill patients in nursing homes, who are not classified as psychiatric cases, the total number indicated is indeed large. Small communities, small towns, and rural areas, as well as metropolitan sections of the United States, have plenty of reason for concern and need for appropriate action.

In neither Marion County nor in Holton were systematic efforts made to ascertain the number of persons sixty-five-and-over who were classified as mentally ill. General observations indicated that a substantial number in the various local institutional facilities were either seriously withdrawn or markedly hostile. When the local facilities no longer sufficed or the families of the patients were unable to cope with the situation, the patients usually went to a State hospital, but frequently remained there for a short time only. To make beds available for patients who can profit most from hospital treatment and to return patients who can profit most from residence outside a State hospital, many older patients were returned to their home communities. This situation, as well as the evidence of mental illness in younger age groups, led to discussions of the possibility of establishing a mental health clinic to serve three counties. Several years later such a clinic became a reality with the president of the county-wide organization of older people assuming major responsibility for the promotional activities in Marion County.

One small community study of the health of its aging citizens specifically tried, by self-ratings, to assess the state of mental health. The Pennsylvania study (Montgomery, 1965, pp. 11–14), attempted a self assessment of 508 subjects. Of this number, 37 percent rated their own mental health as good; 32 percent as fair, and 31 percent as poor. The findings indicated that more men than women considered their mental health to be good and a favorable socioeconomic status was significantly related to a positive mental health evaluation.

In Marion County especially we saw examples of creative activity that appeared to improve mental health. One patient who had spent some time in a mental hospital and who had been encouraged to work with ceramics had acquired genuine proficiency and skill. She took much pride in her workmanship, her designs, and her colors. Those who knew her best attributed much of her serenity and pleasure in living to her hobby. For one woman, her hobby seemed not only to restore positive mental health, but also to maintain it.

> I happened to meet Mrs. Carruth by accident—merely to ask directions. She invited me in. On that particular day, she was dressing dolls, a whole wedding party of them. Using discarded nylon hose from which she had extracted all the original color and which she had redyed in beautiful soft pastel shades, she fashioned dresses, coats, and even perfectly formed miniature corsages. She had painted the dolls' faces with water colors. The bride was beaming ecstatically, the mother was about to shed tears. Mischief was reflected in the little boy's face. With his cap on the back of his head, and one pant leg pulled up and the other down, he obviously represented a nuisance, a "Dennis the Menace" to his big sister. Mrs. Carruth explained how she became interested in her hobby. She and her husband were operating a grocery store which burned to the ground. Insurance covered only a small portion of the loss. Very shortly thereafter, and quite unexpectedly, their only son died of a heart attack. For Mrs. Carruth her "world went all to pieces." Then someone showed her how to make paper flowers. One experience led to another. Now she not only has a satisfying outlet for her artistic talents but also she is realizing a small income from her activities. She herself recognizes the greatest rewards of her efforts, "I give away most of what I make. I get so much pleasure from making other people happy, I have no time to think evil of anybody."

The fact that in Holton participation in community betterment projects made for higher morale would seem to indicate that such activity has the effect of maintaining good mental outlook and at times, no doubt, preventing breakdown. Lowenthal, Berkman, and associates (1967) did find that low morale or "demoralization does not inevitably precede mental illness [p. 259]."

Mental breakdown in older people, rural or urban, cannot be simply explained by the stereotyped notion that cognitive and affective deterioration are inherent in the aging process. Though no final conclusions have been reached to date, there is increasing evidence to refute the widely prevalent theory that both mind and body decrease in potential capacity as the individual grows older. Thumin and Boernke (1966, pp. 369–371), among others, throw doubts on the theory: their research, which focused on female job applicants, revealed ". . . somewhat surprising [results] in that the decrements which one generally expects with advancing age did not occur on four of the six ability tests: in fact, performance improved significantly on the tests of verbal comprehension and typing speed." In the light of current gerontological knowledge and our present awareness of the conditions of old persons in small communities, it would seem safe to conclude that intellectual capacities do not necessarily deteriorate and affective abilities are not necessarily stunted because of age. Their use and what remains of physical resources may do much to retain or restore mental health. Both creative and empathic expressions of potential would seem to be particularly useful in safeguarding a positive self-image, an essential element in good mental health.

FINANCIAL STATUS

Poor health, retirement, and reduced role and status, frequently, although not always, concomitants of the later years of life, tend to undermine the self-image of the aging. Usually accompanying them is a lowered income, which, along with other forces, presses down hard on the concept of importance and worth of self. A basic requirement of life is that one be able to live decently and to pay for essentials so that physical and psychological wants can be met. Lack of food and other comforts will cause ill health. The cost of illness will further reduce the financial resources of the individual and will lead to insecurity, worry and still more complications. The psychological effects, too, are many. In both rural and urban settings one's income and accumulated material possessions are important indices of one's success. What a man's money buys may be paraded as evidence of his status, and his position in life will be lowered when his income is reduced. Among the elderly are some who are rich enough to live, not merely well, but luxuriously. Some have summer and winter homes, travel extensively, own yachts

and other symbols of affluence. For most older Americans, and especially for those on farms, in villages, towns, and small cities, such
ways of life and the expenditures they entail are very much out of
the question.

Thanks to a network of legislative and administrative provisions, such as Medicaid, Medicare, Social Security benefits, and
Old Age Assistance, persons sixty-five and over in the United States
should fare better in the future, particularly the lower income group.
This does not mean, however, that many old people are no longer
poor: they are.

Medicaid (medical care, administered by states under Title
XIX of the Social Security legislation, for which persons of all
groups on Public Assistance and persons with low incomes who are
medically indigent are eligible) is available to persons sixty-five and
over when Medicare (a federal program of medical aid for persons
sixty-five and over) and other funds do not meet hospital, physicians', and other health fees. By the end of 1967 Medicare was paying hospital bills for five million persons and physicians' bills for
seven million. In 1967 Social Security payments amounted to $21.4
billion. For an aged, retired individual the average monthly grant
was $85; for a couple, $128. (The grants referred to here are those
made available to persons sixty-five and over through Old Age and
Survivors' Insurance. Employer, employee, and the federal government pay into the fund.) In 1967 two million persons sixty-five and
over received Old Age Assistance grants averaging $68 per person.
(Old Age or Public Assistance is administered according to need
from funds provided by federal, state, and local governments.) Another eighty-four thousand persons, a large number of whom were
over sixty-five, received Aid to the Blind, for which the average
grant was $87 (Peerboom, 1968, pp. 19–20).

The median income of families headed by persons sixty-five-
and-over was $3,928 a year in 1967. Of the 4,250,000 couples who
did not live on farms in 1966, two out of five had incomes of less than
$2,675 a year. Two out of three individuals sixty-five-years-and-over
who lived alone and not on farms had incomes of less than $1,900
annually (U.S., Senate, 1969a, pp. 8–10). For most older persons
residing on farms and in smaller communities incomes are consistently lower than in urban areas. Even ten years ago the per capita

income of the farm population, including that of persons engaged actively in agriculture and in other occupations, was less than half of the income of the total nonfarm population (Slocum, 1962, p. 164). In 1959 Youmans (1963, p. 6) found that, in Kentucky, among rural men of all ages the median incomes of the youngest and oldest were $1,104 and $668, respectively. At that same time, the median incomes of the youngest and oldest urban men of all ages were $3,333 and $1,339, respectively. In the entire United States the median income in 1966 for farm families headed by a person aged sixty-five-and-over was $2,989; for aged individuals without a family it was $1,354 (U.S., Senate, 1969b).

Variations exist among both rural and urban populations, but, except for a short period immediately following World War II, the average per capita income of the farm family has always been lower than of its nonfarm counterpart (Slocum, 1962, p. 164). Recently older persons have had lower incomes than younger persons. An increase in income between 1965 and 1968 for all persons residing outside institutions substantially decreased the number of persons with a yearly income below the established poverty line, which in 1966 denoted an annual income of less than $1,975 for a husband and wife; of less than $1,565 for a person living alone. Brotman (1968a) observes that increase of income for all age groups has not affected older people substantially. But the percentage of persons under sixty-five whose incomes were below the poverty line declined from 16 to 14 percent. During 1968, 9.3 percent of the total population who were not in institutions and 18.1 percent of the total population living below the poverty line were sixty-five years of age or older.

Old Age and Survivors Insurance benefits have become available to farmers at a much later date than to most nonagricultural workers. "Prior to the 1950 amendments of the Social Security Act, farmers could qualify for [Old Age and Survivors] insurance only by working off the farm. The 1950 revisions extended this coverage to approximately eight hundred fifty thousand agricultural workers. Amendments to the Social Security Laws in 1954 extended coverage to many groups of farmers not previously eligible and their families" (Loomis and Beegle, 1957, p. 394). Obviously, a good many persons now past seventy-five were retired before the new law was put into effect and consequently are not included in its benefits.

In rural communities, nonwhites particularly seem to have a hard time. Of all persons receiving less than $2,000 in 1966, 7.4 percent were white and 18.3 percent nonwhite (U.S., Bureau of the Census, 1969, p. 330). A study, made in Chickasaw County, Mississippi, to determine the impact upon a low-income, rural community of a new industrial plant illustrates the discrimination. Although 29 percent of the household heads in that community were nonwhite, none was employed in the newly established furniture factory (Wilber and Maitland, 1963).

Inflation affects old people everywhere. The usual stationary income of retirants simply does not buy what it did when it was set aside. The value of savings shrivels and the monthly dividend check buys less and less. One wag commented with much truth: "The nest egg has become chicken feed." With the purchasing value of the dollar decreasing and prices spiraling rapidly, the older person does not face the comfortable future that he anticipated. Increases in the Social Security grants and the government provisions for health care have helped, but they scarcely offset the loss in value of personal financial arrangements. Furthermore, as Kreps (1963, p. 209) points out, savings are expected to stretch over a much longer period of time than was true of an earlier era. A man of sixty has to make his accumulated savings last almost three times as long after he retires as had the man of sixty in 1900. The income of an older adult, urban and rural, white and nonwhite, has an enormous impact on his way of life. His food, his housing, his activities, his associations with others are all vitally affected. To a large extent his income determines how he lives, who his friends are, and what kind of a dwelling place he has.

HOUSING ARRANGEMENTS

Sooner or later old people must face decisions about their living arrangements: whether to remain in the home currently occupied and, perhaps, remodel it, or whether to move to a new abode. Their moving may mean building, buying, or renting more suitable quarters in the same or in another community; moving to an apartment, into the home of a middle-aged child, a grandchild, or some other member of the family; or arranging for someone to move in with them. It may mean their moving into a residence in a retirement village or in a low-cost government housing project, a personal care home, nursing home, hospital, or some other facility. If the aged person lives on a farm, the marriage of a daughter or new work opportunities for a son may necessitate a move of either the young family or of the grandparents. The aging father may find the farm work too heavy for his declining health, or the old couple may need health facilities to be more accessible. The move may be precipitated by chronic illness or by disabilities, such as decreasing vision, which make driving dangerous or impossible. Should a spouse die, it may be inadvisable for the widowed person to remain in the old home, with neighbors living some distance away. In villages, towns, and small cities, similar conditions prevail. Without commercial transport, banks, stores, doctors' offices, churches, and the like may be almost as inaccessible in small towns, if one is unable to drive a car, as they are in the open country.

Whatever the reason for moving, the results are likely to be markedly different from anything that the parents of the present generation of old people would have done. Then the parents often continued to live with their children. On the farm they sometimes built a second house for themselves or the children. At other times they bought or rented a place in a nearby town, leaving the children on the farm. If one parent were widowed the other might make his home with his children, or continue to live alone. When ill or disabled, he invariably was cared for by one of his children. Seldom did either consider the possibility of the old persons' moving into an institution. In fact, few institutions for old people were in existence. The few church homes had waiting lists and usually admitted only those without children. The very poor were admitted to the county poor farm when no other arrangements could be made. Some mentally disturbed parents were sent to the hospitals for the mentally ill, but only if their children could no longer cope. As a last resort, physically ill old people went to a hospital. However, it was generally accepted that they moved there to die. A move to an apartment or to a retirement village was almost unheard of. Conditions have changed. The rapid increase of institutional facilities in small communities for older people attests to the fact that more and more aging persons seek residence in an institution. However, even now, the percentage of older persons living in such facilities is relatively small. Of the 2,907,000 men and 4,211,000 women seventy-five-years-old and older in 1967, it was only 7 percent. Of the men, 75 percent lived in families, most of them with their wives. Twenty percent lived alone. Of the women, 60 percent lived in families, most of them in the home of a relative, and 33.3 percent lived alone (Brotman, 1968c).

Studies of the living arrangements of older people in small communities describe their housing in some detail. A survey by Cowles (1956) of Wisconsin showed that most older men and women continued to be able to live together, particularly in the earlier years of their old age. Thirty-seven percent were living with their children; 4.4 percent of the men and 11.5 percent of the women were living alone. Crowding was most critical among the eighty-three respondents who were living with a son or daughter. Typically, these were cases where the household included children, and often entailed lack of privacy for the grandparent and the rest of the family and caused various problems in family relationships and family finances.

Agan and Anderson (1961), in a study of fifteen Kansas counties, found 20 percent of the old persons who were interviewed living with children and grandchildren. Aging persons in towns of 2,500 or less and in the homes of children or grandchildren were, on the average, older than those living in one-generation households in the open country. Of the old persons living on farms 83 percent owned property; in towns, 80 percent owned property, usually the homes in which they lived.

Many of the town residents had retired from farms, and their housing was more satisfactory (for example, more homes had central heating) than that of respondents who either had always lived in the town or who continued to live on the farm. On the farm, heating stoves were generally the source of warmth; for old people with circulatory problems and cold feet, the resulting cold floors were, no doubt, uncomfortable. Largely because of rural electrification, 92 percent of the older persons living in the open country used electricity which not only provided light but also refrigeration and television.

A study (also of persons sixty-five and over) of another rural county in Wisconsin by Loeb, Pincus and Mueller (1963, pp. 14–15) found 21 percent of 905 respondents living alone, 389 or 42.9 percent with a spouse, and 20.4 percent with children, grandchildren, and other relatives. Six hundred nineteen persons possessed a home when they were interviewed, and another 195 had owned a home at one time in the past. Only 6 percent of the 905 had never owned their homes.

In both Marion County and in Holton, older people almost without exception seemed to prefer to live in the family home, despite the fact that often it was large and rambling and without the arrangements and conveniences designed to make life comfortable. Actually, the great emphasis in some quarters on arrangements and equipment specifically planned for old people did not seem to make much of an impression on older persons in the two communities, particularly on those of Marion County. If the shelf were out of reach, it simply became a depository for items never used. Homemade devices were invented for making equipment in bathrooms more easily and safely used. The large kitchen continued to require many steps, but somehow the old grandmother seemed able to manage them. Some persons, after moving into a well-organized and equipped apartment, thoroughly enjoyed the new dwelling, but generally expressed their appreciation only after they had actually lived there. When his residence no longer meets his needs, an old person's move to a new dwelling place is likely to be painful. Usually it means his giving up a house in which children and perhaps grandchildren have been reared and which has many cherished memories. Furniture, household items of all kinds, pictures, books, and other possessions may have taken on special meanings. They may have been acquired over a long period of time and as a result of much planning and effort. Usually the new dwelling has less space so many items have to be sold or discarded. If he moves to an institution, even a favorite chair or a picture may have to be sacrificed, and, if he is widowed or single, he may be obliged to share a room. For those who treasure privacy the adjustment may be difficult. The opportunity to entertain relatives and friends is missed, perhaps most of all.

Of all moves to other housing, the one most dreaded is that

to an institution. The older person who needs institutional care often resists leaving his own home in order to postpone the time when he is admitted to a "place within four walls." Sometimes, it seems, he hopes to be able to live with a son or daughter instead. Aging men and women may refer to the time when they themselves took care of their own parents. They dread the prospect of institutional care because some see it as the end of what little independence they have. Certainly, what remained of freedom is likely to vanish once a person is inside institutional walls. If the prospective admission is to a county home or hospital for the mentally ill, their youthful memory of and the stigma attached to going "over the hill to the poor house" or to the "insane asylum" may serve as a deterrent. Some may recall vividly the visits they made as children to old relatives in a county home or hospital for the mentally ill: the long hard benches, the separation of husband and wife, the drab walls, the institutional smells, the moanings and groanings of sick patients, or perhaps the laughter of the insane may stand out very clearly. Such memories may provoke resistance even to institutions with adequate programs, especially when the community and the children appear "not to care." Other arrangements to enable older people to stay in their own homes, such as hot delivered meals and handyman, home health and homemaker services, are still too new and often nonexistent in most small communities to be accepted, or even understood. The same is true of foster homes for the aging.

EDUCATION

Most of the older persons in Holton and in Marion County who assumed positions of community leadership had had a better than average formal education. This was less true of persons who were engaged in creative activities. The 100 taped interviews of the Holton study reflected a high priority accorded to formal education. Discussions of unsatisfied ambitions frequently included regrets about the limited educational opportunities available. In both communities the achievements in school of sons and daughters and of grandchildren were reported with pride. "Good marks" and "graduation" were the basis for much conversation. The alumni of a defunct college in Holton, who were now all in their later years of life, would look forward to their yearly celebration.

In 1967, the median school grade completed by persons sixty-five-years-old and older in the United States was 8.7 in metropolitan and 8.4 in rural areas (U.S. Bureau of the Census, 1968). In the past twenty years the educational gap between rural and urban residents has narrowed markedly for most age groups. In fact, in "some sections of the United States there is now little difference between farm and nonfarm people with respect to the percentage of school age children enrolled in school [Slocum, 1962, p. 164]." This, however, does not apply to persons who are now old. For the older man of today who in his youth lived on a farm or in a small town even high school education was hard to come by. For girls it was even harder. High schools tended to be situated in larger centers only, country roads were often impassable during winter, and the formal education of rural and small town youth was considered less important by the community than it is now. In many small communities formal education beyond the first eight grades was regarded as unnecessary and could not begin to compete with the value of hard work. The attitude affected girls and boys in both white and nonwhite families. The improvement seen today is largely found in families of farmers and nonfarm workers. For whites and nonwhites who are hired farm laborers, little has improved.

RELIGION

Whatever the physical, economic, or educational circumstances of an individual elderly adult may be, his religion, or lack of it, also plays an important role in his life. In Holton and in Marion County interest in and preoccupation with religion were evident. For example, in describing the activities of a typical day, many respondents in the Holton study referred to their daily Bible reading and to their listening to religious radio programs. Their description of a typical Sunday almost invariably included worship in church and very often attendance at Sunday School classes when they were physically able. In fact the importance and meaning of religious activities almost matched that of their relationships with their children. Informal visits with older persons in Marion County provoked similar responses. However, there were differences between communities in the county, both in number and kind of religious activities, and among individuals in the same community. Interest was manifested in many ways. As older people tried to interpret the meaning of their religious faith, variations from individual to individual were evident. For some, it provided a reason for accepting a difficult situation: "It is God's will." Others found in their religion courage for a renewal of effort to be more adequate in what they thought was their role: "God wants me to be useful or He would not let me continue to live." Some were preoccupied with the meaning of life and with their own place in it and seemed to seek an opportunity to discuss their concerns. Others talked about death and the hereafter. Clearly, for quite a number of elderly persons in both communities, religion seemed to be an integrating and stabilizing force. It should be added that in the realm of his religious faith the elderly person sometimes tended in his discussion to be cautious. He seemed to test out his listener. Many persons in Marion County and in Holton revealed a highly personal relationship to their God and their faith. It appeared to serve them well under many conditions, including times of bereavement. This was true regardless of their denominational affiliations.

To questions about their religious attitudes asked of 905 respondents in Wisconsin (Loeb, Pincus and Mueller, 1963, p. 63), 4.5 percent replied that "Religion is and has been the fulfillment of life for me." Another 38 percent responded in the affirmative to the two statements: "Religion is important to me" and "Religion is and should be important to everyone, including me, and has been of particular importance or help to me." To the statement that religion "is important when older, and particularly helpful in stressful situations" 9.8 percent replied positively. No information was received from 15.6 percent of the respondents. The remainder seemed less positive about the value of religion, with 11.7 percent (eighty-three men and twenty-three women) replying: "Religion means nothing to me."

A stereotyped notion that the elderly and old people sit in rocking chairs contemplating the end of life and what comes thereafter may not be justified. Death may be considered a highly personal matter and to share attitudes toward it may be difficult. It would not seem to be the kind of information that would be made readily available by systematic research. Nevertheless, some studies have been made and the results at this time would seem to indicate

that the old are less preoccupied with death than is commonly be-
lieved (Cumming and Henry, 1961, p. 71; Iowa Commission,
1960, p. 4; Parsons, 1962, p. 26), an indication well supported
by experiences in Holton and Marion County where old people did
talk about death but not much more than did persons of other ages.
Very few expressed fear of death. Religious pursuits in small communities, for many older people, not only produce spiritual satisfaction but also nurture social relationships. Opportunities to meet
friends and exchange news about one another and about mutual
acquaintances are important. Sympathy, support, pleasantries, encouragement, and jokes find expression and the older person experiences warmth and reassurance as he feels himself one of the
group. Unkind and thoughtless statements also are made from time
to time and critical attitudes are displayed. Even though a positive
feeling seemed definitely to predominate in both communities,
there was some evidence of harshness.

About the church as an institution and its meaning to older
people, it suffices to say that many of them referred to the importance of the church as a place of worship and spiritual benefit and
obviously found the church of value in their social lives as well.
Church buildings, both Protestant and Catholic, were used for
social and ecumenical gatherings. Church members visited invalid
old people, though often rather spasmodically. For years one man
with multiple sclerosis was provided daily with a hot meal in his
home. Some older people seemed apathetic about church activities
and some were critical. Miss Brown said, somewhat bitterly: "I was
always active in my church and, like my father before me, I always
contributed when I was able. Now that I am poor, and cannot
make donations, my church seems to have no use for me. Sometimes
not one member visits me for over a year and our minister [who
had been in town for two years] has never come to see me." Loeb,
Pincus, and Mueller (1963) concluded: "There is reason to believe
that many older people think the church neglects them. Only 30
percent of the population have been visited recently by a minister
[p. 74]." Regional, denominational, and individual differences, no
doubt, make for a variety of findings. However, needs of elderly
and old men and women in small communities that are not met
by the churches appear to be voiced frequently enough to pose

some genuine challenges for the members and ministers of rural, town, and small city churches. The facts that people constitute the church and that the members are the church would seem to need greater emphasis in small communities.

DEMOGRAPHY

Of the 18,796,000 persons sixty-five years and over in the United States on July 1, 1967, 8,101,000 were men, 10,695,000 were women. Whites numbered 17,327,000, nonwhites 1,469,000 (U.S. Bureau of Census, 1968). In 1968, 39.8 percent of the population aged sixty-five-and-over lived in nonmetropolitan areas (U.S., Senate, 1969b). The total number in that age group is increasing rapidly. Brotman (1968c) notes that at the beginning of the twentieth century every twenty-fifth American was sixty-five-and-over and present trends indicate that by 1990 "at least every tenth American will be sixty-five-plus [p. 4]." The differences in the numbers of men and women are continuing. The men aged sixty-five-years-and-older outnumbered women in 1900 but even then the sex ratio for seventy-five-years-and-over was 104 women to 100 men. According to Brotman's forecast (1967), in 1990 women seventy-five-and-over will outnumber men 170 to 100. At present the older age category represents 6.1 percent of the total nonwhite population, whereas the older group white and nonwhite comprises over 9 percent of the total population. As the economic, educational, and health conditions of nonwhites improve, a large increase in the number of persons sixty-five-and-over can be expected. In 1960 most persons sixty-five-and-over were living in Iowa, Missouri, Nebraska, Kansas, and Arkansas—all Midwestern states with relatively high rural and small town populations (*The Older American*, 1963). Of these states, Iowa ranked first, with 12 percent of its population being sixty-five years old and older. The states' averages, although high, scarcely pinpoint the marked concentration of older people in small communities. In Kansas, where the sixty-five-and-over population in 1960 was slightly over 11 percent of the total, one rural county with a total population of 3,048 persons had 21.3 percent in the sixty-five-and-over group. Twenty-five percent of Holton's 325 residents were over sixty-five.

Small communities have disproportionate numbers of old

people mainly because young people all over the United States have left the small communities, and because the elderly, in Florida and Arizona particularly, have moved into small towns in rural areas. In the twenty years between 1940 and 1960, the population of Mills County, Texas, declined by 44 percent. So many of those who left were between twenty and twenty-nine years old that more than half of the total population of the town was fifty to fifty-nine years old. The decreasing birthrate will make Mills County more than ever a county of elderly and old residents (U.S., Department of Agriculture, 1963, pp. 24–25).

In 1960, the median age of the United States' total population was 28.6 years for men and 30.4 years for women. For urban men the median age was 29.3 years, for urban women 31.3. The rural nonfarm man's median age was 26.0 and the woman's 27.5 years; the rural farm man's was 29.2 and the woman's 30 years (U.S. Bureau of the Census, 1960). Older persons in nonmetropolitan areas in 1966 numbered 7.3 million (Brotman, 1967), of which 10.7 percent represented nonfarm persons and 10.2 percent farm persons. Since 1960 the metropolitan population has grown, and the farm population has decreased. Brotman (1967) points to the fact that "for the older population, the areas that grew faster [since 1960] than the 13.5 percent increase in the total 65-plus population were the nonfarm portions of the suburbs around the central cities (24.4 percent increase) and the nonfarm portion of the nonmetropolitan areas (plus 14.5 percent)."

These statistics represent the old and not so old, in the United States, and many of them live in small communities. Each has his own capacities and limitations, each has his own way of dealing with life's opportunities and disappointments. On farms, in villages, towns, and small cities, these aging persons may have lost all purpose in living, or they may find satisfaction in pursuing old or new objectives and goals in life. Some become passive and resigned; others struggle valiantly to make life worthwhile. Some have physical disabilities and succumb to them; others mobilize what they have left and use the remnants of health and energy in surprisingly constructive ways. Some retain excellent health and remain mentally alert until they die; others become permanently disabled. How well the old person mobilizes what remains of his potential capacities is determined partly by his pattern for coping with what comes, a pattern that has been established throughout life, and partly by the pressures on the remnants of potential (Neugarten and associates, 1964). These pressures come in the form of pain, debilitating illness, sensory deterioration, and such vicissitudes of life as the loss of a mate, children, friends, income, home, and important human associates and valued material possessions. The use of potential strengths also depends on the opportunities available for discovering, mobilizing, and using them. Herein lies the challenge to members of an old person's family, friends, and others in the community, and particularly the social worker. If he can learn or sense what the capacities are, or how much of former abilities remains, and encourage and support their development, he may, as did the nursing home administrator, help people like Maggie find the harmonica that will enable them to talk again.

Families

4

The well-being of a family group or of individual persons may range all the way from excellent to poor. As a family the Johnsons found happiness; the Mertons did not. The ties in the one were strong, in the other weak. In each case a family image determined to a large extent the behavior of family members and their relationships to one another. The effects may be illustrated in a letter from Grandfather Johnson and an encounter with Ellen Merton.

Dear Mary:
  I certainly thank you for the good wishes on my ninetieth birthday . . .
  I had a wonderful celebration for my birthday, put on at Jane's. It was attended by all the children and grandchildren who could reach Jane's at one time, seventeen in all. They simply surged in on me, all at once. I was, of course, tremendously surprised and, I might say, flabbergasted.
  The crowd had never all been together at one time before, so the visiting continued all day. At noon there was a

69

luncheon, specially arranged, which was very good. I ate
my share.

There were many pictures taken during and following
the luncheon—black and white, color, slides, and a Polaroid
which are available a minute after exposure. . . . They
created a great amount of merriment. I think the one which
was of the most interest was that when I tried to blow out
ninety candles on a big cake all at once. That is preserved
as an especially interesting one. All in all, I think this was
the most interesting day of my life.

He continued with the activities of each of his four children and
their respective families. Pride is reflected in every sentence. When
he came to Malcolm, John's second boy, he added:

Malcolm is employed by the Australian government on a
wild animal survey where he will be for about a year. I
have always thought a lot of Malcolm. On my birthday he
sent me the following cablegram: "Birthday greetings to a
great grandpa from Australia on your ninetieth birthday.
Malcolm." I shall always keep this and cherish it as long as
I live.

John came for me by plane from Centerville where, as
you know, I live alone. I stayed with them for a couple of
months and then came to Jane's where I have been most of
the time since. I was, however, also at Bert's for ten days.

The Merton family—Ellen, her father, her stepmother, and
her grandmother—have, it would seem, little to keep them together.

Ellen came into the office and stood there. One might
have thought she was seventeen or eighteen years old instead of actually only fifteen. Her red hair was neatly done
up in braids. However, she wore heavy makeup, was care-
lessly dressed and seemed to make an effort to present an
image of "a woman of the world."

The social worker knew that Ellen had left home and she
was trying to find work and a place to live. She also knew
that several times Ellen had been summoned into Juvenile
Court, both for playing truant and on a charge of shoplift-
ing. Her father on these occasions appeared in her behalf,
but seemed to consider the responsibility of having her pa-
roled to him something of a burden. Several years ago the

grandmother came with the father. She seemed to have little sympathy for her granddaughter.

Hesitatingly and somewhat belligerently, Ellen responded to questions. Yes, she is trying to find work, but not just any kind of work. She wants to be treated decently, not shoved around and stepped on like when she was on that awful job at Mike's Cafe. No, she does not have a place to stay. She would like an apartment where she can be her own boss and have friends. But that would cost too much. But one thing is sure, she will never go home again, no, never! That she knows for sure. As long as her father lives with "that woman, Maggie" she will never set foot in his house again. Maggie, her stepmother, always accuses her of everything that goes wrong. She just keeps telling Ellen she is "rotten to the core."

Maggie came into the home two years ago. When she came in, Ellen's grandmother got out. Her grandmother did not want Ellen's father to marry Maggie and made a terrible scene when he told her that the marriage had already taken place. Ellen always knew what kind of a woman Maggie was. Even before Ellen's mother died, Maggie had her "clutches" on Dad. Ellen always was afraid that he would marry Maggie, just as he finally did. He would have done so sooner if Ellen's grandmother had not raised such a fuss.

Ellen was six when her mother died. Things were good with her mother in the home. Her grandmother kept house for the family until her father remarried. According to Ellen the grandmother is very strict and bossy. She even bosses Ellen's father.

Grandmother does not come to the home and Ellen does not visit her. Ellen is not even sure where grandmother lives. Ellen doesn't much care. Her grandmother never made a decent home for the family—not like the other girls have. Ellen recalled the occasions when she had left home before. She always returned when she could not find work. But never again! No, never will she go home again!

IMAGES

Family members have images of their own group; the community has a notion of what the family is like. The extent to which these images are in line with what individual members desire varies greatly. The Johnsons, no doubt, found theirs satisfying. Certainly the grandfather did. The family-image contributed to his own positive self-concept, and his children and grandchildren probably experienced similar benefits. Neither Ellen nor her grandmother is happy to be of the Merton family. Ellen's father and Maggie, too, may have reservations. As individual members no one in the family has much to gain from belonging to the group.

Family-images contribute to the unique family life styles and behavior patterns that, despite many modifications, continue through time (Weiss, 1962, pp. 111–114). They influence the behavior of individual members. Conversely, the way of life and characteristic behavior of family members result in family-images held in and out of the kinship group. Sentiments, values, and goals become integrated into family self-concepts and family behavior through verbal and written communication and through other forms of interaction. For the family of the ninety-year-old grandfather the integration of behavior and of affection, values and aspirations is such that a celebration is not just a commemoration of a birthday but of membership in the father's and grandfather's family. For each member the family-image has genuine value; it is positive in the eyes of all and, therefore, membership is treasured. Other families, too, who are acquainted with the relationships which exist think highly of the grandfather and his children and grandchildren.

The Mertons, by contrast, would seem to have very little to celebrate. The family-image is poor and the members do not find the family pattern useful. There is no pride in their identification with each other and little inclination to feel that "come what may, we, the Mertons, stick together." The values and goals of the family, both individually and as a group, are weakly integrated. There is disparity in what they may vaguely wish the family were like and what in reality it proves to be. Ellen apparently wants a home like that of other girls she knows, but the Mertons cannot offer it. The family pattern is predictable only in that it is sure not to offer an anchor to which its members can cling in time of trouble or a source of enthusiastic response when there are joys and achievements to be shared. It is unlikely that other families in the neighborhood place much confidence in the group.

The two families are moving in their own separate ways. The one has achieved a high degree of family unity and is confidently steering in the direction of continuing strong family ties.

Words and deeds of the other family reflect separateness and dis-
unity. Bitterness, jealousy and strife mar their relationships. They
are moving away from, rather than toward, the goal of greater
family self-fulfillment. Yet, whether recognized or not, each and
every Merton, including the grandmother, is finding hopes thwarted
without the support of the other members of the group. Bowman
(1964) suggests that "in a sense people do not live as individuals,
they live as members of a variety of clusters. The basic cluster of
which the individual is a member is the family [p. 9]."

Seventy-five to a hundred years ago the family-image in
small communities was of utmost concern. When all or most of the
family tended to live in one geographic area, when the neighbors
included uncles and aunts, cousins and second cousins, when one's
intimate friends lived close by, the community's assessment of the
activities and behavior of family groups, and their reputation generally were extremely important. Much of this attitude still exists in
rural areas and small towns, especially among older persons. Sometimes more effort seems to be made to protect the family-image than
to ensure the well-being of individual members. For example, Mr.
Brown's daughter lived in a small village where her husband was
employed as cashier in a bank. He was the only paid employee of
the bank and, as such, he was respected in the community. There
were three children: one about to enter college, a girl age twelve,
and a four-year-old boy. Her parents and an unmarried brother lived
on a farm. The husband and wife of the young family were having
marital problems, aggravated apparently by his occasional drinking
sprees with other men. This kind of behavior was accepted in the
town, but the aftermath tended to make him irritable and even
abusive at home. The wife had taken the first steps toward obtaining a divorce when her father intervened. She had contemplated
returning to her parents' home, but was forced to give up her plans
for a divorce when her father's intervention included his making
clear to her that she and her children could not live on the farm.
Apparently the chief concern of Mr. Brown, Sr. was that "in the
history of the Brown family" there had never been divorces. "We
are known as people who stick to their bargains." There was no
divorce and the Browns, no doubt, continued to be known as a
family who kept promises. Whether, from the point of view of the

welfare of all the members of the family, the decision was wise remains obscure.

If the family-image in the small community does not meet the standards of the residents, the family members, particularly the elderly and the children, may feel the effects of community disapproval in a special way. In school, church, and other groups, they may be slighted, either openly or covertly. For example, where public assistance is stigmatized the children of mothers receiving Aid to Families of Dependent Children and the old who are on Old Age Assistance may be the butt of unkind remarks and may be denied participation in cherished activities. They may be included with an air of benevolence and condescension which may hurt and irritate. Said one woman of seventy-eight: "I was always respected in town and my parents before me. But since I have had to take 'welfare' no one seems to have any time for me. They all think they are better than I am. If they do include me they have such a 'holier than thou' attitude that I can hardly bear it." Attempts to keep public assistance grants confidential have little effect in rural communities and small towns. Checks have to be cashed and the public welfare worker's car is identifiable, and is quite likely to cause the neighbors to conclude that the family in front of whose home it is parked "is on welfare." The family's stock goes down accordingly. Sometimes members of a family who consider the image held by others to be unfair may deliberately flaunt their "evil ways." "I just gave the neighbors something to holler about. They begrudge me my measly small welfare check and so on pay day I paraded down the street in a 'new' dress for all to see. They didn't know my sister sent it because it no longer fits her. The neighbors all think my son should provide for me. But he has his own family to support and doesn't make much. Anyhow he gives me a room in his home and that is all I can ask." Members who care about their family image, for whatever reason, have some potential for solidarity. It may be the motivation for presenting a united front. Among themselves they may disagree, but the importance of the approval of the neighbors may outweigh personal differences.

The self-concept and the assessment of the family by others in the community is closely related to the group's search for identity. The residents in Grandfather Johnson's home town, where his sons and daughter grew up and his wife had died about ten years earlier, accorded the family as a group a highly respected place. The children and grandchildren could take pride in being identified with the Johnsons. Conversely, it may be safely assumed that neither did the Mertons feel a family identity, at least not with any pride, nor did the community identify the family group as being able to assume a positive role toward its individual members or toward others in the community.

In the last decade, professional literature has increasingly attested to social workers' recurring awareness of the importance of understanding the social milieu in which persons as individuals and in groups grow and develop. The family as a functioning unit and the environment that it provides for its members has had particular attention. The family's strengths and weaknesses have been assessed. The effects of the family upon persons who come to social workers have been increasingly recognized, especially in the case of the child or the young adult. But the family unit will also affect the older person. Mrs. McGovern explains how she was affected by her family.

I was new in town and did not know her story. Her crutches were by her side. Her cheeks were round and rosy. A twinkle hovered about her eyes. Her very Scotch brogue left no doubt about her ancestry. We exchanged pleasantries. Then she pointed to her crutches and told her story. She was serious now.

"Two years ago it happened. I fell and broke my hip. An infection set in. They had to amputate my leg at my hip. I was in the hospital a long time. A woman over eighty does not heal fast. I wanted to die. What was there to live for? I knew I could never again be in my little cottage where my husband and I were happy for many years. The children understood. They are fine lads. You see, I have two, and they have good lasses. They said, 'Mother, you won't always have to stay in the hospital. You can go home sometime. You will learn to walk on crutches.' I did not believe them, but they were so kind and sweet, I just pretended. Then they took me home. After they had gone I just sat. After a while I cried—a long, hard cry. But then I said to myself, 'This cannot go on. I must learn to walk.' I did, but it took a long time. I tried not to let the children see me discouraged. They were so good. They brought in my food and they cleaned my house. Now I cook my own food. I can keep my house clean, too. I lay the crutches aside and crawl about on the floor and scrub. I can do most anything but climb a tree." Her chuckles shook her whole body.

In Holton and in Marion County many Mrs. McGoverns and Mr. Johnsons seemed to be a part of family groups. They received affection and support from their children and grandchildren and, in turn, they played a positive part in the family life. Grandmother Mertons were also in evidence, more in Marion County than in Holton, no doubt because in the former we came to know a more representative group of older people. In Holton the focus was on individuals who had answered a mail questionnaire, which tended to produce a sample of persons in good, or at least fair, health and, since the purpose of the project was to mobilize the resources of the aging for community service, of persons with more than a casual potential concern for other people. In both communities there were Grandmother Mertons who lived with their children and grandchildren and others who lived away from them. Some were demanding, critical, and irritating. Sometimes the old and the young family members seemed to be aware of the basis for unhappy relationships but to be unaware of the remedy. For example, a young man, who had always lived with his widowed mother, brought his new bride into the family home. His young wife found little opportunity to establish her identity as a housewife and later as a mother. The chairs had to remain exactly in their long-established place, and the household duties had to be carried on in their long-established manner. The young husband shrugged off the complaints of both his wife and his mother as being "nothing but differences between two females." When the daughter-in-law suggested changes, her mother-in-law wept and accused her of ingratitude. Yet when the situation was discussed with the social worker, the mother-in-law seemed clearly to appreciate her daughter-in-law's desire to establish her own home. Mothers at times have difficulty recognizing that their daughters have grown into mature women and that they have a right and capability to make a decision when, for example, "the baby has a cold." Some mothers continue to plan the meals and direct the household duties; sometimes a mother or mother-in-law may relate in detail how self-sufficient she was when a young wife and mother. This happens regardless of whether the home belongs to the parent or to the young nuclear family.

Old men, too, can be domineering and critical. They may not approve of the pattern of grocery shopping or of the arrangement for family credit. They may criticize the behavior of the grandchildren or the paternal permission to drive the family car. More serious than his querulousness may be the effects of a grandparent's invalidism on the family. One case, besides taking up much of the mother's energy and time, meant that the children had to be abnormally quiet and they could not bring home their friends when they wished. In other cases, a widowed daughter sacrificed her own health to take care of her father, a chronic invalid, and a single daughter gave up a cherished career to nurse her mother. Yet a nursing home seemed out of the question in both cases. The aged parent felt, or was thought to feel, that he or she should be personally cared for by one of the children, and anyway funds were inadequate. Usually both parents and children preferred to live separately, an arrangement that seemed to dilute some of the potential tensions. It was observed, however, that quite often when the parent was living alone, and especially when he was in poor health or became disabled, members of the younger family would encourage him to move into their own home—an action, no doubt, ordinarily motivated by genuine concern for the parent's welfare, but at times perhaps by fear of condemnation by other relatives or friends in the community.

Burgess and Locke (1945) describe the family as a "group of persons united by the ties of marriage, blood or adoption, constituting a single household; interacting and communicating with each other in their respective social roles of husband and wife, mother and father, son and daughter, brother and sister; and creating and maintaining a common culture [p. 8]." A family group that serves its members well, as each one pursues his own and common familial concerns—loving, playing, learning, teaching, worshiping, dating, marrying, working, dying, all the experiences that involve the support, approval, and sometimes disapproval, of others in the kinship group—has in its image a guide for the behavior of all those who belong to it. In some ways every family concept is unique to a particular group, or at least to families in one neighborhood or community. In other ways it is like all family concepts of all families of a larger society. Individual family images may be challenged and altered by changes in the community and in the familial institution.

A distinction is being made between *a* family as a small group and *the* family as a social institution. According to Bierstedt (1963), *a* family is an associational group with all the dimensions of an association: "consciousness of kind, social interaction, and social organization" (p. 347). Each one of the elements of social organization is present: "a specific function or purpose, associational norms, associational statuses, authority, tests of membership, property, and a name or identifying symbols" (p. 280). Anyone's family is a group or unit of which the elderly person and every other member is a part. *The* family, as, for example, Mead (1948, pp. 453–459) views the present American family, is a way of life, or a crystallized pattern of choice of mate, marriage ceremony, kinship, social role and status, system of norms, values and sentiments, plan of household management, and other accepted ways of feeling, thinking, and doing. These accepted ways represent traditional modes of behavior and, to some extent, apply to families in large and small communities, to upper, middle and lower class families, and to families in apartments and in ranch houses. Yet in their details, these ways of life may not fit any one family. *A* family is a part of the familial institutional pattern of a community or of a society, but one family or kinship group is not *the* family institution. *A* family is a cluster of persons similar to, and yet different from, any other family.

FAMILY AS A SOCIAL INSTITUTION

For years much was written about the early history of the American family, which most of the time was described as predominantly preindustrial. It was broadly delineated as an extended family with the older generation living in the same dwelling with the young members, usually with other kinfolk as well. When the relatives did not live in the same home, they often lived in the neighborhood. This type of extended family has been repeatedly described as having gradually been transformed into a nuclear structure, that is, changed into a group that consists only of the parents and their children. This particular analysis has recently been challenged. Kent (1965, pp. 51–56) has pointed out that even in the very earliest period in our history, young people left their parents in the old country and came to America to establish a new family, quite separate from their families of orientation.[1] The same thing happened when the young couple moved further west and the parents were left at home in the eastern part of the country. In other words, in American life the nuclear family living separately from other members of the extended family is not a new phenomenon. Litwak (1960a,b) was among the first to suggest that a new type of extended family is emerging. In studying families in a housing project in Buffalo (the respondents included 920 housewives) he found that, even though members of the older generation did not live with the younger parents and their children, there was much communication with them and in many instances a close relationship. The extensive research of Shanas (1961, 1962) supports and elaborates Litwak's findings. Her data would seem to indicate that children keep in close touch with their parents even though they may not live under the same roof. She also discovered that a good many of the older and younger generations, even today, live together, and that when they do not, at least one child often lives near the parents. Her findings apply to the entire population of the United States regardless of community size.

In both Marion County and Holton we found evidence of such threads of kinship, marriage, and association. Middle-aged children referred frequently to their parents, and vice versa; much was said about grandchildren, great-grandchildren, and, occasionally, even great-great-grandchildren. Most of the comments reflected interest, pride or concern. Ninety-year-old Mrs. Matson who was visited by her grandchildren and, in turn, visited them on the East coast, talked often of her big family. She even remembered the names, ages, and birthdays of two great-great-grandchildren. The local papers of both communities abounded in reports of family gatherings. In summer, family picnics, with sometimes more than a

---

[1] Families of orientation are the nuclear families of the parents of the husband and wife, the families in which the husband and wife grew up.

hundred attending, were common. Distances in both communities often prohibited all but occasional visits. Even long distance telephone calls were too expensive for many. One mother, for example, confided that except on very special occasions she could not telephone her daughter who lived on a farm in the same county: the twenty-cent charge that was added to her monthly bill was too much. But she and her daughter could and did write. In fact, one mother said she preferred receiving letters to long distance calls because she could reread the letters. Correspondence with relatives seemed to occupy much of the older people's time, particularly for the women. Letters and photographs were treasured and shown. Visits from children or grandchildren were the topics of much planning and conversation beforehand. A visit from other relatives was often discussed in great detail afterwards.

Thus, the extended family continues to exist, in a modified form. Since originally it was largely a preindustrial phenomenon and thrived in an agricultural society, one might well expect to see clear remnants of the earlier pattern in a small community: one did. In certain farming neighborhoods earlier patterns were very marked. For example, in one Slavic farming community, in which very few persons who were born in Europe are still living, it is possible to see an old grandfather make decisions about the crops to be planted and the farm machinery to be purchased, despite the fact that a son does all the work. In several families the oldest son was reported to be the heir apparent to the family property and responsibilities of the aged father. Until he died, however, even when the son had married and had children, the old grandfather remained the undisputed decision-maker. Thus, in varying forms, the current small-community family retains characteristics of the earlier European extended family. Persons related by blood are likely to keep in touch with one another through three or four generations. Brothers and sisters and even cousins communicate with each other. Three generations or unmarried brothers and sisters may share the same residence. However, the practice of old and young families living together in the same household is no longer as common as it was. It usually occurs, at least in Holton and Marion County, when an elderly parent becomes ill or disabled and is unable, or thought to be unable, to care for himself.

Basic remaining features of the extended family (such as the kin's being included in the recognized membership of a family related by blood and marriage and the determination of who may live together, especially in time of need) pertain not only to the family structure but also to the expected activities, functions and responsibilities of the members. Major changes have taken place in these functions, even in small communities, and sociologists for at least four decades have studied the changes (Ogburn and Tibbitts, 1933, Ch. 13; Groves, 1940). Important responsibilities and activities of the family group such as health services, protection, education, recreation, economic production, religious activities, and other functions that formerly lodged almost exclusively within the family home and on the farm, are now shared by community agencies.

In the present trend toward shared function, the family in small communities definitely continues to maintain the responsibility of being a unit through which other institutions and organizations operate. The family encourages or discourages its members to use services offered by community agencies. This responsibility assumed by the family is a dynamic force in the community as evidenced by the approach of Agricultural Extension workers to rural families. Recognizing that a farmer is not likely to adopt new farm practices until his wife has also accepted the need for change and that a woman will not consider new ideas in household improvements until her husband approves, the Agricultural Extension Service initiated the Farm and Home Development Program by which the husband and wife are now consulted together. Some salesmen of farm commodities use a similar approach for the same reason (Rogers, 1960).

Regardless of the size of the community, the family has always had an important role in socializing its members. Families on farms, in villages and small towns have a greater effect on the social activities of their members than do their counterparts in large centers. The family traditionally has been and still is the source of important values and goals. It is the family that transmits the societal folkways and mores, helps to establish individual patterns of behavior toward other persons and groups, nurtures and limits the development of the capacities of family members to give and receive affection, and promotes or hinders patterns of dependency, patterns that play a mighty big part in the adjustments that have to be made to old age (Goldfarb, 1965, pp. 10–45).

CHANGES IN RURAL LIFE

The degree to which the earlier institutional structure and function of the family persists varies greatly in a community, as does the extent to which old and new patterns merge. The transition occurs at different speeds and the family's acceptance of and resistance to new patterns differ. That changes affecting the whole institutional structure and the family's traditional and customary activities would create tensions and strains among its members would seem inevitable. Social changes will benefit some members of society and hurt others. In the transition of the family to a youth-centered institution, the older generation has paid a price in the loss of role and status. This has affected its self-esteem and purpose in life.

The effects on the whole family and on its individual members are more clearly evident and understood when certain other major community changes are kept in mind. New inventions and methods of farming have reduced drudgery and introduced formerly unheard of living comforts. Scientific farming, specialization and expensive machinery, labor saving devices, the greatly increased cost of production and the subsequent threat to the small family farm have played havoc with many of the duties performed earlier by the aged and by children. The grain cradle, hand rake, and one-horse plow have vanished and with them the elderly men and women, and the children who used to work in the fields and around the barns. Work horses and mules no longer have to be fed and cared for and the hoe does not have to be wielded. There is no further need for the elderly parent or uncle or aunt to tie the bundles of grain cradled by the farmer. Other chores, such as feeding chickens, slopping pigs, churning butter by hand, and turning the handle of the washing machine, have also ceased to be a part of rural and small town family life. Factory-made clothing supplants in large part dresses and shirts made from yard goods bought at country stores. If there are gardens, the peas and lima beans are likely to be hulled by gadgets. This leaves the aged men and women of the farm and village without their former duties (Wilkening, 1964, pp.

1–17). As folk beliefs and practical experience have been super-
seded by scientific knowledge the young graduates of agricultural
courses taught in colleges and even in high schools have learned
more about producing abundant good quality crops or breeding
marketable livestock than had their granddads through many years
of experience. Hence, the grandfather may no longer manage the
farm and his advice is no longer sought. Similarly, the grandmother's experience in gardening, preserving food, raising chickens, and
sewing has been supplanted by new and modern ways of living.
Residents of small towns and villages were and are so closely associated with farm life that the change for them is about the same
as it is for persons living on the farm. Taylor *et al.* (1949, pp. 522–
523) describe fourteen trends of change taking place in agriculture.

Unless the older person has accumulated enough money to
be useful to younger members of the family, the hard truth to be
faced by the aging parent, both on the farm and in town, is that
few economic advantages result from his presence in the home of
his middle-aged children or, for that matter, anywhere else. One
major exception found in Holton and Marion County was the situation of a grandmother, sometimes both grandparents, who cared
for the children so that their mother could go out to work. Motiva-
tions for the interest and concern of the rest of the family are hard
to assess. However, from observations in a variety of small communities, the conclusion that most adult children genuinely care about
their parents, regardless of financial considerations, seems justified.
That does not mean, however, that when financial aid or personal
service is extended, some children may not consider their role a benevolent one, an attitude reflected in the terminology used in referring to financial aid and services to aged relatives by members of
the family or by the community through its variety of programs.
Frequently, the service is referred to as being either "for" or "to"
the aged person. The assistance usually is necessary and the source
of help appropriate. However, the philosophy underlying aid to
elderly persons, on either an individual or a community basis, might
well be "by," "of," or at least "with" the older person. Then, too,
as long as one hears in small communities comments such as: "Old
people are just like small children," and can observe treatment governed by this attitude, with the potential contributions of the old

people completely ignored, the chances are that the elderly may tend to behave accordingly.

In fairness to middle-aged children of aged parents, general observations would lead one to conclude that many adult sons and daughters seem to have reached a high state of "filial maturity," that is, they have become really adult, ". . . with a new role and a different love, seeing him [the old parent] for the first time as an individual with his own rights, needs, limitations, and a life history that, to a large extent, made him the person he is long before his child existed" (Blenkner, 1965, p. 58). The parent who himself is also mature, and whose relationships with his children are good is indeed fortunate. If financial help or personal service is rendered, the attitude will not be condescending. Moreover, such sons and daughters are capable of giving the emotional support that is necessary in crises, such as when illness strikes, the marital partner dies, or the parent becomes blind, deaf, or physically crippled. However, even under favorable circumstances, the aged parent, particularly the father, may have his moments of feeling useless, inadequate and even rejected, if not by his children then by his community. After all, his memories remain, memories of the productive role of his own parents and grandparents and of his own satisfaction in his hard work, particularly if he managed a farm or small business or had a position of authority and responsibility.

Literature on the aged often refers to their loss of family status. The change is attributed not only directly to their loss of a productive economic role because of ill health or retirement, but also to the less prominent part they have in family decisions of all kinds (Burgess, 1960). On farms, even while the father is still working, sons and daughters when old enough to be gainfully employed, much more often than not find work elsewhere. The farmer's wife in these days of specialization on family farms and with her household tasks reduced, may work in a nearby town. In 1958, 26 percent of the women on farms in the United States were gainfully employed outside the home; in 1950, 17 percent (Rogers, 1960, p. 167). Hence, the family members are no longer part of the farm operations as they were at the beginning of the century. In towns and small communities, even more frequently than in the open country, children and mothers find employment outside of the home. All of this means that old men on farms or in small towns, who have lost the role of decision-maker more recently than have their metropolitan counterparts, may feel more keenly the lowered esteem in which they are held. To them it may mean evidence of inadequacy as fathers, husbands, providers, and citizens of the community. Cumming (1964), who analyzes the disengagement of the aging individual from the positions he has held in the past and the parts he played in those positions, defines instrumental roles in any given social system as "those primarily concerned with active adaptation to the world outside the system during the pursuit of system goals . . . socio-emotional roles are concerned with the inner integration of the social system and the maintenance of the value patterns that reform the goals [p. 11]."

This interpretation of changes in roles with advancing age from "instrumental" to "socio-emotional" fits the small community older man exceedingly well. Traditionally his chief responsibility was to cope with the forces of the "outside world." This coping produced the cash that supported the group and provided other security as well. With it came influence and authority. In contrast, his wife on the farm, town, or small city nurtured affectional and other family ties, and saw to it that value patterns were adhered to and family goals pursued or changed as the situation required. Thus in her old age, unless perhaps she was also gainfully employed, she faces few changes in her roles, whereas her aging husband faces many, and seldom do they improve his status.

New and constantly improved transport and communication facilities have significantly affected small communities. Many persons now in their late sixties, seventies, eighties and nineties can remember facilities that were introduced in their own families and that have become obsolete in their own lifetime. For example, the covered carriage, which replaced the open farm or spring wagon, was introduced to and disappeared from small communities in the space of a lifetime. The aged remember the introduction of the telephone and rural free delivery service of newspapers and magazines, mail order catalogs and other advertising material. Automobiles, air mail, radio, television, and rural electrification appeared on the scene. As a result of today's new conveniences every aspect of family life is different from what it was in the early youth of today's old

people. The introduction of members of a small-community family
to the material and nonmaterial culture of metropolitan areas must
have produced some of the most significant differences. In retrospect, the very rapid changes that have resulted are more visible to
old persons than to their children and grandchildren and the impact
may be deeper. The many changes in small communities that are
affecting older residents today could be described in much greater
detail. What has been said is sufficient to present a glimpse of why
old people of today may face problems that have grown out of tran-
sitions in American society. Even though not limited to rural areas
and small towns, these problems may be more poignantly felt there
than in large cities.

FAMILY LIFE

It is within the changed and changing farm and small town
community that, some fifty or more years ago, a family unit of persons now old had its origins. Later families of their children and
more recently of their children's children emerged and developed.
In every decade, the families emerged in terms of existing values
and ways of life. Modern transport and communication facilities
permitted interaction of persons now old with the familial institution in transition and with other forces both in the community and
in the larger society as well (Nye and Berardo, 1966, pp. 97–
129). Out of the interaction of forces within and without the kinship group, emerged family norms and values, hopes and expectations, roles and status structure, affectional ties and degrees of family
solidarity. As in the cases of the Johnsons and Mertons, family life
styles and characteristic ways of coping with the ups and downs of
life, good and bad, evolved. The family pattern became the basis
for the manner in which members of each generation viewed their
kinship group and the way in which others viewed them. The
family image provided goals and aspirations and served as guides
to family behavior. Some aspirations and goals were limited; others
were equal to the potential capacities of the family members. All
the families that emerged during the same period and in the same
community had much in common and much that differed. Each
family had potentials for creative, empathic growth toward greater
family self fulfillment; all had some decrements, and probably no

two families originating five or six decades ago in the same measure or in the same balance.

As reflected in the example of the several Slavic families described earlier, the communication and interaction that fashioned the three-generational families now residing in small communities vary in different cultures and, within the same culture, in different generations. They also vary in the different life cycles of an individual nuclear family and of the whole kinship group. A family group, both nuclear and extended, differs from all other clusters of people identified as a group, in a number of significant ways. It is bound by blood and marriage. The marriage ties may be severed by divorce, and other personal ties by separation or in other ways, but the blood ties are permanent: biological heritage cannot be eliminated. Membership, unlike that in most other groups in our society, is completely involuntary except for the husband and wife, who had a choice of marital partners. Even membership through adoption is conferred without the child's consent. Communication among peers is precluded by the wide disparity in age, even in a nuclear family and certainly in a three- or four-generational family. Sex and age, statuses and roles of the various members all produce differences.

A family unit is often referred to as a primary group—in the manner conceived many years ago by Cooley (1929, Ch. 3), in which the contacts are intimate and face to face. The same is true of some other small groups. However, the communication in other groups is seldom as intimate as in families, nor as personal; neither is the relationship sustained for as long a period of time. People who live in close proximity and share as many personal experiences as families on farms and in villages normally do, develop definite patterns of communication and interaction. Given a similar circumstance, the response and forms of response—replies, gestures, words, silences, chuckles, tones of voice, and so forth—can be anticipated. One man recalled: "When mother yelled, we paid little attention; when her voice got lower and lower, we stopped to listen." The pattern is likely to become so well established that the whole interaction process, including the outcome, can often be predicted. This may make family living monotonous, but it contributes to the comfortableness, security and stability of the individual's life. It becomes an integral, continuous part of the family style of communication. The affectional ties that emerge and are nurtured in intimate and personal interaction cement a family together. Those ties may be weak or strong; predominantly warm and loving or intermingled with hostility. That old members can pursue goals in their own best interests when the affectional ties of a family are strong is illustrated in the story of Mrs. McGovern and in the letter from Grandfather Johnson. The interaction of the members provided support and stimulation. The older generation can also strengthen and support the younger members of a kinship group as was shown by the account of Mr. and Mrs. Osborn.

Both family images and family interactional patterns have, as well as continuity and durability, variations and changes, evident at different periods in the life span of a kinship group. Interaction in terms of family self-concepts begins before a nuclear family is established. In the choice of mate and before the marriage ceremony, the positions and responsibilities of husband and wife are beginning to be defined in terms of images based on patterns of both families of orientation, on knowledge of the ways of life of other families, and on the images accepted in the community. Expectations are likely to be shared and values and goals tested; common attitudes and aspirations are discovered and agreed upon.

After the marriage ceremony, new responsibilities and experiences develop. Positions and roles are redefined and probably modified. With the advent of children, more changes occur both in the kind of communication between husband and wife and in what is conveyed, and in their relationships as parents. Husband and wife acquire images of themselves as mates, as parents, and as family members in their kinship group and in the larger community. In the meantime, the children, largely through interaction with their parents, with one another and later in play groups and in school, also develop norms, values and positions in the family with the expected and attendant behavior patterns. Their values and positions are reinforced or modified through contacts with other cultural carriers, such as television, church, school, and 4-H clubs. In the process, perceptions are formed of how the children see themselves, what they are, how they behave or should behave, and how they think others view them. The process of being and becoming continues as the children grow to be teen-agers, go off to college or to work and then, as young adults, establish their own family groups.

Interaction between adult and growing children and the aging parents and grandparents continues throughout the life spans of the members. It changes as the family and other forces in the community change, and as the intergenerational group reaches different stages of maturity, not just of physical growth and strength, or of intellectual development, but also of empathic capacity. A child plays more and works less, a middle-aged parent plays less and works more, and an aged person may play either more or less depending upon his physical condition and his work habits. The child gradually leans less upon his parents for physical and economic support and protection and in many ways, though not necessarily in every way, the grandparent, if he lives long enough, becomes more dependent upon his middle-aged child. What is needed in the way of affection and what an individual member is capable of giving is not necessarily a matter of chronological age. The fourth-grader, Manuel (a language barrier may account for his poor English) had a storehouse of affection as may be seen in a letter he wrote to a Midwest social welfare agency:

> Dear Case Worker:
> I am 11 I go to school to Lawfetete grade school I am in the 4 grade.
> Of all the things I wanted most for Xmos was a grandmother. Eddie my friend lives across the street has one so has Johnnie & I go some times with them but its not like having one of my really own. Please find me a grandmother.
> My mother never had no family her folks died when she was 2. My father has no family. I got a dog a pet squarril. My pet lezard died. I could make her lots of things. I could visit her or even push her wheel chair, or she could visit me. My mom has a car. I feel sad when Johnnie talks about his grandmother all the time & I don't have any So today in Sonday School I told my teacher & she gave me this address to write to.
> Please send me a grandmother its all right with my mom. I am ½ Indian and ½ Spanish my father is a policeman I have a big sister May who is 16 My big brother is in the Mariens—he's a doctor. I have a baby sister who is 5 she

bothers me all the time to play dolls with her I promise club
scouts honor to be good to her. Im not to pretty My hair is
light Brown I have black eyes and I sure like to play Base-
ball I played last year and I like to fight to. Well that is all
I can thank to write about myself I hope I pass the adopa-
lionins. I don't know how to Spell that Word. It means to
adopt some one I just hope I pass & can get a grandmother
to love. Thank you.

Your friend,
Manuel

Many grandparents, too, notwithstanding their lack of physical strength and failing memories, have a great capacity for loving
and being loved. They and the Manuels should get together. As
old people may have to take increased financial support and physical care from their adult children, they may be able to reciprocate
with a large measure of unselfish affection—that is, if they themselves and their middle-aged children have resolved some of their
own conflicts of independence and dependence. Then giving and
taking can be mutually very satisfying.

Parsons' theory (1953, pp. 92–128) that the extended family as an institution, including its intergenerational communication,
does not meet the requirements of occupational and geographic
mobility in an industrial society was challenged in a number of empirical findings and, on theoretical grounds, was questioned by Litwak (1960a). Yet, as Litwak himself observed, occupational mobility tends to include changes in social status. If the social status
of the young man as he advances in his job increases, and that of
the old man remains stationary or is lowered, potential tensions may
arise. In the new situation, the elderly of today, who have always
lived on farms or in small towns, may feel less comfortable than do
their urban counterparts if their visit to the son's or son-in-law's
home should coincide with the boss' coming for dinner. Parsons'
theory that our present industrial society, which calls for geographic
and occupational mobility and accompanying changes in status, fa-
vors a nuclear family system may well be valid. However, despite
tensions that may be created in such situations, communication between members of the larger kinship group continues and the extended family, even though in modified form, remains as an integral
part of American culture.

In communication between a family group with other families of the same or different kinship groups, the interactional process lacks the close personal association and intimacy to be found in the immediate family. However, rural neighborhoods, small towns and villages often give evidence of much personal contact, affection and emotion. The tragedies and joys of one family group are likely to be shared by other families, though one may also find indifference, strife, and conflicts so pervasive that what happens to any one family may be of little concern to others. The quantity and quality of communication between neighbors vary greatly in different communities. In the vicinity of Holton two small villages of the same size presented very different patterns of relationships and mutual aid. In the one, the people were said to enjoy one another's company and to linger over their coffee in the local cafe. Financial difficulties, breakdown of parent-child relationships, illness, death or some other tragedy became the concern of neighbors and friends, and aid was prompt and sure. In the other community, the owner was said to encourage customers to leave the cafe. People did not seem to care what happened to others. The researchers could find no reason for the contrast. Attempts to attribute the indifference of the second community to its many natural calamities, such as fire and floods, seemed pointless when it was found that in one of the Marion County towns in which major tragedies had occurred, the residents had responded with marked compassion and desire to help. In some small communities one may still find residues of other patterns of mutual aid, such as neighbors getting together to bale hay or drive cattle to market. A neighbor may nurse a sick friend, or stay overnight with a family recently bereaved. However, with more and more reliance on farm machines and upon factory produced articles, and with the much greater use of hospitals and mortuaries, these reasons for contacts have greatly declined (Slocum, 1962, pp. 247–250).

The virtual disappearance from rural communities of the local country school, which often served as a neighborhood center, has also reduced the contacts between small-community people as family groups. In one rural neighborhood less than twenty years ago, the one-room schoolhouse was the center for neighborhood family activities. Friday nights were designated "family nights" on which two families would usually "take turns" together and pool their talents and give performances ranging from harmonica quartets to plays in which parents and children took part. Grandparents were always present in the audience, often coming from nearby towns. The events elicited much response; fun and satisfaction were derived from what, for them, were creative efforts. Today, some of these family activities may continue in farm organizations and small-community churches. However, the trend is for them to take on greater educational overtones, and even when the purpose is primarily social, the programs tend more and more to be planned by professionals.

The content of communication with women and between women of a few decades ago differed from that of small-community women of today. There was little concern with the scientific way of growing flowers, or with principles of artistic floral arrangement, balanced menus, the theories about child care, or other topics of similar intellectual quality, which are currently often subjects for discussion. The woman was respected as housewife and mother if her activities were accompanied by orderliness and cleanliness. She was expected to be a good neighbor and friend and, when needed, to help with the work on the farm or with the business in the small town.

In the Midwest the business of farming has changed. Now farms may be quite large, consisting of both the family farm owned earlier by deceased or retired parents and, in order to make the enterprise pay, of a number of rented farms. The farm operator may also be a tenant. Corporation farms, too, increasingly affect small communities. A corporation farm, like any other corporate enterprise, has a board of directors and a manager, who may or may not reside on the farm. According to the policies of the board, the manager employs hired men or tenants or both. Most corporation farms, sometimes called "factories in the fields," produce specialty crops, such as wheat, sugar beets, potatoes, and cotton (Loomis and Beegle, 1957, p. 153). The standard of living of the manager and his family, whether he lives in the open country or in town, is likely to be higher than that of other residents. In contrast, that of the farm laborer is definitely low and has not kept pace with other employment categories in small communities. Many laborers on corporation farms have seasonal work and their incomes are uncertain. The life of the itinerant seasonal farmhand and his family is well known to county welfare workers in small communities. Traveling in old cars that have a way of breaking down, the family is often stranded without money for repairs or for oil or gas. The children's school attendance has been irregular for years. They may be sent from door to door to ask for food and other items. Some members are often in poor health, and sometimes need to go to the hospital. At best, the standard of living of the itinerant laborer's family is very low and many social problems are inherent in its way of life. Though he may have more stability the income of the hired man on family farms is low. The life of the elderly in such circumstances is physically hard and, from a middle-class viewpoint, bleak and scarcely worth living.

The increased mechanization of farming has reduced the number of farm laborers markedly (Kolb and Brunner, 1952, pp. 94–97). With the usual limited education of both parents and children and their lack of occupational skills, many who would formerly have had employment as farm laborers, though often only seasonally, are now unemployed. Others are eking out an existence in cities and small towns as unskilled laborers. Because of union activities, unemployment compensation, and low cost public housing projects, their existence may be slightly better than the farm laborer's. However, in small towns and cities the former farm laborer is likely to live in a substandard house and find employment only sporadically. Certainly he has little to look forward to in old age.

Sed Thompson had not completed the eighth grade, and until six years ago had traveled with his family over the country in search of seasonal farm work. To improve the family situation, Sed decided to settle in a small town. Unable to find a house into which to move his wife and six children, Sed built a shed-like shelter out of old lumber which he found, begged and bought on credit. In the winter the one-room home was heated by a wood stove. A coal oil stove was used for family cooking.

The oil stove was old and smelly. One day, for some unknown reason, it exploded. The fire that followed destroyed the house and all of its contents. The much more tragic outcome, however, was that two of the children died in the fire and another suffered such severe burns that complete recovery is quite unlikely. On the following day, Sed and his wife, Nell, numbly viewed the scene of destruction. What now? Small towns and rural areas, too, have pockets of poverty.

The fate of the Thompsons as they reach the age of sixty is not difficult to visualize. Their children most assuredly will not be in a position to take care of them. Until 1968, when the Supreme Court struck down the archaic provisions, Public Assistance was unavailable to those who could not comply with state residence laws. The irregular income of families like the Thompsons and government requirements in many communities to deduct all income, regular and irregular, from the budgetary needs of a family in order to determine the family's budgetary deficiencies also create difficulties.

In small communities the families of operators or employees in business, of farm managers, farm operators, of tenants and laborers continue to be dependent upon one another or upon their neighbors. Even up to very old age, people in areas of sparse population try to hold on to relatives and former friends until for some reason, usually death, a permanent break occurs. For old people such separations may mean much more than a loss of a friend. It may also mean that the old man or woman loses another role, another source of prestige, another social support—and part of himself (Rose, 1963). Thus, the opportunity to communicate with friends as long as possible is important. However, public transport is decreasing and personal contacts may be difficult. The decline in public transport has tended to deprive the elderly of one important source of comfort and satisfaction. Fortunately, other forms of communication, such as telephones and the postal service, are still available.

When the spouse dies, after perhaps a half century of their living together as a couple, the most meaningful source of interaction is terminated for the widowed mate. Repeatedly heard in Holton and Marion County was the remark: "Life has never been the same since my husband (or wife) passed away"—the implication being that life has not been as good as it was before. Certainly after weathering the vicissitudes of rearing a family, and together assuming all the responsibilities that must be faced through the years, many husbands and wives develop much dependence upon each other. Their verbal and nonverbal communication becomes an established way of life. There may not always be harmony but the interaction develops into a pattern which, in many cases, assures a comfortable stability and security. The disintegration of a long established pattern, particularly one permeated with love and affection, causes a loss and loneliness that can be, and often is, devastating. Hink (1966) found in his small sample that men who lost mates were much less socially active and lonelier than widows. He suggested that men rely on their wives to arrange social activities and the average man is at a loss when get-togethers are no longer arranged nor friendships supported and maintained. Wives may be more dependent in monetary matters than their husbands but more independent in social activities. In the normal course of the life span of a family, from marriage through the sequence of childbearing, child leaving home, and later retirement, the death of the widowed grandparent or great-grandparent finally completes the cycle (Glick, 1947, pp. 164–174; Loomis and Beegle, 1950, pp. 77–87).

INCREMENTS AND DECREMENTS

In many ways members of a family in a small community have advantages, particularly the aged member. Even if none of his children is close at hand to help take care of personal needs, nieces, nephews, and cousins or other relatives are likely to live nearby. Neighbors are ready to help. If the old person becomes senile and wanders off, whether he lives alone, in the home of relatives, in a foster home or in a personal care or nursing home in the community, he is not automatically referred to the police or sheriff. People know him, help him and notify his relatives or friends. The old person in a small town or in the country may be able to drive his car longer than is possible for his large city counterpart. If he is handicapped in any way, perhaps by failing hearing or vision, the fact is likely to be known when he comes along in his car, and people will react accordingly. Before he reaches a possibly deteriorated mental state or becomes a driving hazard he has more opportunities to perform useful tasks than he would have in a large city. With space available for gardens and often for a cow and farm fowls, he may even be economically productive. His own self-esteem may be less threatened. His ties with neighbors and friends may be stronger than they would be in densely populated areas. Common values and concerns may be more easily shared.

Decrements are found in the small community. Organized facilities to meet the needs that have grown out of contemporary change have not kept pace with growing demands. Often there is little to fill the gaps for all members of the family. Young people complain of having no place to go for recreation; the old people wish they had more income to enable them to be less dependent on their children. When nursing home care is indicated, and even when everybody consents to the plan, waiting lists are long and in many cases services are inadequate. Values of young people, when they leave a small community home, may change drastically and the intergenerational gap between old and young can become great. The role, status structure, and the goals of a family unit have undergone great changes and continue to do so. With the family's consisting of members of different ages, their tasks and positions, assumed and assigned, shift according to physical stamina and amount of experience. The special dilemma of the old member in today's family is closely related to the decline of his physical stamina which parallels the rise of his fund of experience. His status in the family tends to decrease as the tasks which he performs in the group become less useful. Whether he lives in the home of his children or they in his, or whether he has his abode elsewhere, the inevitable situation he has to face, if his children and grandchildren are to be free to pursue their own lives, is that instead of being the independent member who is responsible for dependent members, he becomes more dependent while the other members become more independent. The major changes of modern life, which have been felt more recently by the aged in rural areas than by those in urban areas, make a strong impact at this juncture in history.

Such is the family of the small community which the social worker who wishes to be of service to the older family member meets. He does well to focus on activities which aid the members as a group to maintain and increase what strengths—usually many— the family unit possesses. He should also try to preserve and increase the positive elements in family relationships. This means that he must recognize the ultimate interdependence of old and young, and the ultimate independence of each member.

Interest Groups

5

Some groups have strength and vitality and members find satisfaction in their interaction with each other. Common interests and goals are recognized and group positions and roles are assigned or achieved. The members develop group norms and values and the group becomes a cohesive whole with its functions clearly defined and understood. It has an identity, develops a collective self-image and, for a time at least, it moves along serving its members. Then there are aggregations of people that can scarcely be called groups. People come together but communicate little. They may derive some comfort from knowing that others are around, others with similar problems and experiences; they may communicate even in the silences. Yet there is little group structure and what happens to the whole group may barely concern them. Each man is a separate entity. There is little fusion of member interest and aspirations and little identification with other persons. A gathering of old people who find satisfaction in sharing a meal and an afternoon's entertainment is the embodiment of a group with its own identity.

They had come together from farms and from the town. There were nearly fifty of them, men and women ranging in age from sixty-four to ninety-one. They came at noon to share a potluck meal and to participate in and enjoy the program. Before dinner, as the noon meal was called, the committee—a different one for every meeting—made the coffee and arranged the meat, vegetables, casseroles, salads, pies, cakes, puddings, hot rolls, spreads, and every other conceivable item of food on a side table. Knives and forks were placed on a long table in the center. In the front of the long hall were the men and women, some standing, some sitting. Small groups were clustered around the edge. Some women were moving about admiring the display of needlework arranged near the walls. The men were interested in the garden vegetables on a small table in the corner, especially in one very large turnip.

Mrs. Ireland was wiping her eyes. Two months before her husband had died. Very sudden it was. Mrs. Baden and Mrs. Stamm listened sympathetically. Both were widows. "We know," they said. "Time will heal," soothed Mrs. Baden. And then she added: "You will never get over it, not altogether, no never."

I turned. I heard Mr. Sample with amusement in his face and voice tell of the antics of his great-grandson. "A chip off the old block, hey, Sam?" commented his listener.

And now it was time to eat. There was a hush. "Bless our fellowship together and grant that we may be worthy of Thy great bounty," prayed the president. Some made the sign of the cross. A few echoed the "Amen." Solicitously the wives handed plates and cups to their husbands. Joshing and laughter accompanied the warnings not to eat too much. They ate with concentrated relish. The committee refilled the cups and plates. I sat across from Grandma Matson. She was the ninety-one-year-old in the group. Earlier she had insisted on getting in line and serving herself. Somehow she managed both plate and cane. Her plate was heaped when she sat down, but now it was empty. "Would you like something more?" one of the committee asked. "You can bring me some more cake and pie," was her unabashed reply. To me she explained, "I like to come here where I get good things to eat. At home I cook just one thing. If I cook more I have to eat leftovers all week." I nodded. Silently I wondered about her digestion. But only I worried. She didn't.

The meal ended; the program started. A pianist, two violinists, and an accordionist left the table and went into action. The walls shook. Then there were folk songs and hymns. The audience joined in. After a while Mrs. Haynes was introduced. She "gave a reading" complete with gestures. She had talent for mimicry and her own delight and humor were infectious. There was much laughter.

She was followed by Mr. Schwartz who recited a poem he had written himself. He described the countryside. To him the trees and the skies, the land with its wheat and corn, and the cattle grazing in the hills represented something close to paradise. His audience agreed and applauded him well.

By way of a contrast, Kwok-Wha Lai (a second-year graduate student in social work at the University of Kansas) describes a group that is no more than an aggregation of persons, totally lacking in any identity of its own.

Every time, and any time of the day, when I pass through the Chinatown park, I see a big crowd of aged Oriental men gathered together there. Approximately 90 percent are Chinese. My uncle is one of them. They sit around the park to have a sun bath, to obtain fresh air, and to kill their time. These aged people are sitting, taking a nap, smoking or looking around; but very few are talking. They seem not to communicate even though they are sitting close together. My uncle says to him all faces are familiar for they see each other every day since the park was established two years ago. They do not know much about each other but their nicknames: Uncle Wong, Old See, or Grandpa Chan.

These men live around Chinatown in an inexpensive hotel. They immigrated to the United States forty or fifty years ago, when they were strong young men. They were unable to earn a living in China and so they took a chance on the other side of the world and many found jobs as farm laborers. They worked hard and for long hours. As soon as they had a good amount of savings for a trip back to China and to finance a wedding, they returned home to get married. Chinese females were rare in the States, therefore they had to spend a great amount of time and money to marry a Chinese woman rather than marry a 'foreigner.' Very soon after they were home the wedding was prepared and the bride was chosen by their parents. Approximately one month to a year after they had married they had to return to the old place and hard life. For sure, they were unable to understand their bride. My uncle returned when his son was ten days old. They supported their families faithfully, sending a sizable amount twice or four times a year. Since they were not educated or even some were illiterate, they could not have much communication with their families.

They always hoped to save enough to return in their late forties and perhaps start a little business in China. Few were that lucky, and many lost communication with their families during World War II. They grow old alone, though married. They see the world cold. They have received no affection, warmth and sympathy from anybody. Years ago some might have immigrated into this country illegally and there is the constant fear that some day they may be deported.

Groups may mean much to persons in their sixties, seventies, eighties, and even in their nineties. A group may be the device for relieving the monotony and lonesomeness of daily living. It may offer opportunities to share joys and sorrows. It may serve as an occasion for eating well in the company of others. A group experience may consist of their joking with one another; it may provide the opportunity for persons of different faiths to pray together. New achievements may be shared; something pleasant and interesting may be anticipated.

Social workers, slow to recognize the importance of group participation for persons of all ages, have in recent years begun to take notice. "It is a paradox that a profession known for its interest in helping people with problems of relationships within their intimate circle of family, peers, work associates and neighbors should be discovering the group . . . yet the group as a unit of social work services has become of interest to more than social group workers . . . it has opened a new range of services in a wide variety of social problems" (Ray, 1958). Perhaps, in analyzing the benefits that Grandma Matson and her friends derived from their meeting, one might add that participation in group activities may prevent social problems from occurring, and may even lead to the development of experiences hitherto unrealized and to expressions of concern for others. Interest in clusters of people has been greatly stimulated in American social work by the increasing concern for older persons. Current literature seems to reflect that as much, perhaps more, work is being done with groups than with individual older people. Even articles on casework with the elderly may refer to the importance of their group experiences (Falck, 1963, pp. 63–67). However, as Goldstein (1963, pp. 34–42) pointed out, the concern of social workers has been largely with the small group. Larger groups also deserve attention though they have not had much to date.

THE GROUP DEFINED

Interest groups and associations are clusters of people whose interests, individually and collectively, are served through interaction among members and through the combined interaction of all the members with other clusters of people. According to Bierstedt (1963, Ch. 10, 11), an aggregation of persons constitutes a social group only when there is common interest. Hence, in a sense, all social groups are interest groups. He goes on to say when groups are organized they become associations. The "two concepts, association and organized groups, are precisely synonymous." He lists seven criteria of an association or organized group. It will have "a specific function or purpose, associational norms, associational statuses, authority, tests of membership, property, and a name and other identifying symbols." Social groups may meet all of the seven criteria or only some of them. In other words, all associations are social groups but not all social groups are associations.

Interest groups and associations with which persons in their later years may be affiliated, are of many varieties. They range widely in size, purpose, kind, and complexity of organization, locus of authority, eligibility requirements of members, values and goals, group role and status structure and all other elements and dimensions that make of a collection of persons a group or an association. Interest groups in small communities may consist of two or more persons who call one another the first thing in the morning and the last thing at night to make sure that all is well with the person living alone. They may include county-wide organizations of older persons numbering five hundred or more. They may serve a single purpose or have many reasons for existence. They may be loosely organized or have a formal structure with written policies and procedures.

Some groups and associations of the elderly or those in which the elderly have an interest are autonomous. The members themselves are responsible for the policies and procedures. If a professional person assumes responsibilities for the program or for some other activity of such a group, he does so either as a member or as an employee of the group or association. In other, and in frequent instances in small communities the members rely on finances, policies and professional services of larger associations, whose activities exceed local boundaries. In either case, decision-making may range from the autocratic to the democratic. The group may consist only of older persons, or may include younger people, perhaps whole family groups with members of all ages. Membership may or may not be differentiated by sex, social status, work experiences, hobby interests. The group may identify with one another and have common values and goals, or may have little group loyalty and much strife.

In this chapter, interest groups are considered to consist of the informal but recognizable friendship groups described by Loomis and Beegle (1957, pp. 103–104) and of more definitely organized associations. Included are groups consisting of peers of older people and of nonpeers, groups with close or remote personal relationships, groups with and without clearly recognizable roles and status. Interest groups and associations of older people or including older members may consist of subgroups. The institutional structure as a whole, of the church, school, Grange, Farm Bureau, Farmers' Union, and other agencies, is excluded.

LIFE STYLE OF THE GROUP

Various disciplines are currently preoccupied with systematic studies of small and associational groups; for example, Goberlienski (1962) has analyzed fifteen hundred research studies on the behavior of small groups; the bibliography in Blau and Scott (1962) illustrates the considerable interest in the formally organized associational group. However, until recently the research, particularly into small group dynamics, has been so partialized and the findings so discrete (Cartwright and Zander, 1953; Hare, Borgatta, and Bales, 1955; Coyle, 1962, p. 349) that all the activity has not been very useful for the practicing social workers. Moreover, the studies have been cast in different frames of reference with comparably little effort made to show the relationships among them or the practical application of the various theories. Olmsted (1959) discussed three different theories of the behavior of small groups: Homan's theory, Lewin's Group Dynamics—sometimes called the Field Theory—and the Interaction Process Analysis to which Bales is an important contributor.

The frame of reference within which groups described in this chapter have been defined has evolved from social work teaching and practice. It has largely grown out of pragmatic experience but also owes much to the literature about small and associational groups, which until the 1930s accumulated only slowly. No effort has been made to summarize existing theories, nor any attempt to present what might be regarded as an eclectic view based on existing studies. A group will develop a life style or pattern as unique as is that of an individual or of a family. As in the individual and in the family, this pattern changes and keeps on changing, yet also has a sameness. Members of their own groups and members of other groups in the community recognize this pattern and react to it as they perceive it. The pattern may or may not satisfy member needs. If not, however, membership in an interest group is more easily withdrawn than membership in the biological family.

A group or association comes into being and attains form and stability in a recognizable sequence. It usually begins when for some reason a number of people get together. Coincidence may bring them to the same place at the same time, such as when two men drop into a cafe for a cup of coffee and, since only one booth is vacant, they occupy the same table. They start talking; they discover that each has recently retired and is somewhat bored; they learn that they both like to play pinochle. No room in the cafe is available for pinochle games, so one suggests that the janitor in the courthouse may let them play in the basement. Each one has a friend who also likes to play pinochle. Within a short time a card club is in existence. People may assemble on the invitation of one person who has either a selfish or an altruistic interest, or a mixture of both. Elderly Mrs. Jones, for instance, who plays the piano, may invite a number of persons who play different musical instruments into her home. They enjoy the experience of playing together and invite others. A small musical group or even a band or orchestra is the result. An invitation may be issued by an organization. The church minister may announce a meeting of all who wish to make cancer pads for a nearby hospital. In time an organization of women making all kinds of hospital supplies may emerge. No matter who makes up an assembly of persons or why they get together, a group may emerge if communication between potential members occurs. As indicated by the scene in the Chinatown park, their propinquity and continuity do not necessarily make a group out of a collection of people. If, through communication or interaction, some common interests are uncovered, particularly interests better served by collective than by individual action, or if the assumed or assigned leadership has sufficient prestige or authority, future meetings and additional interaction may be assured and a group or association result.

At the beginning of a group's development the members tend to behave and act in terms of their own interests and self-images and of what they consider appropriate in the light of their previous experiences. However, in the course of interaction, conceptions of common values and the expectations of others emerge. Common interests and values manifest themselves; but common behavior patterns or norms evolve. As the interactional process continues, positions and responsibilities are assigned or assumed. If, in addition to providing satisfactory goals, the group facilitates an effective meshing of roles and the members find satisfaction in enacting their roles, a high group morale is likely to be evident. From dissatisfaction or frustration, dissension and conflict may well develop, especially in members whose roles are often classified as group task, group maintenance and composite roles. For a discussion of group roles see *Adult Leadership,* January, 1953.

In formally organized associations, procedures for group action are usually outlined in a constitution and/or bylaws. The vested authority is made clear and a hierarchical division of labor is arranged. Not only is a name given the association but also symbols, such as insignia or songs, are developed. Provisions are made for the admission and exclusion of persons as members, as well as for the acceptance and disposal of finances or property. Some place from which the group or its representatives may operate is decided upon. In the early stages of a group's existence, the social structure, including its material components, is often inadequate. Thus one or a few persons deeply committed to the goals of the association often contribute an extraordinary share of thought, energy, and even finance. Their leadership is likely to be charismatic and may present some obstacles when a more organized structure and approach are desirable.[1] When a group is led by someone with much authority and a desire to exercise it, and when he has preconceived goals for the group, the interactional process may be highly controlled. Group positions and responsibilities are autocratically assigned rather than bestowed upon or assumed by members, and the group's norms and values are dictated by the leader. Participation may be encouraged by the leader's emphasizing the attractiveness of the association's goals and by rewarding participation. Fear may affect the participation of members in groups that have a pronounced dictatorial leadership.

In time, the structure of the group and the behavior of its members may become firmly set. The same pattern of group roles and status continues and the policies which govern the program become deeply entrenched. Gardner (1965, p. 20) suggests that, "like people and plants, organizations have a life cycle. They have a green and supple youth, a time for flourishing strength and gnarled old age." Though not always true, ossification or rigidities in structure and behavior tend to develop in time, and the focus tends toward the group's meeting needs of a minority of individual members and the perpetuation of the association for its own sake rather than for the purpose for which it was originally organized. Unless the goals, program, structure, and reorganization are reevaluated and the purpose renewed, decline and even death follow. The life span of a group without formal structure tends to be short; while an association may last months, years, or centuries. However, groups without formal structure, particularly if their activities are surrounded by tradition, may last a long time.

SELF-CONCEPT OF THE GROUP

For members individually and collectively to contribute to and receive benefits from a group or an association, they must have faith in the worth of the unit as an entity. They must respect them-

---

[1] For a discussion of Weber's theory of the relationship between authority, and charisma and bureaucracy, see Blau and Scott (1962, pp. 30–33).

selves as interacting persons, their behavior toward one another within and outside the total group or association, their group image as they see it and believe others to perceive it, and their group goals and methods of accomplishing them. When the unit's shared concepts are positive, a feeling of pride and satisfaction exists. When the assessment is shared by persons, groups, and associations outside the members' own circle, the satisfactions increase. Participation is willing and enthusiastic, esprit de corps is good, group morale high —all of which promote individual development as well. The group will have a collective positive self-concept if the purposes for its existence are understood and wanted; when its member roles are acceptable and mesh well. In a group with a positive self-image there are relatively few noncontributing members. Not only are the group's norms and values acceptable to the individual members, but its short-term and long-term goals harmonize with the norms of a large proportion of the members. So the members are willing to work for the goals and their achievement, in the minds of the majority, adds to the stature of all and reflects the worth of individual members. Their being together and working together is likely to stimulate greater participation.

Sometimes the leader, who may have been self-appointed, selected by the group or appointed from outside by a central agency, may not be able to inspire the members to participate enthusiastically. He may lack skill; his values may be out of tune with those of the group, he may not be able to relate to the group. Criticism of his leadership begins and the members are less enthusiastic about a previously acceptable goal. Their assessment of their own worth, as a collective interacting unit, declines. They begin to take sides: some support, others denigrate the leader's efforts. In the resulting conflict the movement of the group has gone into reverse. This reversal can happen when, although the leader may continue to serve satisfactorily, a member who has performed a specific task leaves the group. Perhaps he played the part of the group morale builder exceedingly well: he pointed to the progress made, recognized the contributions of other members without fail, spoke optimistically, yet realistically, about what they could accomplish by working together and, at appropriate moments, relieved group tensions with his well-placed sense of humor. Neither he, nor others, may have been aware of his particular contribution and the effects of his absence may not be clearly understood. However, unless the void is filled group lethargy, lack of interest, and loss of group spirit or even destructive opposition and dissension are likely to follow. The withdrawal of financial support, a critical report by the agency that sets the standards, a central governing policy unacceptable to the local group, change in outside supervisory or advisory personnel, the organization of another group with a similar but more appealing program may upset a group's morale. Subsequent interaction merely erodes the feeling of self-worth. As in the case of the individual aging adult and in the family group, the collective creative and empathic potential of the interacting members may stem the tide of declining group self-esteem, but such a reversal will usually be difficult.

The members' morale, the group's self-image, and the cohesiveness of a group or association are all closely interrelated and interdependent. If all the members have a positive concept of the group, morale will be high; high morale promotes cohesion. This is not simply one sequence of cause and effect. A high morale will also nurture self-esteem, and the group's cohesiveness may affect both its self-esteem and morale.

GROUPS IN SMALL COMMUNITIES

Small groups and associations are numerous in small communities and increasing. Hausknecht (1962, p. 26) states that they are more numerous in small villages and towns, especially those with populations of between 2,500 and 50,000, than in metropolitan areas. As in urban areas, interest groups on farms, in villages and small towns "arise out of likenesses and differences in age, sex, occupation, tradition, experience, choice, propensity, intent, and so on. They may be contrasted with locality groups, which have lateral or geographic dimensions, whereas interest groups have perpendicular or voluntary dimensions" (Kolb and Brunner, 1952, p. 239). Certainly interest groups may have geographic boundaries, but their primary reasons for being and becoming are perpendicular rather than lateral. The members are motivated by common interests or concerns rather than merely by the fact that they live within a certain locality. The geographic boundaries may determine who is to be a member and what kind of structure the group is to have.

Lindstrom (1961), doing a study of nine hundred forty-seven rural interest groups in Illinois, found some significant current trends. He noted that now most interest groups are subdivisions of larger groups. However, the local group membership is not large, at least large numbers of members do not attend the meetings which tend to be face-to-face encounters. Despite their affiliation with larger social systems, the Illinois interest groups retained considerable authority for policy determination. They tended to have broad objectives, even though they were originally organized to serve a narrow purpose.

Membership in small-community interest groups dwindles in the later years of life. Associations of peers of aging persons are few. "Practically no special associations for the elderly are found in rural areas and small towns, although some rural people are nominal members of national voluntary associations with political purposes" (Rose, 1963, p. 14). Bauder (1958) summarizes "most studies" as indicating "a precipitous decline in social participation [in groups] with the approach of occupational retirement and with the reduction in occupational roles [p. 149]." As is perhaps implied by Bauder, it is not only the number of members but also the degree and kind of participation in interest groups by older persons in small communities that should be explored.

One might explore the expectations that both old and young have of participation by the elderly in community affairs. Interviews with 487 persons in a small Pennsylvania community revealed that "participation was generally approved, especially by the better educated and higher status respondents and valued for benefits to older persons themselves as well as to others." Only 4 percent of those interviewed felt that older people should not participate. Those who said, "They're too old, let the young people take over," tended to be in the older age group themselves (Britton, Mather and Lansing, 1962, pp. 387–396). In a similar study in Marion County the results were significant in that a larger number of the "younger respondents considered their older townsmen capable of participation in community affairs than was anticipated by the older respondents. However, (contrary to the Pennsylvania findings) more young than old persons had reservations about their potential contributions." (Wylie, 1963.)

Britton, Mather and Lansing, and a series of research projects conducted at an earlier date by members of the staff of Pennsylvania State University (1954a, b), have shown that the relationship "between age and social participation" is influenced by social status, employment, education, and to some degree, sex. Expectations about participation in small communities were positively correlated with high status, "white collar" jobs and education. Women generally seemed more inclined than men to regard participation in community groups favorably.

At the beginning of the Marion County project, ninety-eight interest groups and associations to which older people could belong were delineated. Church groups, of which there were many, were not included. It was observed (with notable exceptions) that few older persons held leadership positions. This was as true of women's organizations, such as study clubs and the "work, eat and gossip" groups, as of men's service and veterans groups. When older men held positions as president or high office, they usually were persons with superior educational advantages and were retired or partially retired from "white collar" jobs. Older women who held such positions usually had husbands with jobs of some prestige. For family, economic, or other reasons, both men and women who served as leaders tended to have high social status in the community.

Havighurst and Albrecht (1953), in their study of Prairie City, "a small community where the agricultural and the industrial economy overlay at many corners" (p. 7), found that "practically no older person joins an organization as a new member . . ." and "in the Study Sample only one person (one percent) over sixty-five held a leading office in an organization." The authors conclude that "the principal need in Prairie City, if one should undertake to develop social organizations for older people, is for the kind of association that will appeal to lower-status people. While upper and upper-middle [class] people have relatively easy access to social clubs, those in the three lower status groups, especially men, do not participate much in existing associations" (p. 7). Since, in Marion County, there was no dearth of interest groups for which older people were at least eligible nominally, and since minimal participation seemed to be characteristic of the people in their later years, the reasons for their not participating were examined. Explanations advanced most frequently by the older men and women themselves included: poor health or physical disabilities, such as loss of hearing or sight, lack of transport, prohibitive expenses, lack of information about time and place of meetings, inappropriate or uninteresting programs, and a feeling of not being welcome. One woman of eighty, who was in poor health and frequently in no condition to attend meetings, observed, "When I do feel like going, they really don't want me. They never visit me." Certainly all of these reasons are credible. Poor health—heart ailments, arthritis, fractures, deafness, blindness and similar disabilities—are genuine barriers to participation in groups. Yet of the more than 1,000 persons interviewed, a large majority stated that, from their point of view, their health was good or fair.

Lack of transport is particularly deterring in a county of 960 square miles, with no commercial taxicabs operating in the villages and towns, and with train and bus services of little value to either rural or town residents. Private cars may be the solution for some. However, car ownership often entails prohibitive expenses and many older women in small communities have never learned to drive a car. Both men and women who have driven cars in the past may not be physically able in their later years. Participation in organizations does cost money. There are membership fees, appeals for special causes, expenses for meals, refreshments or entertainment in homes, and other items that may strain the financial resources of the elderly. Perhaps the inappropriate and uninteresting meetings, lack of information about them, and the lack of evidence of being welcome may also have some basis of reality. With many the interest groups increasingly becoming subgroups of larger associations and with programs suggested by professionals working in cities some distances away, it may be possible that the special interests of older people in small and rural communities are neither understood nor met. Younger residents of rural areas and small towns are much better oriented to the centrally planned programs of both governmental and voluntary agencies and associations. They were brought up with them. It is possible that local young people may recognize the inappropriateness of suggested programs for the older residents and therefore discourage, or at least fail to encourage, participation by them.

Yet as Rose (1963, pp. 9–11) and Bloedow (1963, pp. 117–123) observed in Minnesota, and as experienced in Marion County, opportunities for group participation produce enthusiastic response. In five localities out of six in Marion County, when groups of older persons were invited to meet and to indicate how the project might serve them best, the one suggestion offered promptly and unanimously was the establishment of a club or organization of persons of their own age. In the sixth small town, the older people themselves, and largely on their own initiative, organized a club less than a year later.[2]

As in rural Minnesota, the clubs in Marion County seemed to serve desired objectives. Interest and willingness to participate was evident in the fact that 500 persons attended the third annual meeting of the county-wide association of the local Golden Years organizations. Approximately 250 other persons were present during the day, participating in the event in some way or another. Considering the distances that many had to travel, and the fact that there were only about 2,000 persons sixty-five-and-over in the county as a whole, one feels that the large attendance reflected more than a passing interest in group associations.

Perhaps since status, occupation, and, in particular, formal education assume importance for group involvement, the homogeneity of status, occupation and education (all important in groups) of older people on farms and in rural villages means that participation in groups made up of contemporaries offers fewer threats to self-esteem than in groups that include younger persons. Many persons now in their later years did not expect a college or even a high school education. The present generation does. Like their urban counterparts, rural young and middle-aged persons of today are accustomed to participating in group discussions and in other group activities, and they do so with poise and self-confidence. Not so the men and women of the older generation. They are not good

[2] Considerable argument for and against peer group associations of older people, and a clear demonstration of the importance of association for older people, not only with their families, but also with their peers, may be found in Rosow (1967).

matches for the younger group. They may hesitate to speak up, especially on subjects with which they are not completely familiar. Yet there are older persons who prefer membership in mixed age groups. Some in Marion County indicated that groups containing younger members proved more stimulating. Some commented they did not feel "old enough to associate only with old people." These usually were the younger persons aged sixty-five-and-over or those who continued to be alert and active.

Church groups were not included in the total number listed for Marion County. Perhaps it should be noted, however, that with the high concentration of old persons in villages, towns, and small cities, the membership in many small-community churches is predominantly of older people, especially of older women. Sunday School classes and other church organizations may consist mostly of older people. The extent to which programs are planned by and with them seems to differ in different churches. The older people and their middle-aged children seem concerned that youth should have first consideration. Yet some older people, when they cannot participate actively, seem to feel ignored.

PURPOSE OF INTEREST GROUPS

If it is true that the aging process makes for disengagement from life initiated either by the older person himself or by persons or social institutions surrounding him, or by a combination of the sources, it should logically follow that interest groups and associations of all kinds would serve little purpose. Actually, Cumming (1964, p. 5), a co-author of the disengagement theory as originally presented, herself has stated that she would expect a certain number of disengaging persons to seek group affiliation. She hypothesizes that some older persons will test out their own self-images through interaction with others. They use the responses of others to confirm the correctness of inferences made by themselves. If the responses are unexpected other persons are tested out. Some older men and women might be much more passive. They wait for cues that confirm their self-concepts. When what others seem to think of them does not coincide with their own image, they change their self-concept. These reasons may well be valid. Not all older people seek group membership, and those who do are not all equally interested and vigorous.

The interaction of older persons with others in a group serves a variety of specific purposes.

For example, the Senior Citizens Club, a meeting of which Grandma Matson attended, has grown in the last ten years phenomenally. To be sure such groups have been nurtured by recreation workers and other group-work leaders, although some have been organized on the initiative of the elderly themselves. The continuation of such groups has depended upon the participation of elderly persons and that participation itself provides evidence that the peer group serves a purpose, one that is related to the strengthening, clarification, or maintenance of a self-concept. The names of such groups reflect their purpose. Often euphemistic—Golden Age, Over Fifty, Senior Citizen—they seem to call attention, perhaps with some defiance, if not with conviction, that old age is golden, perhaps beautiful, that old persons retain their citizenship, and that old age includes people who are not so old—only fifty or perhaps sixty or sixty-five. The extent to which the older persons themselves have coined these phrases, or have been coined by younger persons mindful of the self-concept of the elderly is not known. In many instances the old have continued to use such and many similar terms persist in spite of objections. The Senior Citizens club meeting indicates other ways in which peer groups strengthen self-image and the concept of worth. It may offer opportunities, real or hoped for, for a desired role and status: somebody has to be president. Someone may ask the blessing before the meal and call the meeting to order. If he is president, he also has the responsibility inherent in his position to preside over business meetings, appoint committees, and assume other duties. Others may gain satisfaction from holding other offices. The duties that accompany the serving of potluck meals may give women in rural areas and small towns a chance to display their cooking, baking, and serving outside their own kitchens and homes. The expression of verbal appreciation and requests for more no doubt help to nurture a feeling of self-worth. An opportunity to display the fruits of labor, such as needlework, flowers, or a big turnip, may also strengthen

or maintain a favorable self-image, as will the effect of telling others
with pride of a grandson who is recognized to be "a chip off the
old block." Peer groups also provide a chance to share pleasant
and unpleasant, happy and sad experiences. Only with a group
of contemporaries is it possible for old persons to find so many
other men and women who have lost mates, whose children have
moved away and who may be living on reduced incomes. "We
know," said Mrs. Baden and Mrs. Stamm. They, too, were widows.
They could sympathize and comfort. "Time will heal," they said.

In small communities, as elsewhere, eating seems very important. When two or more people meet, they often have a meal,
at home and at meetings outside of the home. The uninhibited
abandon with which Grandma Matson ate the food on her heaped-
up plate and accepted more when it was offered reflects the appreciation with which some old persons living alone consume a variety
of food. Her reason for attending the club meetings is valid. If
a person living alone prepares more than one dish to give variety
to the meal, the chances are that he will be eating leftovers for
the rest of the week. The opportunity to eat with others also provides satisfaction. One statement frequently heard after a marital
partner had died is, "The hardest thing about living alone is to
have no one with whom to eat." Peer groups may encourage creative activity. An elderly man in a small town or village may hesitate to try to carve, paint, act, dance, play music or experiment in
handcrafts when young people "who have so many advantages today" are about. But to attempt skills in the company of other older
people is quite another story. The competition is less formidable or
so it seems. A group of peers may also provide an opportunity to
serve others. Visiting sick or shut-in members, providing a card
shower for hospital patients, taking responsibility for community
improvements, such as, for example, a beautification project in Holton, and similar activities are all feasible for clubs of the elderly.
One group in Marion County always sent attractive plates of food
to members who, because of illness, were unable to attend meetings.
Another group took a basket of food to residents of the County
Home. In small towns and villages such acts usually depend completely on volunteer leadership, and their regularity and continuity
are determined by the interest, time, energy, health, transport facili-

ties and other resources and limitations of the group and its leaders.

In many respects retirement and care homes serve some of the same purposes as Golden Age or Senior Citizen clubs, particularly if they have communal dining rooms. However, the intermingling with other people is more regular and frequent. The problem of eating alone is solved. That does not mean, however, that meals served regularly will satisfy all the food eccentricities, including those of individual health needs, which are likely to exist among older persons. Nor does it mean that the food is attractively served or designed to stimulate appetites.

Social interaction in retirement homes and in Senior Citizen or Golden Age clubs serves in various ways as an antidote to loneliness and boredom. Close affective ties may be formed, some leading to marriage. Romances seem quite common and perhaps should be listed as one of the purposes served by peer groups in and outside institutions. Perhaps the major purpose served by social groups is to help satisfy the need for identity. Membership in a group does that. If his contributions are recognized, an older person can take pride in who and what he is. If he is singled out because of his birthday, certainly something his very own, he may bask in his own identity. Perhaps it is largely for this reason that birthdays seem to be so important among older people in small communities.

The fact that some older people prefer membership in groups made up of persons other than their peers attests to their value. If elderly men and women have opportunities for productive participation in mixed-age groups, they may well derive many benefits, including that of being in close touch with the point of view and changing attitudes of a younger generation. Neighbors United, an association for mobilizing the resources of older people for community service in Holton, consists of representatives of the different organizations in the town with members ranging in age from the early thirties to over eighty. Difference in age seems no deterrent. One did hear, however, older men and women comment that, in the past, church, farm and other groups and associations that included younger members used to provide satisfaction, but do so no longer. One woman in a small town remarked that church activities were informal when she was active. Now the programs are administered by committees with plans suggested by personnel in national headquarters. She felt lost and no longer enjoys her membership.

Few local groups and associations established to provide services extend them to the elderly. Early in the Marion County project, at a meeting of the presidents of the various organizations not affiliated with churches all offered some services, none primarily or permanently for health and welfare. Reports of activities showed little concern for the aged:

> There is no phase of this work that pertains to older people in the community.
>
> There is no special service to older people in the community.
>
> There is no program for older people in the community except as they are in need of special service.
>
> This organization is a service organization and its program is directed toward children.
>
> The primary function of this organization is an educational one and the group is geared to high school students who may be potential college students.
>
> This organization at Christmas time does something for needy people and sometimes this does include some of the older people.

Older people, and particularly the handicapped, may have little to look forward to except the sound of "Gabriel's horn." Since there is not a clear-cut role for the aged many old persons have little in the way of a present. Events and occasions that may be anticipated may give some meaning to the present, may help to mobilize energies and to obliterate pain, if only for short moments. This may be true even when the person cannot directly participate in the group activities.

> Mrs. Ross was in a wheelchair, sitting erect and stately despite her arthritis and her eighty-seven years. She was not expecting company but her white hair was carefully combed and she wore a necklace. She told me about her family and her illness. She was crocheting because it keeps her hands from getting stiff. She showed me three of her afghans, each one most exquisitely done. She talked about color combinations, stitches, designs, and the nieces who would be the recipients of her handiwork.

"Would you like to show your afghans at a county-wide hobby display?" I asked.

She was not sure. She would be unable to go herself and the afghans might get lost. "Perhaps Jane (a friend and neighbor) would bring them and be responsible for them," I suggested.

Jane would and did. The display of afghans won a special award. Even now, over a year later, people talk about the beautiful work.

When I brought her the plaque with her name engraved on it, Mrs. Ross was very pleased. "Will you have another display next year?" she asked.

"Would you like to show some more of your needle-work?"

She hesitated, then said, "I don't suppose I could show the same afghans?"

"No, I don't think you should," I replied.

"Well," she said, "I'll make another." And then, with a chuckle and her characteristic humor, she added, "If anyone asks you my age, just say I am over forty."

Actually, Mrs. Ross has two events that may add zest and meaning to the present: the visits from her nieces when she will have an opportunity to present her gifts to them and the work on another afghan to display a year hence.

In Marion County the churches played a major role in the activities of older people. Service and social programs in which elderly men and women participated were largely organized on denominational lines. This had much meaning for many. But they were interested in meeting persons from other churches. One old man, a loyal church member, offered his explanation for the growth in Marion County of Golden Year clubs, which were not affiliated with any of the churches, during the time our project was developing: "These group meetings have caught fire because they are the only means we old people have of getting together, especially with members of other churches." As greater variation in cultural background and religious affiliations existed in the Marion County community than in most areas in the state, it was noteworthy that the priest of a Catholic parish, speaking in a United Brethren Church, with many Mennonites and persons of other faiths present, commented that the most important by-product of the three-year Marion County project was to make possible the meeting in one place of older people of all faiths.

Even though for many older persons in small communities benefits derived from affiliations with small interest groups and associations cannot compensate completely for the loss of a productive economic role and the decreased status that accompanied the loss of the role and cannot take the place of a deceased marital partner and of friends who have moved away or died, the groups can serve useful purposes. A social worker in a small community does well to be aware of the existing interest groups and associations, the objectives they have, their members, the membership requirements, the leaders, their methods of operating, their programs, how much group spirit there is, the group's self-image, and how it is viewed in the community. With such knowledge the social worker is able to aid the elderly persons wishing to join a group. If he is to organize a group, the social worker will also need to understand the emergence and behavior of groups. The person who wishes to be of maximum service in a small community needs a genuine interest in and concern for the isolated and unhappy individual for whom life is very difficult, as well as for the older person who has many advantages but needs opportunities to mobilize and use his potential. He must be interested in mentally ill and retarded old persons as well as those physically well and mentally alert. This does not mean that every person should be encouraged unduly to become involved in group activities. In fact, just sitting in a park on a summer day, or watching television without interaction with others may be what some people need. However, every human being requires opportunities to experience the interest and warmth of others and their encouragement and support, opportunities that should be made available much more frequently in small towns and rural areas than they are.

Service Agencies

6

The effect a social welfare agency has upon its beneficiaries, apart from the results of any financial or concrete material help, will be strongly determined by public and private images—of the agency, the beneficiaries, and the communities in which the agencies function. Physical facilities and institutional regulations will influence the image, but the basic and most dynamic effect will be stimulated, or extinguished, by two people: the social worker and her client.

Jim, her neighbor, had stopped at the corner to make the turn to Scott's Hatchery. Mrs. Craig was glad to get out and walk the six blocks to the courthouse. She was light on her feet despite her plumpness, and she liked to walk—especially this morning. She had to get her thinking straightened out before she faced her caseworker, Mrs. Bunce. Mrs. Craig had seen her only a few times. All day yesterday she thought about what she would say to get some extra money included in her budget. Mrs. Craig's round face was serious. She walked slowly to give herself more time to think. Now if she still had her old caseworker she could tell her the truth. She smiled. Yes, that caseworker was nice. She even asked her, Mrs. Craig, for advice. She wanted some quilting done and Mrs. Craig told her about Amy White, who quilts "by the spool." Mrs. Craig did not know just how much Amy would charge per spool. The caseworker wrote Mrs. Craig later and thanked her! Just to thank her, Mrs. Craig! That *was nice!*

But all this wasn't doing her any good now. Mrs. Craig came back to the problem at hand. In a short while she would have to talk to Mrs. Bunce. What would she tell her? Well, she would give her an account of her last month's expenses. She had them all written down. Item by item she recalled the list in her mind, checking each one off on her fingers as she walked along the street. Then came rent! She had not spent the budget allowance for rent and old lady Smith had asked for it several times. Just this morning she was there. When Mrs. Craig did not have it for her, she became nasty. But Mrs. Craig couldn't tell Mrs. Bunce that she spent her rent money to get Larry out of jail. Larry always got into trouble because of his drinking. Yet, what was a mother to do? She couldn't let him rot in that stinking county jail. Not her own flesh and blood! And Larry always was all right. Really. His kids love him and how he plays and carries on with them! Mrs. Craig chuckled at the thought.

But Mrs. Bunce—what would she say? Mrs. Craig had gone over the question again and again. Once more she thought about telling Mrs. Bunce that she had broken her glasses and it cost the rent money to get them fixed. But Mrs. Bunce would ask her for the receipt, and she had no receipt. She had thought of this yesterday. No use to think about that again. Well, she could say her groceries cost more. They did. Mrs. Bunce, though, would think that she spent too much money on food. "What did you buy?" she would ask. "Strawberries in midwinter?" Well now, strawberries! They sure would be good! And with whipped cream! Mrs. Craig patted her rounded stomach. The thought made her feel good inside. She came back to her problem. What could she say to Mrs. Bunce? The old caseworker might not have included the amount in the budget, but she would have said, "Now, Mrs. Craig, let's see what you can do about this?" And always a way was found. Larry liked her, too." He said she was human. What did that preacher say about people being human? Her thoughts

were wandering again. She remembered the day. She did
not go to church much, but that Sunday she went. She liked
what he said. She tried hard to remember. It had to do with
human kindness and milk. Milk of human kindness! That
was it. Milk! "That kind," thought Mrs. Craig, "does not
have to go into the budget." Again, she smiled for a moment.

But what about the rent money? Mrs. Craig had passed
the courthouse and she had better turn back. When she
called Mrs. Bunce yesterday to find out if she could see her,
Mrs. Bunce said, "At ten." Her voice was crisp and definite.
She meant *ten*. And the courthouse clock said five 'til. She
must go in. She pushed open the heavy door to the basement. The familiar disinfectant smell was there. The janitor's snow shovel and broom were there in their accustomed
corner. The hallway seemed dark. Much darker than ever
before. She saw the door with the sign *County Welfare*.
What would Mrs. Bunce say? Her heart pounded. She felt
all stiff inside. She knew she would be flustered. Again the
words flashed through her mind. Human kindness. Budget.
Rent. Slowly Mrs. Craig opened the door.

IMAGE

An agency organized for service is a hierarchical association
of people, with esprit de corps, conflicts, competition, cooperation,
supervision, ideas, goals, frustrations, and achievements. It consists
of buildings, offices, files, typewriters, adding machines, finances,
records, reports, manuals, bulletins, laws, directives, brooms, mops,
wastebaskets, and so forth. To many elderly men and women, especially in small communities, the attitudes of persons affiliated with
an association (often just one or a few caseworkers or one group
leader and a member of the office staff) and the requirements of
the organization that must be met are what makes the service
agency. What the staff member is and does and how he does it
speak loudly for the organization, both in the estimation of persons
who stand to profit from the services rendered and of the public.
Buildings, equipment, washed and unwashed windows also help to
create an image. They may represent the concept of the agency
held by the administrator or the collective image of the staff. They
may influence the public's opinion of the organization. Material
facilities play a lesser part than the attitudes and interests of the

administrators, and may even get in the way if the appearance of buildings and offices becomes more important than the needs and interests of people. Spotlessly clean care homes with windows shining and carefully chosen pictures on the walls may fail completely to satisfy the old man who would much prefer to see his faded print with the cracked frame decorate the room, and his own worn drapes, purchased with money saved over a period of years, keep out some of the bright light that hurts his eyes.

Its self- and public-image is as important to a service association as to an individual elderly person, a family, or an interest group. It helps or hinders the agency's purpose; it determines goals and influences the motivation of paid and volunteer staff; it affects decisions. When the images, of the agency personnel and of the public, including persons who are the primary beneficiaries of the services, are positive and remain positive over a period of time, the program of the association may be considered to have community endorsement, that is, if the public's evaluation is based on adequate information and if approval is actual and not presumed. As with individuals and with other social groups, a satisfactory self-image has to include the element of worth, but more so for associations established specifically to promote health and welfare. The image has to have worth for persons who will benefit from the program, for those who have the primary responsibility for administering it, and for persons and groups who, financially and by other means, support the agency. The image of worth gives confidence, pleasure, and incentive, purse strings tend to loosen, individual and group morale is fostered, and action is spurred. A good image stimulates satisfying, interactional processes and makes interpersonal relationships positive. The process becomes circular: satisfying interpersonal agency relationships create a positive organizational image.

ORIGINS AND DEVELOPMENT

A service association, in its variety, takes time to emerge. In the past, when service agencies were largely unaided by patterns of structure and programs suggested by national and state organizations, and without financial grants from central sources, the process of being and becoming was often long, slow, and arduous. Studies of the origins and early development of service agencies and institutions established during the nineteenth century and the first quarter of the twentieth century show that lack of money and physical facilities, too few employees and too little experience invariably plagued the leaders. The early development of service organizations and institutions in the Greater Kansas City and Topeka areas are reported by Dunham (1960), Hall (1960), and Macy (1961). Most of the agencies were started by one or a few individuals, who were motivated often by their religious convictions. Objectives were tackled with a singleness of purpose and little analysis of the most useful structure or of standards of service. The pioneers saw and met needs in ways that seemed appropriate to them. Their concern was great, their actions at times highly moralistic. Relatively few agencies were the result of an extensive and intensive inquiry into needs and resources and any careful planning of goals. Leaders were influenced by developments elsewhere, but hardly guided by them to the degree that concrete suggestions were followed, such as occurs today in local subsidiary branches of state and federal agencies. Leaders expended much energy and often sizable portions of their meager incomes. Buildings and physical facilities were at a premium, so personal time and effort went into locating and renovating them. Dunham (1960, p. 28) tells of a minister and his wife who, with very little assistance from others, developed a program of continuous institutional services. Having operated the program for ten years, they were obliged to find different quarters. The minister's wife describes the move: "There was much cleaning and repair work to be done over the entire building. My father, who was living with us, my daughter, husband and myself and the other workers spent many weeks in scrubbing, painting, varnishing, papering, etc. Barrel after barrel of whiskey bottles were taken from the attic and basement. Finally, after much hard work, the building was ready to move into . . ." Even though for a while some aged persons were cared for by the minister's agency only a few organizations in the early 1900s were established for that specific purpose. Nor did all aged persons find a safe niche in either an extended or a nuclear family. The county poorhouses and poor farms, available in extreme cases of need, were operated primarily as farm enterprises, at least in a good many states. Hogs and cattle were often more important than the human beings or inmates. Official reports said much about the health of the farm animals, but little about the welfare of the people.[1] In Kansas the decennial statistical reports of the residents of county poor farms were made, by the county assessor, to the State Board of Agriculture rather than to the then Board of Trustees of Charitable Institutions (*Kansas General Statutes*, 1875).

Church, fraternal, and other private homes had waiting lists. In addition to meeting some spiritual needs, church homes in small cities and towns seemed to have been largely custodial. Many were much more humane than most county homes. In fact, church and fraternal institutions were founded because of the unsatisfactory conditions of public establishments. Admission to an institution, church, fraternal, state, or county, spelled for the aging man and woman "the end of the trail."

Had Mrs. Craig required financial assistance a hundred or even sixty years ago, she probably would have been given some temporary aid by neighbors, or possibly even by a township trustee. More than likely, it would have been in the form of food, clothing, or fuel and would not have been available for an extended period of time. Assistance would have been given on the assumption that, if the situation should ever be reversed, she would act in a like manner. At best, aid would have been little. A crisis, such as the one brought on by her son's drinking, might have been met by neighbors. This, however, would have depended upon community attitudes toward drinking, the reputation of both the son and his mother, and the frequency with which the crisis recurred. As long as Mrs. Craig maintained her seemingly good health, neighbors might have tried to help her find work, such as "taking in washings." However, in small communities then, as now, work such as she might be able to do was scarce. Mrs. Craig probably would have faced the prospect of spending the remainder of her life in a poorhouse. If there she found genuine human kindness, she would, indeed, have been fortunate.

Despite the shortcomings of programs and practices, associations and institutions were established to serve people. The em-

[1] See any of the early Biennial Reports made to the Kansas State Welfare Agency, known at different times by different names, now the Kansas Board of Social Welfare.

phasis was primarily on social difficulties. What was wrong was to be relieved, eliminated or hidden away. When the agencies were established, objectives often were broad and all inclusive. Gradually projects were eliminated until one special program remained as happened in the minister's institution; speedily discarded were services to the aged which were doomed with the failure of a financial plan to make the program self-supporting (Dunham, 1960). This, however, was not always the case. Lindstrom (1961) reported a contrasting development of interest groups which started with a single objective and gradually assumed broader purposes. Hall (1960) described the emergence and the many changes of another agency which repeatedly helped develop specialized programs and then encouraged them to become autonomous associations. Many organizations and institutions that had their origins and growth in the nineteenth and early twentieth centuries continue to administer service programs today. In small communities they are limited almost entirely to church and other voluntary and local institutional services: the Salvation Army, Red Cross, and Scouts. Many are subsidiaries of national organizations and most are maintained largely by volunteers. Remnants of the past continue in the programs, or, more often, in the lack of programs for older people. In contrast to the process of emergence of service organizations of the nineteenth century and the first quarter of the twentieth are the growth and development of agencies and institutions since, particularly associations that have had support, guidance, and financial assistance from federal and state governments. Their development has been different and their impact upon communities and upon individuals has been marked.

Public Welfare Departments. Precipitated by the Great Depression of the thirties, three thousand local public welfare departments sprang into being almost overnight and functioned in ways that under the previous conditions of associational growth would have taken a span of generations (Brown, 1940; Altmeyer, 1945; Burns, 1949). States that formerly had been reluctant to assume responsibility for local financial needs, and the federal government, that had followed a hands off policy and let states look after their own, stepped in with legislation, finances, personnel, office equipment, organization plans, policies, records, reports, supervisors, consultants, training programs, philosophies and attitudes. The social security legislation that grew out of the Emergency Relief programs defined the persons to be aided, among whom were the aged and the blind. In only a few years local county welfare departments had become a part of community life. Federal and state funds continued to come. Their expenditure required careful records, audits, and reports, all of which proved more and more time-consuming. Budgets became the handmaidens of staff members.

Personnel for the local agencies whose programs were administered by the state or supervised by the state and administered locally, was recruited, paid, granted sick leave and vacation on the basis of what developed into merit system or civil service requirements. Salaries remained on a par with others in the county courthouse. Salaries higher than local rates, even when paid from federal sources, were unacceptable in the community. To increase substantially the local salaries of all public officials was scarcely possible with the small tax base that each county unit had when the county seats had to be accessible to a man on horseback. Any merger of county units would cause too many vested interests and loyalties to clash. Today many offices remain in the basements of county courthouses or up several flights of stairs. People with heart trouble, arthritis, or with poorly mended hips may have trouble climbing them. Some communities have provided adequate space for the headquarters of the local departments, with some even designated as Family and Community Service Departments. Whether they are in basements, up several flights of stairs, on the first floor or downstairs, whether they have adequate or inadequate offices, the modern agencies disburse financial aid more consistently. Bureaucratic policies and procedures have flourished. Human kindness may be found, but is not necessarily part of the agency. In some offices Mrs. Craig would find much, in others, very little. In some offices she might become aware that straight records are more important than her need to get and to keep her son out of jail. Public welfare workers in many small communities have to assume both kinds of responsibilities. Usually no other organized services to meet the two needs exist. It is a difficult combination of duties. The staff members are referred to as caseworkers and the recipients of the grants are known, even to themselves, as welfare clients. Thus, despite differences in structure and program, adequacy of financial grants, and amount, kind and quality of service, local public welfare organizations in sparsely populated rural centers have the elements of a big city bureaucracy. Public welfare agencies have brought to local small communities a fairly predictable source of financial assistance to those eligible, including the elderly and old. Accompanying the material aid, principally cash payments, has been an emphasis on budgetary management. However, service for the aged has had low priority. When public assistance cases were reclassified in 1964, in Kansas (the author was informed that this type of reclassification applied pretty generally), a large majority of Old Age Assistance recipients were placed in a category for "limited services only." This really meant little service, if any. Many departments visit the aged only to redetermine eligibility, once in six months, or perhaps even less frequently.

In the amazingly short period of time in which the county welfare departments were catapulted into small communities, something happened to mutual aid and neighborliness. Mutual aid was not able to meet the critical needs of the depression of the thirties and would not have sufficed for what has come since. What remained of mutuality and what could have genuinely benefited the local community were not nurtured by the welfare program. What remained of local neighborliness was increasingly relegated to the government agency. Some local workers and other residents were very much aware of this and wished to do something about it but there was little they could do. Changes had to come from the top. When they did not come, conformity was the simpler and perhaps the only course for the local department. But mutuality has not died out completely. This was abundantly clear in both Marion County and Holton. It continues to exist and can be stimulated and harnessed. A very encouraging stimulus to its revival is the Federal Government's present emphasis on recruiting volunteers and indigenous aides who could prove of great benefit to small communities. Many volunteers and aides might well be elderly persons.

The county welfare department is often the hub of other tax-supported and public welfare activities. Few agencies, such as Social Security, Vocational Rehabilitation, Employment Security, State Employment Service, and others have full-time personnel in rural areas. Staff members may spend one day a month in the county seat, or come in on some other part-time arrangement. They may or may not have office space in the welfare headquarters. However, the county department is usually informed about the welfare workers' comings and goings and may even make appointments for them. For state institutions and organizations, such as hospitals for the mentally ill, industrial schools, and institutions for the mentally retarded, the county welfare staff members may prepare social histories and assume follow-up duties, all in addition to working not only with the elderly, but also with other age groups. Governors' commissions on aging and departments for the aging within state welfare and health departments are increasingly available to assist the county worker with the variety of tasks that pertain to the health and welfare of older people. These organizations give valuable information and may help administer some of the program. Even though only at intervals on the scene locally, the state department staff can advise, supervise, and be consulted. Through them federal and state funds, such as those provided by the Older Americans Act, may be obtained. The state agencies, generally, are responsible for promoting the sound development of local programs including those designed to meet the needs of older persons. The effort on all levels of government to administer public welfare effectively and usefully has been enormous. The benefits have been substantial, the funds expended have been huge, and considering their size, accompanied by relatively few sizable national financial scandals.

As in all programs, not just health and welfare, designed to meet the needs of large masses of people, individuals fall by the wayside. In public education the educational needs of some children remain untouched and even special education, health, and counseling programs do not reach all. Welfare programs have provoked much dissatisfaction which has been expressed by both the beneficiaries and by the federal, state and local staff. Some have thought too much money was being spent; others, too little. Some have criticized the multiplicity and the rigidity of policies; others have wanted more rigid laws, more red tape. Some have felt that financial assistance to old people encouraged middle-aged children to neglect their parents; others have recognized the desire of old people to be independent of the financial assistance of their children and have advocated higher grants. Some have argued for more institutional care, others for more services in the home. Some have wanted liens on older persons' property; others have opposed liens. Some have criticized personnel for being hard, cold, and calculating; others have considered them entirely too generous and kind. Most persons have expressed less dissatisfaction when they knew the people of whom they spoke or the individual situation in its wider context. Yet always one hears of the cumbersome array of policies and their destructive effects. "The welfare system is a huge machine which crushes the dignity of human beings." The Welfare Rights Organization has voiced similar comments. Mrs. Craig would have agreed.

Much evidence exists to show that public welfare goals, in particular the emphasis on just, equitable, and humane administration of public assistance, are not being achieved to the extent desired and necessary, and a thorough reevaluation of the programs at various levels of administration seems to be under way in many quarters. In the meantime, major changes made possible through congressional legislation in 1962 and 1967 are beginning to be implemented. Especially important is the emphasis on service, the current effort to divorce the financial and service components, the focus on volunteer and indigenous help. Unfortunately the proposed changes do not appear, at the time of writing, to be simplifying rules and regulations. The situation of the aged is, apparently, not going to change noticeably.

Mental health centers and nursing and care homes have one trait in common with the county welfare department: Funds have been and are available from federal and state sources to stimulate their establishment, and, with financial aid, consultation and guidance. The agents, however, may be more experienced with metropolitan areas than with small communities.

Mental Health Centers. Following the passage of the Mental Health and Mental Retardation Center Act (PL 88–164) in 1963, mental health centers in the United States have had a phenomenal growth.

The 1965 amendments to the act (PL 89–105) provided funds for staffing the centers. Legislation enacted in the fifties stimulated the organization of many mental health clinics. One hundred twenty-three centers serving one or more rural counties were put into operation in forty states by July 11, 1968. Of these centers, twenty-eight served rural counties only.[2] (A rural county is situated "outside a Standard Metropolitan Statistical Area and [had] more than 50 percent of the population in communities of 2,500 or less in 1960.") At the same time many clinics were, to a large extent, financed locally.

Mental health clinics or community psychiatric facilities established outside institutions had made considerable, if slow, progress before 1963. Their early origins are traced by Deutsch (1937, Ch. 15) to the social movements toward mental hygiene and child guidance that began in the early twentieth century, and to the outpatient services of hospitals for the mentally ill. These movements were affected by other forces, such as the public health movement and the growth of social work and its changes, in the late teens and early twenties, to an emphasis on the psychological needs of the individual. Mental health clinics that were not primarily affiliated with hospitals were devoted to the study and treatment of problems of children. Adults, and especially old people, received much less attention. The first clinic, established in Chicago in 1909, became the Institute of Juvenile Research. It was followed by others in which the programs were administered by a team consisting of a psychiatrist, psychologist and one or more social workers. A number of early boosts to the growth of child guidance clinics occurred: the five-year demonstration program sponsored by the Commonwealth Fund in the 1920s, which grew out of a study by the National Committee on Mental Hygiene on problems of school children; the establishment of the American Orthopsychiatric Association in 1924. Hence, the continuous and traditional concern of mental health clinics with the well-being of children could be expected to militate against a similar focus on the psychiatric problems of older people.

Outpatient services of mental hospitals, first introduced in 1885 by the Philadelphia Hospital, were supplemented later in various states by community clinics sponsored by local mental health

[2] Dorothea L. Dolan, 1969, personal communication.

associations, social work agencies, schools or other organizations. Many outpatient services emphasized the diagnosis and treatment of children and members of their families. By the end of 1965, 2,000 psychiatric clinics had been established throughout the country (National Committee Against Mental Illness, 1966, p. 15). With the effort to move older patients who were not profiting from institutional care out of mental hospitals to make room for younger patients with more hopeful prognoses, pressures had begun to be placed on community clinics to serve elderly psychiatric patients. By 1964 only 2 percent of the total clinic population was in the sixty-five-and-over age group (Rosen, Anderson and Bahn, 1967). Only 4 percent of the 2,000 clinics were in rural areas.

With federal funds available for establishing and staffing mental health centers, their development in different communities since 1963 has been rapid but with similar patterns. This is less true of clinics originating before the Mental Health Center Act. A comparative study (McDonald, 1963) of two facilities established in the early fifties in two counties in Kansas, which had sizable rural populations, shows a variety of dissimilarities. One facility grew out of the mental health activities of a men's service club that began almost as early as the child guidance clinic movement. Through the years it operated on a part-time basis. The clinic's present form was precipitated by the untimely death, in 1947, of a highly respected and well-liked community leader who for some time had advocated the organization of such a facility. In fact, he was discussing the need for it when he was stricken. This had the effect of mobilizing community interest. The other clinic was established after a systematic community survey had been made. The county seat, a city of nearly 165,000 people, was surrounded by small towns, villages and farms. The approach to the establishment of the community agency was characteristic of the then current health and welfare efforts in urban centers. The community study and early organizing efforts were sponsored by the local Community Chest and Council and was conducted by the national organization of Chests and Councils. After the report was published, another local group took primary initiative for promoting action. The emphasis, in public health, on prevention and the focus on child guidance affected both clinics, especially the clinic originally sponsored by the men's service club. The same public health officer—a man concerned with mental health—served the community for a number of years. He viewed the objectives of mental health clinics and other community clinics under his administration from the same perspective. Their function was primarily educational and preventive and attention was focused largely on infants and very young children. When they needed further services, patients were referred to local physicians. Hence, their support and cooperation were solicited and the medical profession was well represented in the developments that followed the death of the community leader. Other professional personnel, such as those of a state university in the county and those from the limited number of local health and welfare agencies, were also represented, though not predominantly so. From the beginning and through the years, a sustaining, effective support came from local citizens with strong community service interests.

The focus on infants and young children and the primary concern with the prevention of mental illness gave way to a treatment service for older children and adults when school administrators, the juvenile court judge, and social workers who were faced with teen-age behavior problems exerted pressure. Nevertheless, in viewing the course of growth and change on a local level one sees clearly that, in this particular community, older people would tend to have low priority for psychiatric clinical services.

The other clinic, which was in the larger community, began operating six years after its need was established by the community survey. (Actually, the survey was authorized by the Board of the Community Chest in 1940 but, for lack of staff, was not implemented until about ten years later.) The medical profession was only minimally involved in the early development of this clinic. Social workers and a number of representatives from a variety of professions, and other interested citizens contributed most. This clinic, too, was established primarily to serve children and youth, though with less emphasis on very young children. In time it served people of all ages, without much focus, however, on older patients.

In 1964 an estimated 12,000 elderly patients in the United States were given services designed to reduce some symptomology. Nearly 12 percent were referred to other agencies; about 10 percent were given only an evaluation, either complete or incomplete. The clinic services were found to be similar to care in mental hospitals (Rosen, Anderson and Bahn, 1967). Responses to informal inquiries would seem to indicate that, in 1969, outpatient mental health centers of all kinds include older people as potential patients. In actual practice services to older patients are limited primarily to crises preceding admission to, or release from, a hospital for the mentally ill. The increase in facilities in small communities and the growing interest in the aged would portend an improvement. A major problem for all psychiatric facilities, including mental health outpatient clinics, is the shortage of qualified personnel, despite the colossal increase in the total number of psychiatrists, psychologists, and psychiatrically-trained social workers from 23,000 in 1950 to 65,000 in 1965. The number of National Institute of Mental Health training stipends, the primary reason for the increase, rose from 219 in 1948 to over 9,000 in 1965. The National Committee Against Mental Illness, Inc., estimated that Mental Health Centers, Medicare, and other programs will, by 1975, require between 120,000 and 125,000 psychiatrists, psychologists, social workers, and nurses. In the meantime positions remain vacant, and individual staff members in many instances provide services to more than one facility (Rosen, Anderson, and Bahn, 1967).

Care and Nursing Homes. County homes and church and other private institutions established to serve older people preceded present care and nursing homes. The county homes were a part of state and local poor relief legislation and as such were thoroughly stigmatized. Valiant efforts were made, and instances could be cited of meritorious services for the elderly in religious and fraternal homes designed to improve their lot, but the history of institutional, particularly tax-supported, care for old people is not a happy chapter in social welfare and health annals.

With the passage of the Social Security Act in 1935, which made available monthly incomes to needy older people, and with the federal government's policy of denying grants to persons in public institutions, homes of all kinds administered privately by individuals and groups began to flourish, at least in number. Not much could be said for the quality of many of them. Often they were dilapidated old houses converted into a mixture of care homes and

gradations of nursing homes. The administrators generally were un-
trained, inexperienced and poorly qualified for their jobs, though
some displayed extraordinary insight and understanding and much
concern for their inmates. Financial returns were small, at least
from low-income patients, and with limited funds available, the
employment situation was extremely poor. By 1953, 25,000 homes
accommodating 450,000 patients, most of them elderly, were reported for the country as a whole. Of these, only 7,000 homes were
considered to have skilled nursing facilities (Pollock, Locke and
Kramer, 1961, p. 41). Many of the 25,000 homes were in rural
areas and small towns. Modification of the Hill-Burton Act in 1954
made available federal funds for building nonprofit nursing homes,
and the number of homes increased. By 1963, the United States had
13,514 nursing homes or care homes with nursing services available.
The average ratio was 491.5 employees for every 1,000 patients;
thirty states had fewer staff members than the national average;
two states with large rural populations, Kentucky and South Dakota, averaged less than 400 employees per 1,000 patients (U.S.,
Bureau of Census, 1968, p. 71, table 95). Thus, on the basis of one
criterion, homes in rural areas may not compare very favorably with
those in urban centers.

The physical facilities and quality of services in care and
nursing homes is improving. More state supervision, licensing, and
the availability of federal and state funds upgrade the facilities.
With Medicare and Medicaid being granted only under approved
conditions, homes making available nursing care are particularly
under pressure to upgrade both the physical facilities and the patient care. Classifications of functions are being clarified. Now homes
are designated as care homes if they are designed to serve ambula-
tory patients able to care for their own personal needs, and as various types of nursing homes if they are designed for more extensively
disabled patients. Extended care facilities follow the patient's stay
in a hospital, and when extended care is not necessary, skilled medical nursing homes and intermediate medical nursing homes are designed to meet the need of bedridden patients. Medicare is available
for licensed extended care homes and intermediate skilled medical
institutions and, under some conditions, for the skilled medical nursing home. Currently a major obstacle to the success of nursing

homes, particularly in rural areas, is the shortage of qualified staff, such as registered nurses, physiotherapists, and other professionals. Recent federal housing legislation, in addition to the changes in the Hill-Burton Act, has materially aided the development of care and nursing homes. The National Housing Act of 1968 makes available funds so that "rental and cooperative housing can be built which is designed primarily for occupancy by elderly and handicapped persons and includes cafeterias, or dining halls, community rooms, workshops, infirmaries" (U.S., Dept. of Health, Education and Welfare, 1969c, pp. 9, 23). For the first time, the Federal Housing Authority (FHA) can permit the cost of major equipment used in the nursing home to be included in the mortgage funded by the FHA. When federal funds are used, the current procedure in establishing a care or nursing home may require much time, energy and modification of plans by the sponsors, particularly if they are community groups inadequately informed about the laws and policies of federal housing legislation and federal and state licensing requirements. Despite the delays and disappointments, the present increase in care and nursing homes and the improvement of services is encouraging and, like the recent development of mental health centers, should bode somewhat encouragingly for the future care of old people regardless of whether they live in metropolitan or rural areas.

All three agencies—welfare agencies, community mental health clinics, and care and nursing homes—are currently serving older people, but are otherwise dissimilar. The welfare department, from the beginning of its present structure, has administered Old Age Assistance, and in most instances from the implementation of the Social Security Act, Aid to the Blind, including aid for the elderly blind. The services that have been available in addition to any financial grant have varied greatly in kind and quality from state to state, and within states. In general, services for older persons, especially those who are not blind, have had low priority. Community mental health clinics have historically served children and their immediate families rather than older people. With the current growth of mental health centers, more older patients may expect to be served, but, at present, only 2 percent of the total mental health clinic caseload consists of patients sixty-five years old and older. Nursing and care homes traditionally have been established primarily for older people. In the past most homes rendered custodial care, but as more and better health and welfare services are added, the aged are faring better. Despite some improvement, many homes still have a long way to go before they meet state and federal standards. Burger (1969, pp. 14–17) gives a clear analysis of their defects.

All three agencies continue to be plagued with the lack of personnel, both in number and quality. The most substantial effort to meet the problem has been made in the mental health field with help from the federal government. However, through continuous in-service and educational-leave programs, numerous public welfare administrators, with financial aid from state and federal sources, have made sizable efforts to upgrade their local staff. Nursing and care homes are in the process of evaluating and improving their unsatisfactory personnel conditions. With stimulation from federal and state governments progress is slowly being made. Of the three agencies, local mental health facilities seem to have enjoyed the greatest approval and public support in their quest for qualified personnel, perhaps partly because of their objectives. Earlier developments, with emphasis on qualified staff, may have had an influence, together with the historical focus on the priority of services to children and a commitment to the children's best interests. Many community clinics grew slowly. As did the two Kansas facilities, clinics elsewhere grew out of recognized needs and called for much local effort for their initiation and maintenance. Citizen boards and other groups have had the major responsibility for nurturing them. In the same manner many nursing and care homes have been established by community groups and institutions. A good many proprietary homes were established without the participation of citizens and consequently have lacked community and financial support. County welfare departments in the Great Depression of the thirties were of necessity imposed upon localities, and as federal and state funds largely supported the programs, local residents have done little by way of planning, establishing, or running the public welfare department. Any encouragement of effective advisory boards has been sporadic and at times poorly implemented. The resources of all three agencies, theoretically, at least, are available to older people regardless of the size of the community in which they live. This may be more true of public welfare and nursing and care homes than it is, or has been, of community mental health clinics. The recent rapid growth of clinics should make mental health facilities increasingly available, not only to elderly persons everywhere, but also and quite specifically to the older residents of small communities.

SERVICES

Except for welfare services, mental health clinics, and nursing homes, Medicare, Medicaid, and often, though by no means always, local hospital care, comparatively few organized services are locally available to the elderly in small communities. When services, such as state employment facilities and other state services, are available their representatives are on the scene infrequently. Yet many programs might be administered, and could well make life more comfortable and bearable. Many projects, mostly in urban areas, are partly funded by the Older Americans Act. If small communities needed and wanted these services some financial assistance in establishing them probably would be provided. Other programs, no doubt, could be organized with funds from federal, state, and local sources. Health services, such as those of visiting nurses, homemaker aides, and physiotherapists, might currently be financed with grants provided under Public Law 89–749. Housing needs could in part be met with help from federal sources. With able and committed leadership and adequate citizen interest, a good many services could be provided by volunteers with local funds, and many of them could be performed by the older people themselves. In its first three years of operation the Older Americans Act provided money for almost one thousand community projects designed to serve the elderly (U.S., Department of Health, Education and Welfare, 1969b, pp. 18–19). No small community wants or needs all the possible programs, but many small towns and rural areas might well use a combination of several of them. Certainly, no small community should be without access to every one of them, although many are today.

Of the projects funded in fiscal 1968, recreation and leisure-time activities headed the list: 34 percent of the total number. A large city directory of leisure-time resources would indicate the scope of such programs. The *Directory for Leisure-Time Resources for Older Men and Women in Greater Minneapolis* (1963), for instance, lists sixty-eight clubs and groups sponsoring all kinds of dancing, entertainment, games, music, painting, needlework, crafts, and many other recreational activities. Centers are often established to house recreational and leisure-time programs, and may serve many different purposes. The National Council on Aging (n.d.), in addition to listing possible "social, recreational, educational" activities for such a center, includes "counseling, health, nutrition, employment and voluntary community service components, among others. It can serve as the resource for finding, recruiting and re-motivating isolated, rejected, healthy or problem-ridden older persons. It can help restore their identity and sense of usefulness. It can create employment opportunities both on its own staff and in the community. It can be a focus for coordinating and creating community resources for the elderly poor. It can serve as an agent for change, for understanding, for service and for action [p. 1]."

Centers, simply for recreation, or for other purposes as well, may be established in small communities. The Lutheran Welfare Society of North Dakota is developing multi-purpose activity centers and associated services in twenty-five communities. The program has two full-time staff members who are assigned to geographic areas but relies primarily on the services of volunteers. Lansford, North Dakota, has a center in the Country Club. A small amount of federal money was made available for remodeling, and the Club is responsible for maintenance, but the program, including much of the labor for remodeling, is run by volunteers.[3] Generally, it is assumed that an adequate center program will need an employed administrator; however, particularly when the program is not too ambitious, dedicated volunteer leadership can do much. In

[3] Both North Dakota programs were funded under Title III of the Older Americans Act of 1965. The former is entitled *Senior Adult Volunteer Corps, Project No. O.A.A. 475,* and the grantee is the Lutheran Welfare Society of North Dakota, Fargo, N.D. The latter is entitled *Hi-Neighbor Senior Citizen, Project No. O.A.A. 956,* and the grantee is Lansford Country Club, Lansford, N.D.

establishing centers of activity of older people, rural counties suffer
from too great distances. One center situated, for example, in a
county seat, cannot be presumed to serve all the elderly residents
who live within the boundaries of the county. In fact, only those
residing nearby are likely to use the facility. When not enough centers can be made available, arrangements can often be made to
meet in churches, schools, or other buildings in different settlements
in the geographic area. Such facilities, which served for four of the
six programs in Marion County, may give older persons an opportunity to eat together and visit with each other. This is a limited,
but may prove a worthwhile, service. Volunteer efforts may be
strengthened by a mobile staff unit serving one or more counties.

The second largest number of projects receiving funds from
OAA sources during fiscal 1968 was for community planning. (A
list of cities to which awards were made for planning in the 1968
fiscal year would seem to indicate that few grants were made to
small communities.) To assure the availability of as comprehensive
and coordinated as possible a network of services for and of elderly
persons, councils on aging were organized. In small communities
planning councils often take on administrative duties to help implement planned programs. This definitely happened in Marion
County. The county-wide council, in cooperation with local groups,
assessed needs and planned ways of meeting them. The council
appropriated available funds and its members gave personal assistance from time to time in putting the plans into effect. For example, members of the council assumed the major responsibility for
designing and constructing a county fair float. It also planned
hobby shows and leader workshops and implemented the plans.
In the organization of community councils of and for the aging, on
a county-wide, town, small city or neighborhood basis, it should be
determined whether or not the council should be related to one segment of the population. A council for aging, rather than a community council composed of a variety of groups, spotlights one group
of persons and tends to mobilize interest in that one group. However,
the men and women who are interested in older people may also
be concerned for the mentally ill, for children and youth, for persons afflicted with multiple sclerosis, cancer, blindness, or any other
illness or disability. A number of planning groups with interlocking

interests, manpower, and financial requirements may emerge. Perhaps, if all are placed under the same umbrella, more coordinated planning is possible. Yet each group may suffer from the lack of special attention. In Marion County, it was decided to establish two planning groups, one for the aged and one for mental health. Perhaps when both programs are firmly established they can be coordinated in one council.

Closely related to community planning and often housed in multi-purpose centers are information and referral services. This means that a person, often a volunteer with the appropriate orientation, is available to give older people information when needed. It also means that the aging person may be referred to other sources of information or service. In 1968, 11 percent of the OAA funds were expended for information and referral services.

In Marion County information and referral services were introduced and manned by county welfare staff members. The limited use of the service can probably be attributed to the fact that the information and referral role of county workers was not clearly distinguished in the minds of the public from the responsibilities, of same staff members, for determining eligibility for public assistance. If information and referral programs are to be real sources of help, the purposes must be clearly understood and be acceptable.

A sizable number of projects, approximately 14 percent of the total funded in 1968 by the OAA, were established to provide home care services for older residents in the community. These services included visits from homemakers and other aides, the delivery of hot meals, home maintenance, friendly visiting, telephone assurance, and others designed to enable older people to remain in their own homes. Home care projects are established to meet the needs and interests of older men and women as an alternative to care and nursing homes. Eventually many persons will require nursing home or hospital care. However, most older people prefer to stay in their own homes and in their own neighborhoods for as long as possible. That home care and home health services have not captured the imagination of the public in small communities may be in part because programs administered in family homes are less visible than those in institutions. The physical structure of institutional care can be seen, and a sense of relief may understandably ensue when an old person is safely tucked away in a nursing home where he will have physical attention. Moreover, he will not be conspicuous there, and so will not remind younger people that old age awaits everyone who lives long enough, a condition faced with less than pleasant anticipation by most people.

Among the great variety of home care programs that may be introduced into any community regardless of the density of its population is a homemaker service: "one form of assistance" rendered "when a family or one individual cannot maintain living and household routines during a time of stress or crisis" (Hart, 1965, p. 2). An older person who, for example, is recuperating from a broken hip may continue to live in his own home when he leaves a hospital, provided that a homemaker is there to take care of things. Similarly, if an old man and his wife were to become ill with the flu and hospital care is neither available nor even needed, a homemaker may well tide things over during the emergency. The homemaker needs to be qualified for her job. Hart emphasizes that "those experienced in the field believe that, in selecting homemakers, attention should be focused on an individual's personality, understanding of human behavior, and skills in home management—not on the number of years of her formal education [p. 8]." In other words, it matters much more what kind of a person she is than how much knowledge she has accumulated. Homemakers usually work under the supervision of a health or welfare agency and receive in-service training from their sponsoring agency, which, in small communities, is frequently the county welfare department. The homemaker may be in the family home daily for a few hours for a few days, or all day for a longer period. The service may be paid for wholly or in part by the agency sponsoring the program, or by the individual or family using the services.

Hot meals delivered, often once a day, also help older men and women remain in their own homes. They provide nutritious and tasty meals for homebound elderly persons who are often living alone, and have little motivation or energy to prepare a variety of food. Moreover, as Mrs. Matson remarked, if a variety of food is cooked for one person, leftovers have to be eaten for the rest of the week. Except for calories, older people generally require the essential nutrients in the same amounts as do younger people and, according to Swenson (1964), "ongoing metabolic processes demand that all essential nutrients be present simultaneously in the fluids nourishing the cells." In developing programs of hot delivered meals, the assistance and cooperation of a number of professional persons are essential. These may well include a doctor, nurse, social worker, and nutritionist. Rural Extension Services may often help in rural areas. A local hospital will sometimes prepare the meals. In villages and small towns, volunteers are usually needed and available, both to prepare the food and to deliver it. Besides the benefits derived from the hot meals, the daily contact with a person coming into their homes regularly does much to dispel the loneliness of infirm older people and to keep them in touch. It can become a source of new friendships and interests.

Friendly regular visiting and telephone reassurances can be introduced in any small community, and both programs may be administered entirely by volunteers. Older people themselves can be encouraged to assume much of the responsibility for the visiting and invalids and even bedridden patients may do the telephoning.

Home health service—administered under Medicare and designed specifically to facilitate care in the patient's own home and thus shorten his stay in hospital—and a host of other programs, which were not listed specifically in the report of the distribution of the Older American Act funds, might help the older person to stay in his own home. These could include handyman services, reading for the blind or for persons with poor vision, regular assistance with shopping and banking, support in walking, and other aids. One service rendered by a group of young people and their Sunday School teacher in Marion County proved to be of much help to an older woman who lived alone and had to be either in a wheel chair or in bed. She was able to do her own cooking from the wheel chair, but could not clean her house or take care of her yard. At regular intervals the class of young people and their teacher came from another small town to give the house a good cleaning and to mow and rake the yard.

In both Marion County and in Holton, efforts to solve the transport problems failed. A commercial taxicab service seemed to be the only solution, and in Holton, that plan proved unsuccessful. Three percent of the programs listed in the Older Americans Act

Progress Report were for transport. Whether or not any of the programs were located in small communities is not indicated. The need for transportation in small rural areas and ways of meeting them may well be a subject for more study and experimentation, since adequate transport might enable many an elderly person to live at home at least a while longer.

Six percent of the projects listed were devoted to counseling on personal problems, ranging from questions of budgeting, financial investments, nursing home care, and moving into an apartment, to family quarrels and possible opportunities for employment or what to do about retirement. The counselor does well to remember that many old people have difficulty accepting advice from younger people, and that, just because they are old, people do not necessarily need the counsel of others. As in most counseling efforts, the best approach to old people tends to be one of listening to what they have to say and giving them the support and information they need to arrive at their own decisions.

A great variety of community projects to which older people can contribute or which are administered on their behalf require in-service training, such as homemaker services, friendly visiting, information and referral programs and, perhaps even such services as reading to the blind and aiding older persons who are unsteady on their feet. Certainly, projects such as FIND (described in Series V, *FIND, A Model Community Action Program* prepared by the National Council on Aging), which was designed by the Office of Economic Opportunity to locate friendless, isolated, needy, and disabled older persons, requires some orientation and training as does VISTA,[4] SCORE (Senior Corps of Retired Executives), or other similar programs.

Of the projects funded under Title III of the Older Americans Act, both foster home placement and protective services, in

---

[4] VISTA, a program introduced by the Office of Economic Opportunity, is a citizens volunteer corps. Through VISTA older people have been given opportunities for part-time work in their own communities: been on recreation and cultural enrichment programs for youngsters, teaching adults who seek high school equivalency diplomas, guiding families in poverty to existing health and legal services, showing mothers how to shop wisely on limited incomes, helping to start neighborhood clean-up campaigns, and aiding adults to find and keep jobs.

terms of number of grants, had low priority. Yet each service may be very important in the lives of individual elderly persons. Protective services are indicated when a person is unable to assume responsibility for himself or his property. An older person may be placed in a foster home for a variety of reasons, including the need for protective care. Foster care in a desirable family home may serve an older man or woman when living alone is not possible and institutional care is neither wanted nor needed. *Foster Family Care for the Aged,* which has an Appendix, "Guidelines for the Homefinder" (U.S., Department of Health, Education and Welfare, 1965), defines the purpose of foster home placement: "In contrast to institutional care, a foster family not only provides an easier, less regimented life to an elderly person; it may mean savings in financial and—even more important—human terms [p. 3]." Under desirable conditions these human terms consist of a family home in which the older person receives moral and physical support and affection. He can feel accepted and secure. To the extent possible, he has the opportunity to mingle not only with members of the family but also with others in the community. Obviously foster families need to be carefully selected and a responsible agency (in small communities this usually is the county welfare department) needs to keep in touch with the older person.

Few community programs, spotlighting the needs and potential contributions of older people, have brought as warm a response as that of foster grandparents. The Manuels need grandparents and the grandparents need Manuels. The two can get together in any community and can form a mutually beneficial relationship. This has been done informally for years, but its great possibilities within a locality have never been sensed. In organized form, the United States Office of Economic Opportunity initiated the program in 1965. With the cooperation and assistance of the Administration of Aging, United States Department of Health, Education, and Welfare, the program was developed to provide employment for older people with low incomes. The children were living in institutions. Foster grandparents were assigned only two children each to whom they gave personal attention and affection. The Merrill-Palmer Institute studied in depth a program at the Sarah Fisher Home for Children in Farmington, Michigan, with a control group in Maryland where conditions were about the same. The Institute found (Saltz, 1968) that: "The rich emotional interchange between the foster-grandparents and 'their' children has proven to be, in fact, the most distinctive and important contribution of the foster-grandparents to the institutional routine. The emotional needs and potential satisfactions of the foster-grandparents as employees and those of infants and young children in their care seem to be, in a very unique way, mutual and complementary [p. 5]."

Other foster grandparent projects, supported both by employees and by volunteers, are reported to meet with success. They may or may not be centered primarily in institutions. The older person with a great giving and emotional capacity should be considered a potential contributor and his expressed interest not merely shrugged off with the opinion that "she or he wants to relive his own childhood," an opinion expressed by a person in a position to bring older people and children together. The potential contribution of older persons to children is not confined to infants and children up to six. Elderly men and women may be able to get close to and understand teen-agers, including those who are presenting social problems. Certain experiences, such as those of travel, may prove very interesting to school age children. The County Superintendent of Schools in Marion County visualized the possibility of having older people who had traveled visit geography classes in the local schools and help "make foreign countries become real." Mr. Hostetter, as well as writing verses, helped young children start playing a violin; he exchanged rocks with pen pals in all parts of the world. The opportunities of foster-grandparents are as many as a fertile imagination permits.

What older people, in good or fair health, who live in small communities seem to want more than anything else, that is, if they are not operating farms or businesses or managing a house, is work, both to meet economic requirements and to fulfill the emotional needs arising out of lowered status, diminished social contacts, boredom, and all the other accompaniments of retirement from gainful employment. One man who, after a two-year effort to find work, finally found a part-time paying job, was heard to say with great relief and satisfaction, "Now I feel like a man again." Yet employment full- or part-time in a small community is very difficult to find. Young people leave home because jobs are unavailable. Despite their need for the few opportunities for work that may be had locally, retired parents and grandparents prefer to let their children take the jobs so that the children may remain in the community. Efforts of public and private employment services to identify possible employment and develop job openings for older residents have been centered primarily, though not exclusively, in large cities. Even in metropolitan areas the efforts seem usually to have met with limited success. Nevertheless, they have provided some opportunities and they were worthwhile.

Perhaps what is needed in small cities, towns, and rural areas are concentrated community attempts such as the Office of Economic Opportunity's Senior Action Program (SWAP, described in Series I, *A Model Action Program* prepared by the National Council on Aging). To administer SWAP projects sponsoring groups were composed of representatives from business, labor, the professions, clergy, schools, Agricultural Extension Department, and others. The groups focused on finding part-time employment and on recruiting, training, and placing older people in the jobs. In small communities such a sponsoring organization might well delineate possible work not now in existence and better performed by older men and women than by younger workers. SCORE is an example of a successful program in which the experiences of retired executives are used to help small businessmen. The sponsoring group in Holton had no difficulty producing suggestions for unpaid service projects. If money were available, they could have invented paid jobs equally easily. They possessed the imagination and ability to analyze the need for and find some possible employment opportunities not now existing. Currently nonexistent employment with pay will have to be found and made available to retired workers in rural areas. Among other possibilities, clean-up and beautification projects in small communities would seem to offer the most obvious possibilities. Most small towns have large areas of dilapidated buildings and streets. Not only are they unsightly, but also present health hazards. Such areas can use the gardening and planting as well as the constructing, renovating, and remodeling skills of retired residents. Funds now used for grants in aid to individuals might well pay wages for useful work. Financial investment in older workers' experience would pay dividends, not only in a more satisfying life for the person, but also in benefits for the community. When work with pay is not possible, and even when it is, voluntary efforts, such as the Holton community projects, should be encouraged. They do not add financial income, but do contribute to the participants' positive self-image.

Community service agencies emerge and grow under varying kinds of circumstances and in different ways. Their development in recent years has been greatly influenced by the availability of federal and state funds and by the patterns established by laws, rules, and regulations of central financing and planning organizations. For the most part, structure, function, and procedures have been of urban origins and have not been modified greatly to meet local rural conditions. This has hastened the decline of local efforts consisting largely of unorganized mutual aid. However, some of this aid still exists and can be harnessed. Even though minor efforts have been made by service agencies to solicit the advice and cooperation of local citizens in small communities, generally speaking, little emphasis has been placed on the agencies' working with local citizens as a team, and there has been little focus on the mobilization of the wisdom and concern of neighbors and friends. Community agencies and institutions of all kinds established to render service continue largely to be decrement-geared. Their activities tend to be remedial or palliative. In practice they do not stress prevention or nurture the use of potentials for positive well-being. Changes in focus, even when their merits are recognized, are not easily accomplished. Functions, structures, and procedures become institutionalized and bureaucratized in social welfare organizations just as in other aspects of society. Small community agencies dependent upon central financing and patterns are merely part of the total complex of organizations and have little opportunity to modify either local structure or programs to serve local needs more adequately.

Perhaps funds dispensed under Title III of the Older Americans Act and by the Office of Economic Opportunity and other sources will, as in the past, be available in the future. In any event, the volunteer efforts of small-community citizens, including the elderly, will be essential in the months and years to come. Community agencies established to render services to the aged, like all community associations, have a self- and a public-image, which, if positive, acts as a powerful dynamic in motivating the staff, in satisfying the beneficiaries of the services, and in obtaining the cooperation of the community. When the element of worth has special meaning, the effects on the self-image are particularly significant.

Objectives

7

In small communities the social worker who serves the elderly, their families, and other clusters of people has two basic objectives: to alleviate discomfort and to release potentials. Sometimes one objective takes precedence; sometimes another. Frequently both are involved.

Mr. and Mrs. Tom Brandon ask the welfare worker for information about "homes," within the county or in an adjacent county. They are concerned about Tom's father and hope a home will be a solution.

Last spring Tom's mother died. Tom and Margaret, his wife, simply could not let Mr. Brandon, Sr., "going on eighty," live alone on a farm sixty-five miles away. His vision and hearing were bad, and he had arthritis in his hips. If something had happened to him, no one would have known for hours, perhaps not for days. There was a good chance to sell the farm, and Tom and his wife persuaded his father to sell the land, farm implements, and household furniture. They took him into their own small modern home and gave him the northeast room. It really was Tom

Junior's room but he did not mind moving to the basement. "Not as long as I have plenty to eat," said Tom, grinning. The plan has not worked. Grandfather Brandon, after six months, seems even more unhappy than when he first moved in. At first he helped with the dishes, but then he quit that and "just remains in his room listening to his radio and broods." He leaves his room long enough to come to meals. "But," adds Margaret, "he misses quite a few because he says he isn't hungry." Tom explains that his father is very lonely. He cannot venture out because of his poor eyesight and arthritis, and has no friends in town. All of his old friends are too far away to visit him. A number have died, and others are "in a worse state of health than Dad."

They have tried everything. Margaret takes his meals to his room when he does not feel like coming to the table. Tom tries to visit with him in the evenings. Repeatedly they have invited him to sit in the living room and watch television. He does not seem interested. He brought his old radio with him, and that is on most of the day. It is turned up until the noise is deafening, and it "gets on Margaret's nerves." The only person in the family who seems to get any response from Mr. Brandon, Sr., is Peggy, fifteen. She has her friends and school activities and so cannot devote much time to her grandfather. The Brandons have reluctantly concluded that a home is the solution for Tom's father. Tom's sister Lillian lives in Chicago and cannot take him into her home. However, she and her husband have agreed to contribute to the cost of his care in a home. They think Mr. Brandon, Sr., should have other old people with whom he can visit, and when he needs care, the staff will be better prepared to give it than are Margaret and Tom.

The Brandons ask about probable costs. When the farm was sold, there was still a small mortgage on it. The unencumbered amount was placed in a savings account and draws a little less than fifteen dollars monthly interest. Mr. Brandon's monthly Social Security check is fifty-five dollars. He insists on paying fifty dollars, for room and board. The less than twenty-five dollars that is left supposedly is spent for personal items. However, he seems to manage to slip most of it to Peggy. Tom is a mechanic for the Watson Garage. With careful management the couple makes monthly payments on the home, takes care of two insurance policies to help with some of the anticipated expense of putting Tom Junior and Peggy through college, and pays for one life policy on Tom. They cannot contribute much to the cost of care for Tom's father, but they think Lil and her husband will be quite generous.

They have not talked to Mr. Brandon about his wishes in the matter. "After all," says Margaret, "he is almost eighty years old, and he needs others to plan for him." They do agree, however, that after planning for himself for many years, he may like to be included in the discussion. Would Miss Jones (the social worker) talk with him? She states that she will be willing to but does not want to persuade him to enter a home or to make any other change against his wishes. She suggests that it may be possible for the whole family to discuss the situation with Tom's father since all are affected, and perhaps other solutions can be considered. Tom seems rather to like the idea, but Margaret is reluctant. However, with Tom consenting and Margaret supporting him, they agree to tell Tom's father of their concern about his loneliness and that Miss Jones will visit him to see if a more suitable plan can be worked out. Hesitantly, they also agree to participate in a family conference. When asked about his father's hobbies or interests, Tom comments, "Dad has always worked very hard. He used to read the newspaper, and on Sundays we'd go to church, but I don't think he has ever had any interest other than farming."

When Miss Jones visits Mr. Brandon, Sr., he at first seems determined not to enter into any kind of a discussion. He answers with a curt "no" or "yes" or "hmmm." Some reference to an old chair in which he sits brings forth the comment that it belonged to "mom and me." It was bought secondhand when they "set up housekeeping."

"How long ago was that?" asks Miss Jones.

"Fifty-one years last February." Mr. Brandon is struggling with tears.

"It must be hard to go on without her," comments Miss Jones quietly. Mr. Brandon nods. There is a sob. Miss Jones rises, walks to the bed table and looks closely at a photograph. "Is this she?"

"Yes." Miss Jones sits down again. There is a silence. "There never was a better wife or mother than she." Miss Jones nods sympathetically. "Is the other picture on the table of your granddaughter?" she asks. "There seems to be a resemblance."

"There is," responds Mr. Brandon, and for the first time his face lights up. "She is like my wife, Peggy is. Sometimes she comes into my room and asks me questions. All kinds of fool questions. She'll say, 'Grandpa, how did you meet grandma?' or 'What did you do when you took her out?' or 'Did you and grandma dance at parties?' And when I'll say, 'Yes, but not the kind of dances you kids dance,' she'll get up and do some funny turns and say, 'Was it like this, Grandpa?' I tell her, 'No. We waltzed, and sometimes I jigged.' 'Show me, Grandpa,' she says. And I get up, but these stiff hips of mine won't move like they ought to." Then he becomes silent again.

"Have you seen a doctor about your hips?" asks Miss Jones.

"No. I guess it is rheumatism," says Mr. Brandon. "Most people get that when they are old. You just live with it, I guess."

Miss Jones has tried to talk slowly and distinctly without raising her voice. She notices that Mr. Brandon seems to understand what she says. "Your hearing seems to be pretty good," she ventures.

"It is, when you talk plain like that," he says. "Most people just rattle away too fast and they yell. There's Margaret. She is always in a hurry and talks so fast I can't hear her. I turn up that thing," pointing to the radio, "to remind her I am deaf. I think it makes her mad." There seems to be a hint of an impish grin on his face.

"You aren't very happy here, are you?"

The next comments come like the rush of water through a broken dam. "No, I'm not happy. How can I be? I am just an old man in everybody's way. Oh, perhaps that is not quite true of Peggy. She likes to visit me, I think. But she has many friends. You know how popular young girls are. Tom is a good son. He works hard, and sometimes he comes in to talk to me. But I can tell he would rather read about sports or look at TV."

"How about Tom Junior?" prods Miss Jones.

"Oh, young Tom is like all young fellers. He is so busy going off on hikes and playing ball and the likes, he doesn't know I exist. I have his room. That should not be. The boy needs his own room to keep things like rocks and frogs and snakes." Again, there is that impish expression. Now there can be no mistaking it. "Margaret doesn't like them things in the house, and she's put her foot down about bringing them alive into the basement. She says she has to do the washing down there and she doesn't want the critters around her feet."

"You don't get along too well with Margaret," said Miss Jones.

"Oh, Margaret's all right. She is just too persnickity. When I first came I said, 'Now, Margaret, you let me do the dishes.' She said it would be hard for me to get them clean because I don't see so well. Well, I washed them, and then I saw her wash them over again. I don't see so bad, but I could see what she did." Then, after a short pause, "I am just in the way. I am an old farmer, and I am what I am. Margaret doesn't like the way I eat. When they had fancy company, she said to me, 'Grandpa, would you prefer to eat in your own room? I can fix your dinner on the card table.' I knew the score. She just didn't want me."

After a while Miss Jones asks him if he knows anyone in town besides Tom and his family. "No, all of my friends are out in the country, what is left of them. I can't go out there and they can't come in. Too far."

"And how about church?" asks Miss Jones.

"Mom and I always went to the Methodist Church. Tom and Margaret go to the Christian. Disciples of Christ, they call it. That was Margaret's church. Tom had to be 'ducked' before he could belong." Mr. Brandon does not want to be baptized again. "Once is enough." And he doesn't know anybody. So he stays at home and listens to the radio. Anyhow, his stiff hips can't do those steps very well. "Did you ever like fishing or hunting?" asks Miss Jones. "No, you know, where we lived, there was no water for miles around. And as to hunting, there are jackrabbits and prairie dogs, but I was never one to shoot except to protect the crops."

"When you and your wife had company on Sunday afternoons, what did you men do?" Miss Jones continues her questions.

"Oh, we talked politics and things like that, and looked at crops; and sometimes we played horseshoe," replies Mr. Brandon. "Horseshoe was fun then, but with these hips, it's out of the question." "How about Sunday afternoons in the winter?" Miss Jones is not giving up.

"Well, we played checkers and dominoes and sometimes Flinch."

"Did you enjoy that?" asks Miss Jones.

"Yes." His face brightens. "Hank Brown and I used to play checkers. We played to win. Maggie, that was my wife, and Elizabeth, Hank's wife, had to remind us that the stock had to be fed and we had to go home."

"Would you care to play checkers now, that is, if there were someone to play with you?"

"No. Anyhow, there's nobody to play with."

"There is a Center on Elm Street and retired men get together for checkers and cards. They seem to have fun."

Mr. Brandon shakes his head. "I've heard about the Center, but it does not appeal to me. Anyhow, I won't be in town very long. I overheard Tom and Margaret discuss me. They want me to go into a home." He seems resigned.

"And do you want to go?" Miss Jones keeps on digging.

"Hell, no. But what can an old man like me do? I don't want to stay where I am not wanted. Not me."

"I am not sure that you are not wanted," says Miss Jones. "Why don't you talk it over with Tom and Margaret and tell them how you feel?"

"I couldn't do that," says Mr. Brandon. "Anyhow, what's the use? I shouldn't have blabbered so much to you. I wasn't going to, and then I went and did it anyhow."

"Do you want me to talk to Tom and Margaret and perhaps with Peggy and young Tom present, too?" asks Miss Jones.

"What would Peggy and Young Tom have to do with it?" He is almost shouting. "They are not responsible for me. Not them young kids."

"No, they aren't, but they are a part of the family and they know whether they want you to stay or to leave. I think Peggy, especially, would hate to see you go to a home."

"Well, I'm going and that is that." Mr. Brandon is trembling. "Like I told you, I am not going to be in anybody's way."

"Do you want me to tell you about the homes nearby?" asks Miss Jones.

The answer sounds something like assent. Miss Jones lists the four different kinds of institutions in the county and briefly describes each one. Mr. Brandon is silent. After a while he says, "You sure know about all these things, don't you?"

"It's my business to know," says Miss Jones.

There is another pause. This time it is a long one. "Does Tom know about all of this, I mean all of these homes?"

"Yes," replies Miss Jones, "I told them when they came in to see me."

"And they want me to go?"

"Only Tom and Margaret and Peggy and Tom Junior

can answer that," says Miss Jones. "I do think they would like to see you happier than you have been here."

"Well, I would be! A damn sight happier!" Then, in quite another tone of voice, "Can family visit you in those places? I mean, can young kids come too?"

"Yes, they can, especially during visiting hours."

"What do you have to do with all of this?" he then asks.

"Really very little, Mr. Brandon. We do give information when it is wanted and needed, and sometimes we help with the finances. Most of all we are interested in trying to help families find the best solutions in situations like yours. Tom and Margaret told us they were concerned about you. They know you are lonely and unhappy. They thought a home might be a solution and they asked for information."

"Did they also ask you to come and talk with me?" Mr. Brandon is shouting again.

"Yes. But they understood that I would not try to persuade you to go to a home or do anything else you don't want to do. I think this is up to you and your family."

"And that includes Peggy and Tom Junior?"

"To me it would seem so."

Soon after that, Mr. Brandon comments, "Well, I've got something to think about."

The door to the room was closed during the visit. Margaret had greeted Miss Jones when she arrived and had taken her to Mr. Brandon's room and introduced her. When she left, Margaret again came to the door. They discussed the weather and the need for street repairs nearby; she makes no reference to the conversation with her father-in-law.

Tom comes to the office on the following day. Miss Jones does not repeat what was said, other than to comment that Tom's father seemed to feel that he was "in the way" and that she thought a family conference including Peggy and young Tom might serve a good purpose. She says that she found Mr. Brandon, Sr., quite alert and she thinks capable of participating in planning his own future. Tom thinks Miss Jones is probably right. Perhaps he and Margaret assumed that since his father was old, they should take responsibility for him. There is discussion of the ease with which groups of people, like adolescents and the old, are stereotyped but that actually there are many individual differences. Tom seems to understand. He refers to the difference between his own son and another boy in the neighborhood. He comments that for him it is easy to have his father around. After all, he grew up in his father's home. Also, he is gone most of the time, and things that irritate Margaret, like the loud radio when she is at home all day long, do not bother him. He is not sure about having the whole family sit down together. His dad could get nasty, and he does not wish the children to be witnesses. Moreover, Margaret's feelings might be hurt. Miss Jones comments, "I think really you and Margaret will know best if Peggy and Tom should be present."

Tom says he noticed that his dad was in better spirits last night. Perhaps it did help to talk things over. He wants to talk again with Margaret. Could Miss Jones come and help keep "things on an even keel" if they do decide to meet? Again Miss Jones emphasizes that she is interested in helping the whole family find a satisfactory solution and that only the Brandons, including Tom's father, will be able to find the best way out. She will be willing to participate by raising questions and giving information.

The family conference is held after a telephone call from Tom. The children are included. During the first ten minutes all members, except possibly Peggy, are ill at ease. Margaret sits rigidly with her hands clasped tightly on her lap. Tom tries to open the discussion but has difficulty stating the purpose. At his suggestion Miss Jones elaborates. Peggy responds with, "Oh, good!" Tom Junior fidgets. Mr. Brandon, Sr., had greeted Miss Jones with reserve. Now he seems to go to great lengths to be uncommunicative and unresponsive. Finally, Margaret agrees with Tom that all they want is what is best for his father. "That," says Mr. Brandon, "is just so much 'poppycock.' If you wanted what was best for me, why did you have to go and make me sell the farm? I'd be much better off and happier if you would have let me be. But no, you had to mess in my affairs and treat me as if I were deaf, dumb, and blind."

"Well, you know you can't see well, Dad," says Tom. And Margaret, in a hurt voice, adds, "We were willing to bring you into our home. Junior gave up his room for you."

Junior looks uncomfortable. "Oh, heck, Mom," he says, "I didn't mind that. I just would like a place to put things."

"Things like lizards and snakes. Nothing doing," his mother retorts.

Miss Jones remains quiet. Finally, she wonders aloud, since going back to the farm was impossible, might there be other places besides a home to which grandpa could move? Tom says Lil could not offer him a place. "And I wouldn't go to that darn awful place in Chicago, if she could," shouts his father. "What other places are there?" asks Margaret.

Miss Jones explains about foster family care or perhaps a small apartment could be rented where Mr. Brandon, Sr., could keep house for himself. During this discussion he says little but definitely gives the impression that he doesn't think much of any of the suggestions. Finally, he interrupts. "I'll go to a home. That's what Tom and Margaret want, I know. Only they don't know that I heard them discuss it, but I did. I'm not going to stay here and that's that. I can't please Margaret anyhow." He brings up the dishwashing and other episodes. Margaret and Tom are plainly uncomfortable. When Mr. Brandon focuses on Margaret directly, she begins to defend herself. Then she stops short. It seems as if she catches a glimpse of the predicament of her father-in-law. Her expression softens. Then Peggy comes through, "I don't think grandpa should be anywhere except in our house. Gosh, Grandpa, don't you like us?"

Mr. Brandon, Sr., stays. Eventually he plays checkers at the Center. In fact, he discovers that with his cane he can walk there by himself. At the Center he becomes known as a champion checker player. At his son's home he joins Tom and Margaret in the living room from time to time. The radio takes on a more moderate tone.

Basically, as a family, the Brandons had many strengths. Miss Jones quickly discovered them, and her understanding, support, and obvious faith in them helped the family, individually and as a unit, to utilize their capacities. No doubt, friction and some hurt feelings would occur, but all had the experience of successfully meeting a situation that had become disruptive and threatened to deteriorate fast. They had met one crisis together and could do so again. Undoubtedly they viewed themselves with greater respect afterward, and each one must have had a greater sense of well-being and a stronger attachment to the whole family.

The story of Mr. Brandon, Sr., goes on.

At Miss Jones' suggestion and with her help, appointments were made for Mr. Brandon for medical checkups, including an eye and ear examination. He was found to have a diabetic condition, though not in an advanced stage, and cataracts were developing in both eyes. He did not think much of his diet restrictions, but Margaret and Peggy saw to it that he followed doctor's orders.

His induction into the Center did not proceed without obstacles. As a matter of fact, for a while it appeared that the facility would not be available. As in many communities it was operated by a board of volunteers. Two factions were at odds with each other over the issue of permitting dancing on the premises. One group represented a large religious organization opposed to such activity; the other was in favor. Whatever the decision, the Center was losing members and with them the fifty cents monthly membership dues. Without these contributions, maintenance cost could not be met. Inevitably the program of the Center would have to be sharply curtailed or it might even have to close its doors. Miss Jones was a member of the board. She tried several conciliatory tactics but without success. Finally, to the chairman, she proposed a compromise. Two afternoons a week were to be set aside, one for those who wished to dance, and the other for programs that excluded dancing. The proposal was accepted. Neither group was completely satisfied. For a short time there were more withdrawals. However, the majority continued to pay their dues, and the Center remained open. The members became two distinct groups with each board member representing one of the factions and casting his vote to favor his group rather than to serve the interests of the total membership. Miss Jones, as well as some other members of the board, recognized the unhealthy state of affairs.

Just how the differences in the Center will be resolved is difficult to forecast. No doubt Miss Jones will have opportunities to use whatever skills she possesses in working with groups. Perhaps eventually, directly or indirectly, she or some other member can help the whole board, or even the Center members, to work together toward a common goal, one that is not only acceptable but also genuinely wanted by both groups.

Miss Jones seems to have the job not only of aiding elderly individuals like Mr. Brandon but also of assisting whole families and other groups in their quest for greater well-being. Her role seems to have two major objectives: the elimination, reduction, relief, or acceptance of difficulties that interfere with physical, social, emotional, and spiritual well-being, and the provision of opportunities, encouragement, and support for releasing and mobilizing unused potential. To accomplish these two objectives, resources are available in the older person himself or his family, or in church, social, or other groups, or in a variety of special professional services. When the family or neighbors and friends, individually and collectively, are unable to give the older member what he needs or enough of what he requires or when he cannot use his capacities, the resources of community agencies, established by society to serve him, may help. The agency may reduce the difficulties that the older adult and members of his family have or may free potential and help make opportunities available. Miss Jones did both for the Brandons. The agency may do the same for the interest groups of the older persons, which are organized to serve them and through which they can serve. Sometimes new groups and new community agencies may be established.

The two major objectives of social work—helping people in difficulty and providing them with opportunities to help themselves—use all three traditional social work approaches: casework, group work, and community work. Whichever of the three ways, or a combination of them, is best suited to meet the situation may be employed. With the social difficulties of elderly persons, casework or group therapy or both and perhaps community action are most likely to be relied upon. Casework and some family therapy was used for the Brandons. When the social worker is enhancing well-being already partially enjoyed, she uses the strengths and resources of the older person, his family, and his community. Group experience in the Center helped to release some of Mr. Brandon's latent abilities. Perhaps more emphasis could have been placed on the greater use of talents, not only of the grandfather but also of the whole family.

A focus neither on increments or on decrements cannot ignore the other. Under some conditions one will have primary consideration; under others, the other. Public education offers an example of a focus that is primarily on possibilities for positive development and on strengths to be used. The overriding concern is with the child's potential capacity to learn, not with his limitations. Thus, curriculum, teaching methods, and physical surroundings, all conducive (theoretically, at least) to the development of his abilities, are provided. Only handicaps, such as defective vision or hearing or emotional disturbances that threaten to interfere with the educational process or with the development of potential demand that the primary concern be remedial, palliative, or medical. Clinics, hospitals, and most welfare agencies serve persons and families with difficulties, physical, social, and emotional. Their approach tends to be geared to decrements. The resources of the older person or his family or other segments of the community are mobilized but primarily for remedying or relieving the disability. Ordinarily the objective is not to release potential for the sake of positive growth but to achieve the specific goal of reestablishing health. Sometimes the encouragement of the use of abilities for the sake of positive growth occurs after the person's health is partially or wholly restored. For example, a mentally ill woman who taught ceramics found a new interest, and later her new creative work enabled her to enjoy life much more fully.

It is often possible to encourage the development of capacities without first focusing on an existing problem. The difficulties then resolve themselves, either completely or partially. That is what happened to Maggie with her harmonica. Except to give her a place to sleep and food to eat, the staff could do little to help with her problem of withdrawal. When the administrator of the nursing home discovered her earlier interest in playing the harmonica, gave her one, and encouraged her to play it, her condition improved considerably, at least for a time.

INCREMENTS

Whether concerned with the elderly individuals themselves or their families, interest groups, or the community at large, the social worker in a small community does well to rely heavily on assessing assets and resources and building on them. Liabilities or decrements may be evident, but nothing positive can grow out of them. What exists or remains of potential resources can be used, not what is warped and sick or no longer in existence. A chaplain who was born without arms and hands, who had become skillful and competent in using his feet and toes, and who had developed resources of mind and spirit reminded a class of students to whom he was speaking about working with handicapped patients, "Always greet that which remains of a person, never that which is lost." The older adult often has lost something of what he possessed in his earlier days: vigor, vision, hearing, mobility, mate, friends, employment, status, self-confidence. As long as he lives he has never lost all his capacities. Some of his contributions may be much greater than those he made when he was younger. He may be wiser, he may have more patience, he may have more courage, he may have a greater capacity to be gentle and kind. Younger persons, including social workers, often give verbal recognition to this, but in their actions they may ignore what they profess to believe. Like the public at large, they may resort to stereotyping and condescending benevolence, with an emphasis on liabilities instead of on strengths. They, too, may equate chronological age with decrements. So common is this attitude that old people themselves may think more often of what they do not have than of what they still have. If vision or hearing can be improved or restored, if more appropriate food or even medicine will increase vigor, if surgery will relieve crippling disabilities, if anything will improve what is sick or retrieve what has been lost, by all means the appropriate facilities and opportunities should be made available. Yet the use of what the older person has left is more important and often needs to come first. The same principle applies to families, groups, and the community at large. Usually much more can be gained by recognizing resources and capacities than by dwelling on liabilities. The conflicts within a family group may have to be dealt with; the leadership of a group may have to be strengthened; the sore spots in the community may have to be eliminated; but constant harping on them without some encouragement and support of what there is to mobilize will be of little value. And, as in the individual, conflicts, poor leadership, and community problems frequently will be resolved if there is sufficient awareness of strengths and of occasions and opportunities to use them. Above all, there need to be recognition and encouragement. No individual or group can help himself or itself if there is no feeling of worth and confidence such as stems from activity or from behavior considered to be worthwhile and that, at least occasionally, is recognized.

Focusing on strength or increment will possibly prevent difficulties. The older person may never become withdrawn and apathetic if he has chances for meaningful social contacts. He may never become querulous if he can use his capacities. The conflict within the family may never develop if enough emphasis is placed on the members' common interests and concerns, such as a united effort to help the older member find a suitable role within the family. The tragedies and difficulties of inadequate group leadership may be prevented by the social worker's help in the planning or in the development of adequate leaders. Community social disorganization does not just happen. It emerges and grows, usually over a period of time. Serious situations can be prevented by the social worker's recognizing the symptoms of disaster. For example, proper teen-age facilities may be lacking because so many taxpayers over sixty-five refuse to vote for the property levy to provide the facilities. Because the community does not offer opportunities for constructive achievement, some of the young people will inevitably resort to destructiveness. By involving older persons in planning long before the recommendation to increase the tax is made and by giving them, as well as the younger people, the opportunity to study the situation, more affirmative votes may result. It is possible that alternative better solutions may evolve. To recognize and emphasize the use of potentials is not just to relieve uncomfortable or unendurable conditions, nor to restore health because strengths are used nor just to prevent illness or difficulties. Such recognition and emphasis have the important positive result of promoting greater self-realization, which brings with it happiness and well-being. The challenge to one working with older adults in small communities continues to be what it was for social workers forty-five years ago: to "discover and release the unduplicated excellence," in individuals and in groups. Richmond (1922), who used the phrase, referred to the challenge as "a privilege [p. 158]." It remains a privilege in 1969. The emphasis must be on *discovery* and *release*. Of the two, discovery comes first. The question is, how does one discover the "unduplicated excellence," actual or potential?

First, perhaps one must genuinely believe that every human being, including the older individual, has potentialities which are unduplicated, that every person has capacities, some aspects of which are unique to him. Dubos (1966) referred to the uniqueness as "diversity" and stressed the existence of diversity in each human being and the importance of recognizing and using it. A man's uniqueness would appear to give him his peculiar worth in a society. His diversities have a special value. They would seem to enable him to function differently from everybody else, to be inventive and creative. If diversities are harnessed, they may help to make a better life for the individual himself and for others. The great tragedy is that diversity whether in the old or the young, and especially in the old, too often goes unrecognized and unused. Diversity or uniqueness is frequently frowned upon because it may fail to fit into the accepted pattern of conformity.

People, including the elderly, also have unused capacities which may be like those of others in the community. These, too, can have value and should be recognized. However, it may be necessary for the individual to make use of them in his own way and thus even the capacities he has in common need not be duplicated.

Machines and tests of all kinds tend to be geared to the common traits in people. Even when administered by an expert, they are not attuned to diversity. In small communities testing devices are pretty limited. At best, if they do exist, they tend to be guides to human observation and listening and may supplement or substantiate what a person sees or hears. The sensitive eyes, ears, and mind of the social worker in the small community will discover more than any number of tests, especially tests that are neither administered nor interpreted expertly. This is true if the listening and observation come after the worker has become acquainted with the values and ways of life of the community, regards the community as his for the time during which he works there, and is regarded by the people in the community as one of them. In rural areas and small towns it is not enough for a social worker to be accepted by one segment of the population such as, for example, the elderly. He will have to work with groups, members of which are not all old, with existing organizations, and with the community at large. What his senses perceive and what his mind grasps are directly related to how well he understands what the old and others try to convey to him. Their communication is based on their trust in him and their understanding of what should be communicated.

In small communities, office visits of all kinds are less common than in metropolitan centers. Moreover, visits with older people in their own homes or those of their children, in a care home, or wherever they live, will pay dividends. Not only do such conferences yield results, but also many would never take place if the social worker waited for the elderly to come to the office. When visiting persons in their own homes, or wherever they live, the social worker becomes the guest and the elderly persons the hosts. As hosts, they are in charge of the situation and in their own familiar surroundings. They can control what takes place. Their role as host gives them a feeling of security and tends to add to their status. In small communities the social worker is often treated as a friend and pie, gingerbread, cookies or other food, and coffee and tea may be served when she visits. Her visits enable the housewife to demonstrate her skill in baking and serving, and her husband has an opportunity to play the role of host and carry on the conversation. That the social worker should accept the hospitality goes without question. Just the kind of a setting that this creates may in itself be conducive both to a reassurance of worth and to encouragement for revealing further aspirations and abilities.

Many objects in their surroundings will give clues about the hosts' interests and activities, past and present. Photographs, bits of needlework, a worn violin, a drawing or painting, birdhouses, pieces of restored furniture and innumerable other items point to the values and abilities of the hosts. Some reference to these objects may reveal quite unexpected potential. A reservoir of ideas and abilities may come to light. For example, a conversation that followed a comment about a photograph of a young man, whose framed picture stood prominently on the mantel-piece, revealed that he was engaged in research in a distant university, and that his current interest was in the development of a new psychological test. He was obviously the pride and joy of his widowed mother, a woman in her middle seventies with very little formal education. As the conversation progressed, she raised some thought-provoking questions. Why, she asked, when persons retire, or when they have to leave the farm, as she was obliged to do after her husband died, is it not possible to have one's capacities for volunteer or paid work, either part- or full-time, assessed? Are such tests available, and if not, could they be developed? Would some of the school personnel, or perhaps a state agency, be equipped to administer such tests?

Could not a group of older people organize and man an employment agency in small towns and bring together available jobs and unused capacities, with or without pay? The questions were inspired by her own situation and her interest in her son's activities, and the particular suggestions may not have been practical at the time. They did display, however, genuine ability to think about new ways of doing things. With a mind like hers, she should have been encouraged to explore further the same and other unmet community needs and could have done something about them. The elderly in small communities have many ideas that can be tapped profitably.

Older persons' interest in creative art, particularly when the low level of formal education of many is taken into account, is especially exciting. One wonders why there is the fascination for writing poetry, painting pictures, playing musical instruments, and for all the many ways of expressing feelings and ideas.

> I could not be writing as I do
>   If my time were worth any money;
> I feel as the bees in my hive must feel
>   When they cannot make any honey.
> But bees have the habit of sleeping ten weeks,
>   While I can sleep less than ten hours;
> So I have to read, or grind gems, or make rhymes,
>   While they perhaps dream of sweet flowers.
>
>   *D. H. Hostetter*

Old people sometimes say, "I wanted to paint (or play an organ, or write verse) all my life. I never had time." They might possibly have added, "Neither did I have the courage!" Somehow as people advance in years, "what other people will think" about their performance is viewed from a different perspective and some inhibitions diminish. Persons who have grown old dare to be themselves and are able even to talk about their desire for creative expression. Yet despite the lesser role of inhibitions, many men and women, even in their later years, require encouragement and support before they will disclose their interests and aspirations.

The visits with older persons in their own settings will also show much about their attitudes toward others and their relationships with them. If the elderly man or woman lives in the home of a married child, if an unmarried son or daughter lives with the parents, if children are visiting, the family's behavior reveals much about the relationships of and with the older parent or grandparent or even, in this day of three- and four-generation families, the relationship with a great-grandparent. They may not live under the same roof but they keep in touch with one another. The roles that the older person plays in relation to other members, their attitudes toward him and his toward them, the place that he holds in the group, the values about which they agree and disagree, the way they communicate, all tend to come to light. Neighbors drop by or their activities are discussed. The kind and quality of interaction with them become apparent, as does the relationship with members of the church or with those of other organizations. Whether the elderly person is warm and giving and can extend affection as well as accept it, or if he tends to withdraw, may stand out very clearly. His behavior and conversation may show how he habitually copes with pleasant and unpleasant experiences. The attitudes and behavior of others who interact with him may also be disclosed. If the old person is in a retirement home or incapacitated in a nursing home, visits are revealing and important. What the old person has valued so much that he has brought it with him or what his conversation shows about regrets that certain objects could not be brought or that cherished activities cannot be pursued says much about his interests and may point to his potential capacities. In nursing homes possible abilities and interests seem often to be forgotten or considered useless, and if the patient shares this assessment, the social worker must listen and observe even more sensitively.

Much "going out to," physically and psychologically, is an integral part of working with older people, especially in small communities. Transport and communication are difficult. Older people may not be able to come to offices and clinics, no matter how badly they may wish to do so. In small communities life is usually informal, and activities tend to center in homes rather than in offices. Even if older people occasionally venture forth, they will rarely come to the social worker's office frequently enough for any potentialities to be revealed.

The social worker who attends or participates in group

meetings in the church, neighborhood, or clubs of all kinds can often see clearly the capacities that an elderly person possesses and the role that he or she can play in a group. For example, one lonely widow who seldom left her home, and who stated pathetically that she could not remember the time when anyone had asked her for help, virtually blossomed out when given an opportunity to help serve the meal at a potluck luncheon. She appeared very shy before, but she performed her task with ease and self-assurance. Other members began to rely upon her for this service and she became one of them. In such ways are the discovery and the use of abilities closely interrelated. The social worker who finds potential abilities and who wishes to help provide the "environment and stimuli" (Dubos, 1966) to encourage their use has no "bag of tricks" or even pills or drugs on which to rely. He has himself, however, and how he uses himself determines largely how successfully he discovers and helps mobilize resources. In a small community, the worker's relationships take on particular significance. His integrity is there for all to see. His metropolitan counterpart may keep his personal and professional lives separated. Professionally, he may be known only as he appears in his office, in committee meetings, or perhaps at luncheons. Not so the worker in rural areas and in small towns. Though small communities are not all alike, generally what the social worker in a small town is and what he does become inseparable. His behavior is likely to be discussed and evaluated. If the people approve, or even if they do not entirely like what he says and does but do respect him, as a person and for his professional competence, the evaluation tends to be kind. If his behavior is too far out of line with the conventions of the community, he may run into trouble. One young social worker did: wearing shorts she rode by the largest church in a small town just as the worshippers were emerging from the sanctuary. Such flouting of what the community considered important rules of propriety cost her her job, although this behavior would be tolerated more now than it was when the incident occurred.

Actually, respect for a person or a group dictates that one deal sensitively with patterns of norms and values. It does not require, however, even of the social worker in the most rural of areas, that he subscribe to beliefs or ways of behaving personally or professionally that he cannot honestly accept. A social worker in a small town, which had a sizable elderly Negro population, observed that members of the Senior Citizen club failed to invite Negroes to their meetings. When she raised questions about this omission, she discovered that the majority of the members opposed the inclusion of Negroes in the club. After unsuccessfully bringing the issue before the group, she finally told the executive committee that she could not continue to serve the club as long as people were discriminated against on the basis of race. She pointed out that public funds were supporting the program and that everybody in the community, regardless of race or creed, was obliged to pay taxes. The members reconsidered and revised their policies. Some white leaders in the group rallied strongly to the support of the social worker and also assisted in involving the Negroes who accepted an invitation to a meeting. A few white members resigned but the organization continued to thrive. For her stand the social worker's job was in jeopardy, and she clearly recognized that she might have to leave the community.

The relationships of the worker in the small community can be strengthened in many different ways. By working, eating, singing, playing, dancing, worshipping with the people, he may be looked upon as being "one of us." One citizen with insight called it "walking with the people." A student described it as "swinging with" the community. It makes for acceptance and for mutual understanding and respect. It leads to good communication. Effective communication is always more than a one-way process, not only in the exchange of feelings, ideas, questions, and information with the elderly whose welfare is the focus of interest and concern, but also in interaction with the family of the aging person, with interest groups, with service agencies, and with all the other persons or clusters of people who may be concerned. Communication may consist of anything from silences to long spoken or written statements of policy. Gestures, facial expressions, a handshake and pat on the back, or arm around the shoulder, are all ways of communicating. The worker who is one of the community and is respected for his competence and contribution, is able to share knowledge, give encouragement and support, and perhaps at times, especially in crises, make acceptable recommendations. Most advice is neither wanted nor needed. To enable older persons, individually and in clusters, and even a community of people, to come to their own decisions by listening attentively and responding appropriately, in terms of the capacities that they themselves display, is, ordinarily, more useful. There are other ways to discover and nurture potential. Creativity and empathy have been found to have special possibilities in unlocking the human storehouses of "unduplicated excellence."

Creativity. Professional and personal experiences with older people and with families and other groups and organizations in rural areas indicate not only that a creative experience gives a greater sense of self-identity and worth and leads to greater self-realization, but also that all older people, families, interest groups, and associations have within themselves inventive urges and some potential ability for being creative. Walt Whitman expressed this in the words "One's self I sing, a simple separate person." Capacities for creative expression vary greatly. Many potentialities are dormant, have always been dormant, and though it need not be so, remain dormant. To discover creative abilities and to help older adults, individually and collectively, find and use them is an essential service which the social worker can render. Concern about the meaning of creativity and a definition of the creative process has extended over the centuries. Ghiselin (1952) points out that both Plato and Aristotle discussed the subject and that interest, continuing through the next two thousand years, came to the fore again in the early nineteenth century when "Blake, Wordsworth, Coleridge, Shelley and Keats all had their say [p. 11]." Stein and Heinze (1960) have summarized a major effort made recently to define creativity. Perhaps any definition of creativity would have its limitations; the following has been found to be useful in practical experience. Creativity, or the creative expression of an individual or group, is not limited to the cultural arts. Neither is it necessarily marked by perfection according to professional or objective standards. A creative experience is derived from any form of expression which brings "something new into birth" (May, 1959, p. 57), and which, for the individual, family, group, or association that produces it, takes on a semblance of excellence. The newness may not be absolute but its elements are organized somewhat differently, at least from the point of view of the creator. The housewife who ex-

periments with a new combination of ingredients in a loaf of bread,
the farmer who harvests a new "very good" crop of alfalfa hay
after modifying his former methods of preparing the soil, may have
creative experiences. A new plan or changes in an earlier plan carried to a successful conclusion may give a group a sense of creation.
A family may have a creative experience when, as a unit, its members improve the lawn or make part of the house more livable. An
organization may express itself creatively: joint participation by the
staff, board, and clients of an agency in developing a new policy or
program may become a truly creative activity.

There may be many forms of creative expression. The fresh
perspective which is essential in bringing into being "something
new," may come in many ways and under different circumstances.
It may be the result of a steady, painstaking, and systematic search
for a new element (Hutchinson, 1949). This is predominantly the
way of the scientific researcher. It may come in the wake of "flashes
of insight" which, according to Hutchinson, characterize the philos-
opher and artist, but are not unknown to the scientist. These flashes,
to judge from many documented accounts, have a way of appear-
ing when there has been some serious, though not necessarily systematic, grappling with a problem over a period of time. As far as
is known, very little work has been done to try to discover under
what conditions persons of little formal education, such as one is
likely to find among today's elderly in small communities, have creative experiences. That many have them is apparent in the ideas
and objects which one sees in visiting their homes or in participating
in group activities. Until a better reason is found, it is assumed that
basically the same conditions apply to all persons regardless of the
extent of their formal education. There may have been a persistent
effort to discover a new and better way of doing things; there may
have been an undefined need and desire for this over a period of
time, which on the spur of the moment seems to result in the production of something new and satisfying. The media of creative
interpretation range all the way from the paint brush and keyboard
to the combination of a piece of material and an array of colored
threads, from the typewriter on which is hammered out a poem or
a newly discovered chemical formula to the saw, hammer, and wood

which make up the carpenter's tools and materials. Creativity may be found in discussion at an Old Settlers' meeting or in the handling of a problem in a service agency. Whatever the media, the effect tends to be pleasurable and satisfactory, even if only for the moment, and the result is a movement forward on the way to self-realization.

Creativity uses the resources, or the increments, of an individual or group and, therefore is an experience that motivates growth. Resulting in production it inspires feelings of competence and achievement. Thrills and delight accompany what is produced if the creator thinks it excellent. The irritability and dissatisfaction, to say nothing of symptoms of ill health displayed by many older persons who come to the attention of the social worker, or the conflicts that are often found in small community groups, may be due more frequently to unsatisfied creative urges than to deficient physical health, living quarters, or inadequate policies. Marked changes may be observed in apparently unhealthy older adults and in family groups when their creative energies are released. What appears to be "good adjustment" and satisfaction with the status quo can lead to a routine existence which may eventually give rise to difficulties because new ways are not found to deal with new situations. His potential abilities were released when Mr. Brandon, Sr., found opportunities to play checkers, perhaps for him a creative activity. Judging from experiences with many older persons in small communities, one may speculate that Mr. Brandon has other creative potentialities that remain unrevealed in his case history. They might be discovered in a leisurely conversation about his farm activities, or perhaps about the days when his children were growing up. They might come to light as he talks about his wife, his church or about other interests. The family conference may have had creative aspects for the Brandons as a family unit. Their ties are strong and the members, no doubt, do things together. Perhaps the grandfather at times could be included, and if all the Brandons could feel that something "new" and good were brought "into being" through the contributions of all, the future relationship would be on a sound footing. Tensions are relieved when Mr. Brandon, Sr., leaves the house from time to time and perhaps comes home telling with some excitement about the game he has played. However, a positive integration of the whole family group would seem to require more effort.

In addition to their all planning and working on a particular goal, group cohesiveness would be fostered if all members could take pride in the excellence of their achievement and the quality of "newness" that they had brought into being. Vested interests, adherence to traditions, and other factors have a way of limiting the inventiveness of a group but, when barriers are broken down and potentialities released, the results often defy the imagination of any one member. Through interaction individual members can contribute in ways that would often seem impossible if they were acting alone.

Empathy. The social worker, by discovering creative urges and by supporting and encouraging their use, by supplying, or helping to supply, opportunities and occasions for creative expression, can do much toward assisting older people, or clusters of persons to engage in creative activities. But the individual, family, and group need more than creative self-expression: they need also to feel and to express themselves in relation to others, that is, they desire empathy. Foote and Cottrell (1957) speak of empathy as being marked by "social sensitivity [p. 54]." "It is the capacity to perceive situations from others' standpoints and thus anticipate and predict their behavior." *The American College Dictionary* (1953) defines empathy as an "appreciative perception or understanding" of others. An empathic experience is the result of a person's expressing this perception, of a person's reaching out to others and having the ability to respond to their affective expressions. Nobody can confine his interests to himself and consider only his own requirements for growth and then not develop personality deficiencies. A group or association would be similarly affected. One can readily visualize, for example, the condition of a certain church in France. During World War II the church fathers considered seriously whether or not their group had any responsibility for taking a stand concerning the atrocities committed against the Jews in Germany. They decided they had no such responsibility. Twenty years later, so the story goes, after the tragedies which occurred were thoroughly documented, the same church elders discussed their earlier decision.

Apparently they consoled themselves with the conclusion that "had we taken a stand, our people would have become divided." Such a division might well have resulted in a much greater growth of the church as an institution, and in a much more satisfying contribution of the congregation as persons than, one feels, probably exists.

The capacity for empathy varies with people and with groups. Except for the severely mentally ill, it seems that all human beings have some capacity for "putting themselves in the place of others." Such capacities can be used through opportunities and encouragement for "feeling and doing" with, and sometimes for, others. Personal and cultural values in small communities tend to support such attitudes, so feelings of greater worth, a more acceptable self-image, and a self-esteem imbued with integrity would ensue for the elderly person who is able to express empathy.

Perhaps because the social work profession is so steeped in the philosophy of helping people, many of whom have very serious difficulties, social workers may not always recognize that persons need to give to others as well as to receive from them. An old person who has spent his life giving to his family, to his job, to his community, and to his church cannot just sit back and continue indefinitely to take for himself and still maintain his self-respect. The rigid policy of some agencies that prohibits a staff member from accepting gifts from persons who are receiving service from the organization seems out of place. One reason for such a policy is to prevent bribery. Blackmailing tactics can usually be recognized and sometimes are a response to overly restrictive policies of an organization or of an individual worker. Social workers do need to be willing to receive as well as to give. People must give, particularly old people. Some have to receive before they can give:

> Old Zelda lived alone in a small town. She was in her middle seventies. For eight years she had harbored a grudge against her neighbors for an alleged, and perhaps actual, injustice suffered at their hands. Her bitterness over a long period included not only the people living next door, but all people in the community. She shut herself in and all others out. Knocks on the door simply were not answered. When Old Zelda threw a rock in the window of the neighbor's house, the sheriff was notified. A subsequent mental

examination produced the recommendation that she be encouraged to participate in group activities, a recommendation more easily made than implemented, particularly in a
small community where she was well-known and, because
of her behavior through the years, shunned.

It was difficult to reach her. Her own language difficulties tended through the years to add to the misunderstand-
ing. Fortunately the social worker could speak and understand when Old Zelda spoke in German. This gave her an
opportunity to tell her story not once, but repeatedly, in her
own language. The social worker helped by recognizing Zelda's talent for making paper flowers. For Christmas the social worker presented a small potted plant to her. It was
the first "greenhouse" plant that Zelda had ever received.
Her great delight was pathetic. She reciprocated with homemade cookies and paper flowers, perhaps her first gift to another person in years. She had to experience the assurance
that someone considered her worthy of a gift, one that she
herself valued highly, before she was able to give. After that
incident it was possible to talk with her about making paper
flowers for patients in a nursing home. She had taken a big
step toward feeling respect for herself and some regard for
others.

Channels for older people to share with others and to extend
their services need to be opened continually and systematically.
Valuable resources among the elderly, both individually and in
groups, are not always recognized by social workers. For suggestions,
see Morris, Lambert and Guberman (1963), Ch. 3. Aging men and
women can perform many services, especially as volunteers. For
example, in Holton, elderly persons took a major responsibility for
interviews in a home care study to determine the needs and resources in the county. In small communities social services seem to
pay the largest dividends when there is a close coordination between
professionals and citizens. This calls not only for a recognition and
discovery of "natural neighborly" efforts and activities of persons in
other professional positions, such as ministers, teachers, lawyers,
bankers, and others who give specific help, but also for the extension
of their services, rather than their merely helping the professional
social worker extend his efforts. Extension of services means an increased range of their neighborly acts, or a wider and more frequent use of any special knowledge and skill.

Several years ago in a number of small communities in Kansas, a simple question was asked of different people, "Who in this town is the person, or are the persons, to whom people turn for help when they are in trouble?" The consensus of opinion was marked. Subsequent visits with persons named revealed some interesting common traits: they all had a faith in the potential goodness of people ("I have never seen anyone in whom there was no good"); an ability to listen well ("I don't give much advice—I listen"); an ability to keep confidences ("I don't talk about what I hear"). All small communities seem to have "natural helpers," persons whom people trust and to whom they feel free to go for help. Some are quiet and unobtrusive, those who see capacities in others, listen well, and are able to keep confidences. Others, more active, are on hand in times of crisis. They are resourceful and stand by confidently and with strength when tragedy strikes. When such a person arrives on the scene, "the pieces seem to come together again." In the presence of such a person the future may appear more hopeful.

In urban settings volunteers for direct services have often been trained as semiprofessional social workers. To encourage the volunteer to give service "in one's own way," has much value in rural areas, towns, and small cities. What often needs to be stressed, at least when lonely and disabled persons are involved, is that more people than is customary should help, and that the assistance be consistent and systematic. Perhaps some of the "drying up" of local resources when organized social services are established and the subsequent lessening of interest in and concern for others may be due in part to the professionals' not recognizing the strictly local volunteer activities. The contribution of citizens has a threefold benefit: it helps the individuals or group served, the persons who give the service and, if they listen and observe carefully, the professionals. Opportunities for expressing sympathy may release potentialities that provide an elderly person or even a family group with a genuine reason for living. Self-esteem may be enhanced in the process in a way that nothing else can accomplish. Interest groups may find reasons to continue their existence through services to others.

The emphasis on social well-being of the elderly requires a

recognition and use of capacities, tried and untried, both creative and empathic. Channels and opportunities for such expression are frequently limited. The social worker may help the individual family or group use the facilities that exist or aid in the establishment of new ones.

DECREMENTS

Much of what has been said applies to individuals, families, and groups that are experiencing difficulties. The stresses and strains may resolve themselves when increments are mobilized and put to work. Recovery from any kind of difficulty, physical, mental, emotional, or spiritual, seems impossible unless the potential for growth is tapped. Though probably less often than we think, the social worker must focus first on what is wrong. Amelioration, in part at least, is essential before there can be much release of potential for positive growth and development. The emotionally disturbed Old Zelda, who locked herself inside with all her bitterness and hate, was unable to have the healthy experience of giving to others until she had had the opportunity thoroughly to air her grievances and to receive a genuine gift from another person. The positive social traits of Mr. Jones cannot be used to enable him to enjoy the company of friends or contribute to their amusement from his rich store of anecdotes until his hearing is improved by competent medical care, a well-fitting hearing aid or if he finds some other way of receiving communication. A suggestion to add nutritious meat to the diet of Mr. and Mrs. Smith has little value if they are without cooking facilities or "sans teeth" with which to bite and chew.

In stressing the use of the potential increments of elderly people, no distinctions have been made among persons of different age groups. Capacities may increase or decrease with age and the social worker does well to support or encourage the use of strengths or what remains of them.

In considering the decreased well-being of old people, some classification according to their chronological age would seem to be in order, although stereotyping should be avoided. In older people damage to their self-image, including a deteriorating feeling of self-worth, often comes with retirement, with the most crucial damage occurring immediately before and after that point. Current employment practices most frequently designate the sixties as the time for retirement. In small communities this age is often thought of as indicating an inability to do useful work. Thus during their sixties or, in some cases, their early seventies, men especially need to make a good many adjustments. Retirement from farm work is often involuntary at about this age because of an increasing number of disabilities that interfere with physical labor. To be unproductive, as Mr. Brandon, Sr., was, has for many rural and small town persons the implication of rejection and uselessness. Serious health problems, many of which are chronic, may occur in the sixties, but they tend to increase after the age of seventy-five. Very active eighty-year-olds and the twins who continue, at the age of ninety, to drive their car are exceptions.

In a great variety of ways the social worker in a small community can be of service to older people in trouble. As in cases when the focus is first on strengths, a careful assessment of the situation with the person concerned is necessary. This assessment includes not only the individual, but also persons and groups with whom he interacts, positively or negatively. Limitations and resources are taken into account, with the major emphasis on resources. In many instances the social worker will aid the elderly person and his family to find relief from tensions and stress, or even a solution to the difficulty, by giving them an opportunity to share their troubles, and to some extent to view them in a better perspective. Assistance may also be given in locating resources within the older person and his family and within the community. The social worker gives support and encouragement as steps are taken, often slowly, to meet the situation. When enough progress has been made, ideally the social worker shifts his position to emphasize the release and use of whatever capacities there are, because, at that point, the elderly person or his family or group no longer needs to concentrate on doing something about the original crisis. The movement becomes one toward a greater self-other realization and is no longer focused on difficulties.

UNORGANIZED RESOURCES

Organized community resources are few in areas of sparse population. Unorganized resources, especially volunteer services, can be fruitfully mobilized if the social worker has established a satisfactory place for himself in the community and if he knows how to find and to encourage their use. They exist among family members, neighbors, housewives, doctors, ministers, visiting nurses, high school nutritionists, nursing home administrators, grocers, druggists, lawyers, bankers, and other older people. There is the family member who either takes care of the aged person herself or organizes the family to assume the responsibility (Baran, 1969). In one community a grocer and his wife could be counted upon to deliver orders to the homes of customers and to keep a watchful eye on the feeble and absent-minded Mrs. Scott. When Mr. Brown was sick and unable to get out, a next-door neighbor made sure that food was prepared and brought into his home. The same neighbor assumed responsibility for watching for Mrs. Richardson's window shades to go up at the accustomed hour in the morning. If they were not raised, she would make inquiries. A telephone pal system whereby telephone calls were made regularly to persons living alone was arranged. One of two ladies in their eighties, who called each other the last thing at night and the first thing in the morning, commented, "If Maud does not answer when I call her, I can't go over to see what has happened, but I can telephone others who can." The wife of the small town banker visited elderly and old persons who lived alone and, when indicated, got in touch with their children who lived elsewhere. She and her husband not only made arrangements for a sick neighbor in his eighties to be admitted to a Veterans Hospital, but took him there, a round trip distance of over three hundred miles. The banker himself was a source of help in many different financial problems. He helped families receiving public assistance to fill out social security forms and farmers to complete income tax returns. The whole community, including the social worker, recognized the couple as "natural helpers" or "people to whom you can go when you need help."

Instead of being able to turn to other welfare agencies for special services, the small-community social worker can rely on public school staff, or on groups and persons in the churches, particularly on ministers and priests. A school principal or a teacher may know much about the relationships within a particular family. Though his interest is primarily related to the children, he may also know about the role of the grandparent, his place and his difficulties. A psychologist or school nurse may aid in the assessment of an emotional or physical problem. The minister or priest may assist older persons with their questions and spiritual concerns. One retired minister could always be counted upon to visit any old man or woman without a church affiliation. He also was available to conduct funeral services for the unchurched. If their potentials can be harnessed, church groups provide a reservoir of resources. Mr. Baker, a widower with multiple sclerosis, lived alone in a small village. For several years the women of the church took turns preparing a hot meal for him once a day; their husbands delivered the food and rendered the many personal services that were needed. Church members may take it upon themselves to provide transport to church services and to other events. The lack of transport presents a major problem to many old people in small communities. "Lifts" may be given by friends and neighbors or members of a church group or club, but for a continual and dependable mode of conveyance these do not always suffice. Group members and others who might be expected to volunteer their services seem to fear liability in accidents, particularly when the aged person is physically handicapped. If a commercial taxi service is available, some aid may have to be found for persons for whom the cost would be prohibitive.

Social and civic clubs in small towns and villages will serve in a variety of ways. The members of one women's club assumed responsibility for developing an arts and crafts program in a nursing home, an example that has probably been duplicated in many other communities. Members of a Stitch and Chatter Club or of a church group may take simple needlework, such as the hemming on dish towels, to the bedsides or wheelchairs of elderly women patients and encourage them to join in the activity. In one nursing home such a program is reported to have been in existence for over three years with good therapeutic effects upon apathetic and withdrawn patients. In another nursing home the handicapped men fashioned into toys lumber that had been sawed into small blocks by retired carpenters. An earlier plan to make the toys available to a group of underprivileged children in a nearby city did not materialize because the toys proved so popular locally that they were all sold.

Besides making possible some new activities and new interests for the men, programs of this kind in small towns, usually conducted under volunteer leadership, have the potential merit of providing the patients with opportunities to render services to others. In another community one elderly patient with a serious eye condition was released by a large urban hospital after unsuccessful eye surgery. Though she had little vision before she went into the hospital, she had less when she returned home to her one-room apartment on the second floor of a two-story building. A hospital social worker had suggested to the county welfare department that the patient be referred to the state agency for possible home-teacher service for the blind. The social worker discovered on visiting her home that although the patient could profit from the help of a home-teacher (one was not immediately available), she needed someone at once to help her get around at home and to prepare her food until she had had time to adjust to her almost complete loss of vision. A homemaker service was unavailable but a women's civic club helped find a practical nurse and paid the cost of her services until the home-teacher was able to help the patient become remarkably self-reliant.

Only limits of imagination in interested citizens and the social worker in small communities can circumscribe the many kinds of help that can be offered to elderly people and often by them. Many elderly can make suggestions for the solution of their own volunteer problem. The story is told of an eighty-five-year-old woman in a large eastern city who broke her hip. She lived on the third floor of an apartment building and needed a "sitter." She assured the medical student who was taking care of her that the woman upstairs would help and stay with her. It worked out well although some consternation among the visiting medical team resulted when the "sitter" turned out to be 101 years old!

Interest and talent are to be found among all age groups, not only in organizing and leading groups when everything runs smoothly, but also in supplying understanding and skill for meeting conflict, apathy, and other difficulties within a group. Much disagreement existed, in one church organization, over certain items in the group's budget, items that had already been discussed heatedly for several meetings. A member with insight suggested to the chairman that a change in the place of meeting might be useful and invited the members into his home. Somehow the conversation seemed to drift to a discussion of earlier successful projects of the group. In retrospect, some of the problems of the earlier years looked different. By the time the current budget came up for serious discussion, everybody seemed willing to find a satisfactory solution. Similar hurdles have been known to yield when a highly respected member of the group has been able to restate with clarity the group's goals. The chairman of a community service agency in the process of being established called upon the group's elected officers to meet once again with two professional men who disagreed violently over one particular policy of the new agency. Several meetings of all the board members had already ended in frustration because of the time consumed by the arguments of the two men. Immediately after the group of five assembled, the same argument began. Nothing any of the other three members could say seemed to help. Finally, the oldest member, a woman known for her sharp tongue, her genuine interest in community services, and her excellent sense of humor, told the men that they were hampering the development of the organization by their attitudes. She minced no words, but she did it with so much humor that all burst out in laughter. Needless to say the two men found a solution. Numerous persons, sometimes elderly, have often helped resolve conflicts by saying the right thing at the right time. References to the group's past achievements and aspirations or expressions of pride in holding membership will help overcome serious differences of opinion. Questions and comments offered (in most cases, sparingly but appropriately) by the social worker at a formal meeting of the whole group or to individual members outside, may foster climate that makes it possible to work together in a group.

Active resistance and conflict may be dealt with in a variety of ways. Active resistance usually tends to take on the characteristics of conflict. Those favoring a proposal and those who oppose it take sides and both groups tend to react emotionally. In such cases, sometimes additional information may serve a good purpose; at other times, the mere logic and justice of a proposed course of action will suffice as they did in the "Senior Citizen" club which had barred Negroes. Sometimes a compromise can be achieved. The most complete integration of differing points of view and the best way of meeting resistance seem to come as a result of finding ways in which both groups make an effort to explore the situation together, to establish common goals, and to invent ways of meeting them. A respected citizen leader who recognizes the need for action will play a major role in such procedures.

Apathy of a group or of a whole community may be more difficult to combat than conflict. Some examination, with knowledgeable persons in the community, is necessary to determine what causes apathy. It may stem from past failures, resistance to high costs, lack of awareness of the need for change, fear of change, particularly if cherished values or traditions are at stake, the project's being sponsored by persons who are unpopular in the community. When the welfare of a group of persons is in question, for example, the well-being of elderly men and women, opportunities made available to citizens to view the existing conditions at close range may have a salutary effect. In Marion County, where about half of the 2,200 residents aged sixty-five-and-over were interviewed by local men and women, the study's contributions to general research were minimal but the understanding that the many interviewers gained was invaluable. They referred repeatedly to the experience and the most active participants in the demonstration of the project had been involved in the study.

If the citizens, particularly the highly respected citizens, are enthusiastic, others often seem to feel the spark. When plans for action are considered, persons who are to benefit by them, as well as representatives of the groups who may have to assume major responsibility for implementing the plans, should be given opportunities to participate in the very early stages and throughout the development of the action. Except in emergencies, too much initiative in formulating and attaining goals by either professional or citizen leaders without enough participation by all sectors of the community that have a stake in the developments may prove disastrous. Participation may produce results quite different from those planned by the community leaders or visualized by the social worker. In Marion County meetings of the elderly themselves indicated that, in five out of six small towns and surrounding areas, group activities were preferred to a variety of services for persons in their own homes or referral services distributed over the county. Community leaders had expected home-care service to be given preference. A sixth group, in addition to the five mentioned earlier, was organized later. All the groups were functioning five years later, almost entirely under voluntary leadership. It is doubtful whether they would have survived if the choice of programs had not been dictated by the older people themselves.

Sometimes what appears to be lethargy may be something else. In one small town in which the possibilities of a mental health program had been repeatedly discussed, nothing seemed to happen. Discussions about the best way in which situations peculiar to that town could be met continued. When a group was finally organized, it was very well attended. What appeared to be lethargy was, in fact, slow but sure growth. When nothing seems to move in a group or community it is important to be aware of the residents' way of life. In some isolated rural areas, existing conditions threatening health may be accepted because they have always been a part of life. Some years ago in a small town all the citizens were afflicted with malaria. When the clearance of a swampy part of town was suggested, the most prominent leader, who also had the most formal education, responded, "We all have malaria. We take chill and fever medicine. That takes care of us." Such attitudes, however, are becoming increasingly rare. With radio, television, and other communication media available, isolation and problems, particularly of health, that grow out of isolation, are becoming a part of the past. Yet an almost rigid adherence to the status quo in many areas of life continues in small communities and change takes time. Sometimes even the departure or death of a leader whose influence has kept things "as they always were" must occur before change can take place.

The activities of citizens vary greatly from community to community, and within the same county. In some villages and towns of Marion County, one or, at most, two or three men seemed to be consulted before any decision was made, regardless of the issue. In others, different men and women appeared to be influential, depending largely upon the kind of decision to be made. One group might be consulted about education matters, another about a new business enterprise. In some communities, much more "behind the scene" maneuvering seemed to determine what happened to a community proposal than in others. Communities also differ in the factions or cliques that create resistance or conflicts, and in the spirit of cooperation with which residents approach a community task. In one village, in the same county as Holton, a spirit of neighborliness prevailed; in another, little concern for people in trouble seemed to exist. In some communities the attitude toward the poor or mentally sick is kindly, in others ungenerous. The reasons for the differences might provide an interesting and useful study.

With the many demands today for decision-making opportunity, it would seem possible and profitable in small communities to listen carefully to what is being said and, through their participation, enable groups to direct their efforts constructively. Whether the elderly protest as a group or individually, it is possible and likely, if they are really heard, that they will make useful suggestions, some of which they themselves will be able to implement. "Indigenous" aides involved in community services may, even when they come from the lowest of social strata, render worthwhile service. What is needed most in small towns and rural areas is a faith that older people have potentials and a willingness to "hear them out."

ORGANIZED RESOURCES

When compared with metropolitan centers, rural areas have limited organized welfare, health and recreational facilities, in number and in the variety of services offered. But some do exist, particularly when state and national resources are also taken into account. Much can be accomplished through these facilities if there is sufficient knowledge about them and if they are tapped with initiative, imagination, and skill. When more organized resources are needed, potential opportunities for their development exist. First, the community resources must be known. To know them does not mean merely to be able to list them. Miss Jones, in informing the Brandons about the four homes nearby, included much more than simply their names and locations. She will have told them who in the home they would talk to, where he might be found in the building, the services each of the four homes offered, and the cost.

In Brecher and Brecher (1964) the different levels of care that nursing homes in a community may offer are described. As Brecher and Brecher pointed out clearly, appearance, architecture, and fireproof buildings are important but even more important are the competence and skill of the staff and the atmosphere. The social worker needs to know to what extent the nursing home is focused on the patient. This applies whether the home is tax supported, is under church, fraternal, or other voluntary auspices, or is a proprietary home, that is, operated for private profit. As the Brechers explained, a great range of quality of service and of focus on the patient's interests exists. The question of whether or not the nursing home qualifies for Medicare is of utmost importance. If state institutions or agencies are being considered many might be in urban centers, possibly several hundred miles away, so specific knowledge about eligibility, costs, persons to see, and the hours and days when the facility is open or services are available assumes practical significance. In a large state institution there is a particular staff member who is responsible for prospective admissions. Long and complicated corridors in what may be a complex of buildings may prove very arduous and confusing unless the elderly patient and the person who accompanies him, know the most direct route to the admissions office and are able to find their way without unnecessary exertion. The social worker in small communities not only needs detailed knowledge of the existing organized resources, but also the ability to convey what he knows clearly and satisfactorily to the older person or to his family or friends. Apparently, Miss Jones was able to communicate effectively with Mr. Brandon, Sr. His comment, "You sure know about all these things, don't you?" indicates that he was satisfied with the authenticity of the information he received and with Miss Jones' competence.

The social worker's need for knowledge and an ability to impart it will apply to care homes, all kinds of housing facilities designed for the elderly, and to all organized resources, including those that provide care in the patient's own home or in foster family homes.

As elderly people become older, it is probable that they cannot always continue to assume all responsibility for their own care. Institutional care is then often chosen as the only way out. Actually, if some of the many possible home-care services are available or can be established, many older persons can remain in their own homes, at least for a while, and many will be much happier than if they were in institutions. To organize such facilities with enough paid and qualified staff so that continuous and effective services are available presents an even larger problem in small towns, villages, and farm communities than in urban centers. The special skills such as nursing, and occupational or physical therapy, may be difficult to come by. Persons who need home-care may be widely scattered geographically. One county or regional organization may not be accessible to everybody. Financial support seems always to be lacking or inadequate. Somehow money can be raised for buildings but not for community services. A person desiring to make a bequest can be encouraged much more easily to leave his money for a physical facility or for a wing in such a facility, than for community programs, which, as the Brechers pointed out, can be administered at considerably less cost. Perhaps the relative invisibility of services by agencies administering home-care is responsible for these attitudes. Perhaps relatives and friends feel, as the young Brandons felt, that the elderly person is protected and receives professional care when he needs it if he is in an institution. In any event, voluntary services are always needed to supplement professional and paid programs, particularly in the patient's own home, and also within institutions.

The social worker who has knowledge about organized facilities and can communicate such knowledge to the elderly and to their families and friends needs also the skill and ingenuity and imagination to approach local, regional, or state agencies and institutions that offer services successfully. Perhaps most of all he will need a desire for and an interest in collaboration, the willingness and interest to become involved and to involve others in determining how best the patient's wishes and needs can be met. The social worker must listen carefully to the elderly person and to his family to discover what those wishes are. He must listen to the staff of the organized resources while keeping the discussion focused on the requirements of the elderly person. If the need is presented clearly and cooperatively, a home administrator hesitating to admit an elderly patient who is nearly blind may think of ways of rearranging part of his building to accommodate him. The Salvation Army captain or Extension Service worker may find ways in which services, not ordinarily performed, can be rendered by members of their organizations.

Zeal in making sure that the person in need of help gets it does not obviate the necessity for remembering that the social worker, doctor, nurse, administrator, extension worker, or any other person representing an organized facility does have the prerogative to decide what his agency or institution can or cannot do. However, that does not mean that questions cannot be raised which may lead to less inflexible ways of doing things. Neither does it mean that if one source of help proves unavailable other sources should not be tried. Every effort to meet the need must be made, sometimes by establishing new resources. The procedure that applies to the establishment of new volunteer services applies equally to the establishment and development of organized community services with paid staff: planning agencies, home-care services, institutions, and housing facilities.

COUNTY WELFARE WORKERS

Not all social workers serving farming neighborhoods, villages, towns, and small cities are public welfare staff members. Since the early thirties a large majority have been. Thus, when one thinks in terms of the social worker's freeing the energies and abilities of the older people in small communities or aiding them to minimize or solve their difficulties, as individuals, families, groups and associations, or as part of the community at large, it seems the county public welfare worker is expected to carry the load. Highly respected in a good many small communities, he has taken the brunt of public dissatisfaction and criticisms and been accorded a very low status in numerous others. Usually he has been underpaid and overworked. Much of the time he has "stood alone." He has tried to meet budget deficiencies without the necessary funds. He has been admonished to give service in addition to financial grants and at the same time he has been under pressure to extend the investigations governing the grants. He has been taught to respect the dignity and worth of every person who comes to him for help and he has been encouraged, most often locally, to regard all applicants as suspect, as trying to "get something for nothing." He has been under pressure to cut expenditure; yet at other times the situation has been completely reversed. Instead of criticizing him for spending too much, some individual or group has insisted that he be more liberal than law, policies, or available funds permit.

Because our society places so great a value on financial independence, public assistance has been thoroughly stigmatized and the recipient regarded as unsuccessful and worthless. The old person has found it to be not a "right," as has often been declared, but a source of humiliation. His self-esteem, probably already low, may have deteriorated further. The amount of necessary recording and reporting has done nothing to reduce the stigma. There has been little time to learn the hopes and aspirations of older people and their potential capacities for realizing their hopes. For old men and women who need extra time for communication, perhaps because they are hard of hearing, the hurried and infrequent visits by the welfare worker may have been less than satisfactory. Many county workers have recognized this and have been frustrated by their inability to spend more time with older persons and to make available more adequate financial assistance. Some have managed to serve well despite the limitations. Others have built a crust around themselves and on the surface, at least, give the impression of being hard and unsympathetic individuals, the kind Mrs. Craig wants to avoid.

To help older people mobilize and use their potential abilities not only requires time, understanding, and skill, but also a relationship permeated with mutual trust between the aging person and the social worker. To give or withhold financial assistance, even on the basis of an objective formula, makes a relationship one of authority and submissiveness, even when genuine efforts are made to have the older person participate in the process of determining his own eligibility. The objectives of social work[1] have demanded a

[1] "To assist the individual to develop his capacities for both personal and economic independence and to carry out his appropriate family role; to assist and enable an individual to find and to use his own personal resources

dual role of the social worker, a role that has been difficult to maintain. The service and financial assistance functions are currently being separated, it is felt, to good effect. The many-faceted role of the local worker should be simplified. All change creates tension. Staff competencies are undergoing close scrutiny. Some staff members, who have been able to serve well in both service and financial assistance capacities, would, no doubt, prefer to continue as they have done in the past. Others will fear for their ability to give service without the "crutch" of the grant. Yet county welfare workers through the years have adjusted to changes necessitated by new laws and new policies. Many have been able to adapt amazingly well. They have continued to be the persons in small communities who may have been criticized because of the program they have administered but also have been recognized as being ready to help when needed.

Social work in small communities needs to be focused both on positive social well-being and on social difficulties. Well-being is promoted by the social worker's helping the individual, family, group, or association to discover, assess, mobilize, and use potential capacities, some of which are unique; others are held in common with many individuals and clusters of people. Creativity and empathy are particularly valuable in freeing potentialities and nurturing self-esteem. The former emphasizes the capacity of the individual or group for productivity through the self; the latter focuses on the tried and untried abilities in relation to others. Neither positive well-being nor social difficulties can be ignored in effective social work in small communities. Human resources, many and varied, to nurture increments and to reduce decrements are to be found within the aged themselves, as individuals and as groups. They exist within the families of the elderly and in individuals and groups of all ages and interests in the community. Most of the resources are unorganized and in order to tap them the social worker must locate them. This can be done if he becomes well acquainted with the

---

or the resources of the family and community to meet his needs; to help him maintain his sense of individual dignity and worth; to help him assume his appropriate role as a participating citizen using community services to meet his needs and contributing to community life within his capacity" (Sannes, 1963).

people and is considered to be one of them. Expected to have competence, he tends to be able to help release capacities most effectively if, with his recognized skill, he can stimulate a spirit of mutuality, of "give and take."

Organized resources are available, particularly when state and national organizations and institutions are included. If persons in the community, individually and collectively, are to be given access to them, a thorough knowledge of them is essential. Sometimes the existing organizations do not suffice and new ones are needed. These should be established after their need has been determined with the persons who are to profit from them, and those who are in a position to contribute to their establishment and maintenance. Participation should be at all stages of the inquiry and planning. Currently, most organized social work in small communities is administered by public welfare departments. With stigma attached to the receipt of public assistance grants in the community and in the minds of many of the elderly, and with the time-consuming reports that have to be made and the many records that have to be kept, the local public welfare worker has been hampered in his work. It is particularly difficult to build greater self-esteem in others when one's duties include the granting or withholding of financial assistance. The present development toward a separation of the two functions should prove useful for older people in small communities.

Intervention

8

It appears that when the individual to be served is able to do little, the social worker does much; when the person or group, including its leader, can do much, the social worker does little. However, social work intervention is not that simple. It may take as much of the worker's understanding, knowledge and skill to help, effectively, those who apparently need little support, as it does to help those obviously in need of support.

Her hair was thin and stringy. Apart from a fixed smile, her face seemed almost expressionless. The look in her eyes was far away. Her answers to questions were halting and at times incoherent. She could not remember what, or even if, she had eaten during the day. She could not remember if she had a telephone, yet on a nearby table it was in clear view. Heat poured from an open gas stove. The house was suffocatingly hot. Dishes in the sink were unwashed. The unmade bed was in plain sight.

A neighbor had telephoned the social worker. She reported that for over a year she had been "keeping an eye" on Mrs. Long, now almost eighty-five years old. On some days she seemed quite alert and managed to take care of household duties; sometimes she is very confused. This occurs much more frequently than it used to. On the day of the telephone call she seemed more confused than ever.

Her daughter, a widow with arthritis, lived in a small town nearly a hundred miles away. Therefore, she was unable to visit very often, in fact, not more than once or twice a year. She would write to the neighbor, however, and there have been some long distance telephone calls. The daughter thought her mother should be in a nursing home, but Mrs. Long would have none of it. She wanted to die in her own home just as her husband did. The neighbor thought that the time had come when Mrs. Long should be removed to a nursing home or to a hospital—whether she approved or not—although both the neighbor and Mrs. Long's daughter would much prefer to see her go voluntarily. There was much more about old Mrs. Long. She had dizzy spells and falls. No bones had been broken but she was severely bruised. What would happen if she should fall on the hot gas stove? The neighbor and the social worker shuddered at the thought.

Everybody referred to him affectionately as "Old Ernie." He was slender and his agile movements belied his age, now in the late seventies. His old felt hat seemed as much a part of him as the strands of white hair that showed from underneath.

He stopped the social worker in the street. She had met him at the Old Settlers' picnic where he played his fiddle during part of the program. At the time she had asked about friends and neighbors interested in music. She had wondered if they ever played together.

"Like in a band or orchestra?" Old Ernie had asked.

"Yes."

"Well," Old Ernie had commented, "we have not thought of that." But he went on to say that when he was young he had played in a band and that was something he liked to do. Nothing more had been said, but now Old Ernie wanted to know if the social worker could tell him about a place with a piano where "a half dozen people" could practice. He had talked to Mike and Fred. Mike plays a harmonica, or "used to," and Fred still has his old accordion. Madge Turner, who lives "two miles east down the Wittington Road" plays the piano "right well." Old Ernie knows that Jim, her husband, will drive her to town whenever she wants to go. But he "cannot find a place where they can practice."

"Have you tried the Legion Hall?" asked the social worker.

"Yes. But that place ain't heated and if they have to turn the heat on for an afternoon, the Legion has to have three dollars a throw. That," Ernie said, "is too much."

The social worker thought. "Perhaps Father Dwyer would let you use the Parish Hall on the afternoons when the building has to be heated for night meetings," she suggested.

Old Ernie grinned. "You may have something," he said. "I'll get Mike to ask him. He's Catholic."

Whenever, because of his or her position, a social worker acts to aid a person, a family, or a group to relieve or resolve difficulties or to free capacities for a greater realization of themselves or of others, he intervenes. Intervention may range all the way from helping the neighbor and the daughter to get a legally-appointed guardian for Mrs. Long to merely suggesting to Old Ernie and his friends the possibility of playing together. Intervention extends from acting on medical advice in helping to make plans for Mrs. Long to indicating a possible meeting place for Old Ernie and his fellow musicians to practice. One situation calls for the social worker's assuming a major responsibility in helping to make a decision designed to bring about change and in aiding in implementing the decision; the other seemingly involves very little: Old Ernie and his friends carry the load.

INTERVENTION AND INDIVIDUALS

Even a hurried first glance at Mrs. Long's predicament indicates the need for prompt action. Just how, and to what extent, is a social worker involved in a small community, such as a town of 1,200 persons, in such a situation? What philosophy and principles and what knowledge and skills are essential?

Assuming, though it is unlikely, that the social worker knew nothing about Mrs. Long before the telephone call from the neighbor, she needs to be steeped, even before a home visit is made, in the philosophy that a human being, regardless of age or condition, has a right and a responsibility to direct his own life to the fullest extent possible. For Mrs. Long, this means that a drastic step such as the neighbor suggests can only be taken if the patient's ". . . behavior indicates that he is mentally incapable of adequately caring for himself and his interests, without serious consequences to himself and others; and has no relative or other private individual able and willing to assume the kind and degree of support and supervision required to control the situation (Weber, 1965, p. 3). The definition, used by the Benjamin Rose Institute, itself assumes the validity of the philosophy that the patient herself should be given every opportunity to make plans for herself. It also means that relatives and neighbors should be allowed, and encouraged, to assume responsibility to the extent that they are willing and able. All of this involves genuine respect for the dignity and worth of the patient, even if she is old and her capacities have deteriorated, for members of the family; and for neighbors and friends. All have basic rights and obligations. The philosophy of a professional social worker also includes the recognition of the responsibility of a community, not only to aid its citizens when they are in trouble, but also to prevent plights such as those of Mrs. Long. Awareness of this particular situation came much too late. Moreover, in a town of 1,200, adequate community resources are likely to be lacking. Competent medical services may exist twenty-five, fifty or even a hundred miles away but such services may not be of much use to the old people who do not have transport. Such medical care earlier might have forestalled or lessened Mrs. Long's dizzy spells and her serious memory lapses. Community programs for education and service, such as the availability of a visiting nurse to insist on proper nutrition or the delivery of hot meals, might have prevented or decreased Mrs. Long's present disabilities. Community regulations about unsafe heating devices, particularly in places where old people live alone, and adequate measures to publicize and enforce such regulations, would materially reduce the hazards to safety and health.

Needed, in addition to a firm belief in prevention, would be a recognition of the potential capacities of elderly persons of advanced years and the realization that only when their abilities, or what is left of them, are used can their social well-being be promoted positively and their capacities prevented from deteriorating. The social worker in a small community needs also to possess a goodly amount of knowledge if he or she is to intervene successfully in cases such as Mrs. Long's. She needs to know something about the possible nature and causes of dizzy spells and periodic memory lapses of older people, not to decide what is wrong, but to be alert to the possible seriousness of the symptoms. If someone forgets where a telephone in clear sight is situated in his own home, the social worker must not resort to the simple conclusion that "he does not remember things he does not want to remember." She needs to know when a condition requires medical diagnosis and prognosis and therefore to know what health resources are available and how they can best be used. This may not be simple. The doctor may not be able to pay a professional visit to Mrs. Long except in an emergency. Mrs. Long may, like many patients in small towns, not get in touch with her doctor and he may be unacquainted with her condition. He may have known her in the past but that may have been months or even years ago. Mrs. Long may not be able to go for a checkup in the office on the day when the doctor can see her. She may not recognize the need for going, and may not have the transport to get her there.

Then there is the question, raised by the neighbor and the daughter, about forcible removal to a nursing home. What knowledge is required to act on that suggestion? At the very least the social worker must know if patients can be forcibly removed to nursing homes and under what conditions. Such involuntary removal, in most states, could only be countenanced if Mrs. Long is declared mentally incompetent by a court of law, in which case a legal guardian or conservator would have to assume responsibility.[1] In many small communities the chances are that she would be sent to an institution for the mentally ill. In any event, to be able to consider the patient's wishes and to determine if her condition would be benefited or harmed by forcible commitment, the social worker will need to know all the alternative resources, organized and unorganized, that are available to enable Mrs. Long to remain in her own home or to live in a nursing home. If a nursing home is to be the solution, much needs to be known about costs, availability of Medicare or other medical aid, the health services, resources and conditions

---

[1] *Lake* v. *Cameron* raised many questions about forcible removal. See also Lehmann, 1961; Wasser, 1961; Burr, 1964; Bennett, 1964; Hall, 1966.

of the institution. Then the social worker needs to be adept in working with the patient and with others concerned. She may have to
wait for opportune moments to talk with Mrs. Long during her
more lucid days. If the doctor advises nursing home care, the social
worker may have to go with her to such an institution to give her
an opportunity, if she is able, to assess the facility herself. If she
continues to resist, genuine persuasion may have to be resorted to
by the daughter, neighbor, or worker. Whatever the action is, Mrs.
Long, her daughter and her neighbor, no doubt, will require the
support of the social worker over a period of time.

The most immediate hazard is the open flames in the gas
stove, so the dangers that it presents need to be understood. Not
only may Mrs. Long receive severe burns if she should walk into
the fire or fall on the stove, but in her deteriorated mental state,
she might be unaware of the deadly fumes that will be emitted if,
because of an open door or window, the flame in the stove should
be extinguished. Remedies, even for such obvious hazards, are not
simple. To replace the stove with a safer heating device may not,
in a town of 1,200, be immediately possible; to find someone who
could stay with her day and night might not be the work of a
moment.

If the social worker can help Mrs. Long, her daughter, and
her neighbor meet their problems, what else ought she to do? How
may she intervene to lessen the possibility of comparable conditions
in the future? If there are no regulations about heating devices, or
if they are not enforced, it would seem that Miss Jones must in-
form the authorities. If nothing happens, she, no doubt, will enlist
the help of others who can exert some influence. She will probably
want to determine by communicating with individuals and groups
of older people, if a need and an interest for home-care programs
exist. She may help establish the precise requirements and ways of
meeting them, for which action she will need an understanding of
and skill in community organization and planning. The course of
action Miss Jones might have taken in helping Mrs. Long has been
defined by the National Institute on Protective Services (U.S., Department of Health, Education and Welfare, 1969a, pp. 10–11).
Recognizing that a "comprehensive system of services is needed to
provide protection of older people" and that "such persons require

at different times varying kinds, degrees and combinations of services," the Institute classifies three types of protection services: preventive, supportive and surrogate. Mrs. Long seemed to be needing surrogate protection when the neighbor telephoned. However, supportive and preventive protection are also indicated. In contrast to all of the activity surrounding Mrs. Long is the case of Old Ernie and his friends. When the social worker asked Ernie about playing music with his friends, she obviously initiated a possible change in his life. That the question led to his looking forward to a group experience reflects her sound professional philosophy, understanding, knowledge, and skill, based on keen intuitive insight or on experience and systematic learning or perhaps a combination of all three. If older residents indicate some interest in group activities, different kinds of group experiences should be made available in a community. Peer groups may have great value for members and for the community, especially if interest groups provide opportunities for creativity and community services and if they promote "knowledge and understanding toward the aim of wisdom . . . the distillation from life experiences of guiding principles, spiritual and moral values, understanding of the wonders of the universe and man's role in it" (Maxwell, 1962, p. 7). And, one might add, if that wisdom is ever sought.

There is much more that goes into a question such as the one the social worker asked Old Ernie if the question leads to a release of potential and a greater realization of oneself and of others. The social worker was likely to have been well acquainted with the community in which she was working, possibly even to the extent of knowing something about the interests of Old Ernie and his friends. She was able to assess and interpret the situation accurately by observing him as he played and mingled with others. This knowledge and skill enabled her quickly and effectively to tap his potentials. She also knew the possible resources for practice, and how to mobilize them. Ernie too knew how to use them and so Mike, rather than either the social worker or Ernie himself, made the arrangement for their using the Parish Hall.

In addition to assessing need, interest, and potential capacity sensitively and correctly, the social worker in a small community must maintain a fine balance between inactivity and activity.

Intervention to release potential and to encourage maximum self-direction and self-help requires purposeful inactivity, but enough activity so that the goals desired by Old Ernie and his friends are realized. For Ernie, very little, if anything, should be done. Possible limitations of physical energy and disappointment over the unavailability of the Legion Hall may well call for some encouragement. The important issue is that the interest and goals of Old Ernie and others concerned have been assessed correctly and that the organization of a music group is really what they themselves want and not primarily what the social worker wants. Her activity is governed by how much Ernie and the other players need her support and how she makes it available.

In one small town interest had been expressed by a group in the sponsoring of a program of guides for blind and for other old persons unsteady on their feet. The need for such a project had been established and its administration had been discussed. After the decision was made to establish the program, the social worker remained quite inactive, expecting the group to implement the plans. They said they would, but weeks passed by without action. The social worker from time to time brought up the subject somewhat casually and always a continued interest was expressed. Yet nothing happened. Then she changed her tactics. She brought up the question quite directly with the president and suggested possible first steps. She persisted in doing this, with the result that the project did get "off the ground," launched and administered with enthusiasm. Had the interest of the president and other members of the organization not been genuine, the aggressive intervention of the worker would, no doubt, have been resented.

If a paid staff member is available, individuals and groups in a community may expect him to "take over." For example, Old Ernie may have expected the social worker to locate a "place with a piano." In such cases considerable pressure is often exerted, not only by those who expect to profit directly, but also by others in the community, including board members. Such pressures may be difficult to withstand, especially when the social worker himself would prefer to be active. However, if the objective is to free potential capacities for maximum use by a person, family, or other clusters of persons, purposeful inactivity is essential. This should not be carried so far as to fail to support, encourage, and at times intervene somewhat aggressively and persistently when, for a variety of reasons, movement toward a genuinely desired goal has been halted. In a small community, when the evidence points to the social worker's becoming more and the resident's less active, it is time to stop and assess the situation. The intervention by the social worker in Mrs. Long's case may be said to fall near one end of the continuum of participation, in Old Ernie's case at the other end. The gradations between are determined by the situation and the purposes. Mrs. Long was incapacitated and, at times, was unable to look after herself. Her life was in danger. Old Ernie was capable of self-direction. His need and interest was to make a greater use of his capacity, to prevent deteriorating and to promote optimum well-being. In the process others profited. The intervention consisted of the social worker's encouraging activity in others and ostensibly remaining inactive. The case histories of the Brandons and of Old Zelda represent intervention that falls in between the two extremes. The Brandons had fewer obstacles to their own involvement than did Old Zelda, and the social worker intervened less. Yet the two situations had one thing in common. Before the Brandons or Old Zelda could use their potential capacities for self-direction, the social worker intervened to help them reduce the difficulties that prevented their helping themselves. In both instances some of the tensions, strains, and unhappiness first had to be diluted. The dilutive process for Old Zelda took more outside interference than it did for the Brandons. In fact, the Brandons required little direct intervention from the social worker: having been helped to assess their situation and to reduce their difficulties, they could manage very well by themselves. From that point on the social worker might well focus on freeing the Brandons' potential abilities for greater self-other realization. Before Old Zelda was ready for such a step she required much more active assistance for a much longer period of time.

INTERVENTION AND GROUPS

In social work, intervention with community groups and associations has two basic objectives, each relying upon and supporting the other. The one focuses on the individual members and the values they derive from their affiliation with a group or an association. The other emphasizes the formation of a strong unit, or if the cluster of interacting individuals is already in existence, its reinforcement as a functioning whole. Inherent in such a unit, at least potentially, are benefits for the members and others. Groups and associations are developmental: like all human phenomena, they emerge from what is to what becomes, they keep on becoming throughout their life span. Such growth would seem to indicate that social work intervention to establish a new group needs to take into account eight steps: the assessment of the need for a group or association; the formation of the group; the delineation of its purpose; the development of group structure; the determination of long- and short-term goals; the planning of methods to attain the goals; the implementation of the plan; and periodic analysis of the strength of the group as a unit and of the effectiveness of its efforts. These eight steps do not have a rigid sequence and recur throughout the life span of the group. If growth is the objective, the members must participate in all steps and the social worker must listen sensitively and genuinely to what is said. If an existing group or association is to serve elderly people in a new or extended way, the appropriateness of its programs and the possibility of introducing new ones must be assessed. The current state of the group structure must be evaluated. This evaluation will include an analysis of the leadership and other roles and statuses, of the purposes for which the group was organized and its long- and short-term goals, of its characteristic ways of making plans and implementing them, and above all, of the state of its morale and cohesion. Practical considerations, such as what is possible in the group according to its constitution or by-laws, its finances, and its physical quarters will have to be taken into account. Members and perhaps potential members need to participate in the assessment.

Whether a new group is formed or an existing one used, the social worker's decision to intervene should rest on what the members reveal of their needs, interests, capacities, and desires for a group experience. Such information must come from persons who are alert and are using their capacities and from persons who have regressed and are withdrawn. That the apathetic and deteriorated should have their say, as well as the mentally and physically able and the highly gifted, has been clearly and sensitively depicted by Ferrari (1963, pp. 71–83). How can the interest, need, and ability be determined? The intervener may be a paid social worker or an unpaid volunteer; in either case he must be accepted, whether the respondent is capable of grasping easily the benefits to be derived from participating in a group, or has great difficulty in comprehending.

Becoming accepted may require a number of personal visits with withdrawn, regressed, or hostile patients, such as often are found in nursing and other care homes but not only there. A friendly approach to these patients as individuals is necessary to establish a working relationship sufficient to elicit response. An introduction from a person who is already accepted, such as Mrs. Long's neighbor, helps. Sometimes, to test need, interest, and ability, opportunities have to be made available. Even then, the response may be slow, the withdrawn individuals may choose at first to sit in separate corners in a dark room or in other ways show hesitancy to becoming involved. Relatives, friends, doctors, and nurses may be able to give information that unlocks the doors for the withdrawn person. Some techniques which are useful for alert and highly self-directing individuals are not appropriate for persons with "long gray faces" sitting in "long gray lines." Questionnaires, such as those used successfully in rural Minnesota with older individuals living in their own homes (Bloedow, 1963), would not serve well for the residents in "The Home." Neither would a mailed invitation. Before Old Zelda, Mrs. Long, and many patients in nursing homes could begin to participate in group activities, or even to know if they might like to, they would need much support. Alert elderly persons should also be visited, not only because mutual acceptance is important, but also to ascertain whether they indicate a need for and an interest in new group experiences, and to ensure that at least some of the potential members will have thought about the group's goals and will be able to participate, and perhaps encourage the others to participate, in the early meetings. In initial interviews older people can make practical suggestions about meeting times and places.

Bloedow points out that, since the lives of many rural persons are closely bound to their churches, the public approval of local clergymen often proves helpful. This approval may be expressed by his announcing a proposed meeting in a church bulletin, from the pulpit or in another meeting; offering space in the church or a church building; or personally participating in the meetings. In Marion County, such cooperation and approval were apparent at each one of the first meetings of the six new groups organized. When no minister or priest was present, a recognized church leader played an important role. The first meeting needs to be carefully but flexibly planned with the help of local persons who know the local customs. Discussion of possible programs should include references to interests expressed in personal interviews. For persons who have regressed and for whom the group experience will be primarily therapeutic, the first meeting may consist of the organizers' simply recognizing each person and serving refreshments. If the patients are not yet able to participate, some well known songs or hymns sung by others may afford a pleasant moment. No effort may be indicated to gain verbal participation from any of the members at a first gathering. Perhaps some explanation of the possible values of meeting may be made but it will have to be repeated in subsequent personal visits and in later meetings. If the persons invited to participate are residents of an institution, such as a nursing home, their voluntary attendance should be stressed. It should be made clear, particularly if they are invited by someone from the public welfare agency, that participation is voluntary and not a prerequisite to their receiving or continuing to receive a financial grant. Except perhaps when the participants are very withdrawn, even in the first meeting some group structure begins to be evident. Some persons speak up; others keep silent. Some raise questions; others answer them. In small towns and rural areas the silences can be long. The chairman explains, raises questions, and summarizes what has been said. This may have to be repeated in different ways and, in most instances in rural communities, couched in simple language.

In Marion County, there was little development of formal organization at the first meetings of the six clubs. Because of the roles they played before and during the initial meeting, the persons who presided were accepted as temporary leaders; several of them were selected later as permanent officers and subsequently played im-

portant roles. Various local organizations sponsored the first meetings. The primary role of the sponsors was to greet those attending,
to furnish or arrange refreshments and to serve them. To different
degrees the procedures remained informal even after officers were
elected and a constitution or bylaws adopted. In one group a
systematic effort was made, during its second year of existence,
to learn what tasks the members would like to perform and for
which they would assume responsibility. The local leader who
developed the questionnaire and distributed it said that in addition to
enabling the organizers to learn about existing individual interests,
the tasks listed might indicate the various ways in which the members might participate.

Because possibly little, if any, professional help would be
available to the clubs after the termination of the Ford grant,
and because they were committed to the values of voluntary participation, the organizers made a conscious effort to involve from the
first as many people as possible and to encourage the maximum
voluntary responsibility for leadership. This effort had some major
problems. The leaders, being elderly themselves, might suddenly
be taken ill or have their activities curtailed by the illness or death
of a spouse. Efforts to make members aware of such possibilities
and to groom a deputy were not very successful. Except in one
case, neither was the effort to include younger persons who might
provide support when needed. When such a group of younger
persons was referred to by one local resident as an "Advisory Committee" the indignation expressed at the idea of young people
presuming to advise their elders was considerable. However, in
meetings of four of the six groups to which younger persons came
regularly, it was noted that certain duties performed by them, such
as moving furniture, climbing a ladder to cover windows when slides
were shown, and offering suggestions for programs, were gratefully
received. In one small community, the young minister and his wife
were enthusiastically accepted by Catholics and Protestants in the
group, and their new baby was the pride and joy of the whole
group.

Three centers were established by the clubs of older persons.
Because of financial difficulties and perhaps some lingering after-
effects of the conflict over permitting dancing on Center premises

one center was closed. The other two had limited programs at first, but seemed to serve some desirable purpose. In one, monthly meetings of the club were held and small groups used the quarters for playing cards and for similar purposes. The other in its early days was the center for displaying the creative efforts of its members and also served as a meeting place for small groups engaged in educational pursuits. The headquarters were made available largely through the generosity of the city fathers in one instance and through a civic group in another. The labor required for remodeling the quarters was furnished largely by the members. This resulted in individual and group pride and helped to develop group morale. Later, after the termination of the Ford project, the quarters of one club were further remodeled and a multipurpose center established with funds provided in part by the Older Americans Act. The funds were administered under the supervision of the State Division of Services to the Aging.

One club was formed specifically to bring together the older residents who lived in their own homes in the community and the patients of the care home situated in their midst. After much local planning, in which the administrator of the home as well as the administrator of the local hospital to which the home was attached participated, a meeting was held in the basement of the home. The attendance from the community was of such unexpected proportions that some were reported unable to get in. Later meetings were held in a nearby school. Plans were discussed for systematic visiting to the home and for taking patients for rides and to the homes of members who lived in the small towns and on nearby farms. The group, like the other five, continued to meet after the Ford Foundation grant was terminated. Plans for further systematic intermingling among the patients in the institution and the residents of the community, according to reports, were only partially implemented.

Two major practical difficulties seemed to limit potential growth and development of the clubs of elderly in Marion County: finances and possible meeting places. All six clubs struggled with the problems of finance. Even with some funds available from the Ford Foundation grant, finances were inadequate. Membership fees had to be nominal in order to make possible the attendance of all interested persons. Meals were always of the potluck variety so that each

person or couple was expected to bring one dish only. The membership fees provided money for small items, such as coffee and paper
tablecloths, but at best it was something of a hand-to-mouth existence.
Meeting places in small communities tend to be scarce. Churches
and church halls present the most frequent possibilities. But older
persons in small communities may not be very ecumenically minded;
different Protestant denominational affiliations may militate against
the use of a church facility belonging to a particular denomination.
The division between Protestants and Catholics may pose difficulties, but had no effect on two groups in Marion County, who met
in Catholic facilities, with a Protestant minister attending regularly.
The annual county-wide meeting most often was held in a Men-
nonite Church with a variety of Protestant denominations and the
Roman Catholic Church represented. The dining room facilities of
a small-community church are usually in the basement. The steps,
often dark and difficult, present hazards for men and women who
have poor eyesight and find it difficult to walk.

INTERVENTION AND CHANGE

Any social work intervention presupposes that a possible
change may benefit an individual, family, group, or community.
The profession rests on the assumption that change is possible in
persons, individually and in groups, and in the situations that sur-
round them. The intervention consists of the social worker's helping
to bring about the changes that will reduce or prevent social difficulties and enhance well-being. The need for change may or may
not be recognized at first and the change itself may or may not be
desired immediately. Mrs. Long apparently did not want to change;
the Brandons did, but were unable to find a way. Old Zelda desired
change but she wished for the impossible when she wanted undone
what had been done eight years before. Old Ernie apparently had
not thought of playing his violin in a group, but when the question
was raised, he was ready to act on the suggestion. The desire for
change may be nonexistent, consciously wanted, or latent. The results that a change is expected to bring may be wanted and yet not
wanted; the current situation may provide satisfaction despite its
dissatisfaction. Old Zelda, no doubt, derived some pleasure from
her self-righteous bitterness. The young Brandons may have gained

satisfaction from having Mr. Brandon, Sr., in their home despite the fact that they wanted a change in residence to make him happier. Some goals that changes are to bring about are unattainable, others are within easy reach. Some have not been comprehended; others have been clearly delineated. Often there are uncertainties about the kind of goal to be attained and how to attain it. Under such conditions the social worker may be of help. He may aid individuals and groups to find goals or clarify them by pointing up choices, giving information, raising pertinent questions, and supporting interest in and enthusiasm for ideas for change. But what if the goals are at variance with those of the profession of social work?

In the final analysis, any goal involving change is based on values. In social work, as in a democratic society, these values include a commitment to the principle of self-direction. This applies to the individual elderly person, to his family, to the groups and associations with whom he is affiliated, and to the community as a whole. Thus, social work values stress the principle of the right to self-determination. Mrs. Long's self-determined goal was to stay in her own home and die there. This goal was in harmony with the values of social work, but if it meant a tragic accident or the shortening of her life through lack of attention to her physical needs, the social worker could not stand idly by. The profession is committed not only to the right to self-determination but also to the worth and sacredness of human life. This is clearly demonstrated by efforts to prevent suicide, and in the final analysis, the right to self-determination will take second place. Concern for the greater well-being of Mr. Brandon, Sr., was shared by the family and the social worker. However Mr. Brandon and his son and daughter-in-law were confused as how best to achieve the goal. The social worker made her own preference for a way of clearing up the confusion quite evident. Yet when the parents were unsure about acting upon her suggestion to include the children in a family conference, she gave them the responsibility for decision. The inclusion of the children in a meeting with the grandfather was, no doubt, intended to nurture strong family ties. Had the parents decided against including them, that goal would not have been promoted as much as it was. Nor would it have been attained if the parents had included the children primarily because of pressure from the social worker. In this case the value of the right to self-determination seems to have taken precedence over the value of strong family ties. The family unit could not have been strengthened without the parents' exercising their right and responsibility to make the decision. The professional values of social work dictate that the interests of Old Zelda and of others who are affected by her behavior be served. Old Zelda was trying inappropriately and without a chance for success, to meet her own needs. She did not consider the needs of others. There was a discrepancy between the goals of the social worker and those of Old Zelda, as well as in their ways of attaining them. The right to self-determination is not an absolute right (Bernstein, 1960, pp. 3–8); with it goes responsibility for the rights of others. When the rights of others are flagrantly violated, the social worker cannot condone action based on self-determined goals and ways of attaining them, particularly when they cannot possibly make for greater social well-being, even for the self-directing person. The issues are many and complicated. The decision of which value shall predominate is particularly difficult in a small community. Unlike in a metropolitan center, a social worker in rural towns and villages must become an integral part of the community. But her "being one of the community" poses difficulties when an objective stance is necessary. A social worker in thinly populated areas is confronted with more than merely questions of individual or group rights to self-determination and the accompanying responsibilities. If her intervention is to result in desirable social changes, there are other issues that may have to be faced. People may resist change because they have never known or experienced a better way. Even social workers are not immune to "getting used" to unsavory social conditions, as the anti-poverty program illustrates. No one knew more about the pockets of poverty existing in our communities than did the social workers: they did not like them but seem to have accepted them. It took a Harrington (1962) and televised congressional hearings in 1968–1969 to make them known. Changes are resisted because of an unawareness of the need for change or of ways in which changes can be made profitably. The town of 1,200 in which Mrs. Long lived may not have been conscious of all the many ramifications that the protection of its citizens entailed.

Those in authority or in places of leadership may not have known of the development elsewhere of a variety of home-care and home-health facilities, or may have hesitated to establish them because of the lack of specialized services which are necessary if the programs are to function properly. Physical and occupational therapy, psychiatric, medical and nursing services, nutritionists, transport, and other facilities are discouragingly nonexistent or limited. Social work intervention in the development of home-care or home-health programs to prevent or delay the need for institutional care may meet with limited success when too few professional resources are available.

ASSESSMENT AND INTERVENTION

What determines the nature of intervention and how much is indicated? The first factor is the degree of urgency for change. The need for action in Mrs. Long's case was immediate. Her life was in danger, her health required prompt attention. The dizzy spells that had resulted in falls and bruises were liable to recur at any time. Had the social worker discovered her lying on the floor unconscious because of severe burns or in pain with a broken hip, the decisions would have been made even more quickly than they were. There would have been no time to get in touch with the daughter. A long range plan might be discussed with her, and Mrs. Long if her condition permitted, but this would have had to come after the fact, after the social worker had intervened to change the immediate situation. The social worker's role would have been like that of a teacher when a school room is on fire: he decides which is the safest exit and directs the children to take it. They are not involved in making plans. His action is authoritative and decisive. The response is acquiescence. In Mrs. Long's case, discussion with her, with her neighbor and her daughter, and finally persuasion rather than complete directive responsibility was probably the actual course of intervention pursued. Persuasion is a little less drastic than compulsion but it is authoritative and often decisive. The response, at best, is assent, not consent, at least for the time being. Urgency necessitates immediate decision and prompt intervention. Participation by the person affected is minimal. The degree of urgency determines in part how much participation is possible.

The second factor that influences intervention is the capacity of an individual, family, or group to participate in planning a change. Mrs. Long, when the worker was called, had little capacity to participate; Old Ernie and his friends had much. The case of the latter presented some urgency, the urgency that affects all people of advanced years: life will not continue much longer. If the rewards of a possible change are to be enjoyed, the change should be immediate. Ernie and his friends were quite capable of deciding whether or not they wanted to produce music together, and if so, how soon. The social worker's intervention in their case was facilitating. It made possible their consideration of a particular plan for change, and when they wished to adopt it, she gave them some help. Her approach was to raise a question and briefly discuss the plan. The response was complete acceptance. Ernie and his associates accepted wholeheartedly because not only were their wishes accurately assessed but also they had complete freedom to reject the suggestion.

Intervention that elicits maximum participation in planning change tends to promote satisfaction, if there is sufficient capacity for planning and the contemplated change is realistic and within reach. Perhaps before the social worker spoke to Old Ernie she considered the possibilities and difficulties of her suggestion. The pros and cons should be discussed with the individual or the group to be affected by the change. Out of the discussion might develop short- and long-range goals, and a decision of how to reach the goals. The role of the intervener would be that of an enabler, or facilitator, not of a director.

The third factor that determines intervention is the goal of the intervention. For Mrs. Long the immediate objective was her protection. The development of her potentialities would, it was hoped, follow soon. For the old men interested in music, the mobilization of their unused capacities to promote their development and enhance their well-being was the primary goal. Protection can be promoted by an agent or agents other than the person or group to be protected. Growth, however, is an unfolding process; the urge has to come from within. Intervention cannot be authoritarian. It can reveal opportunities, provide support, encourage self-confidence, and help keep the goal in view. Any pressure to develop too rapidly or out of harmony with the inclination of the individual or group will hamper development. A rosebud with an inner push for life needs time, room, sunshine, and nourishment if a full-blown blossom with all of its possibilities for color, size, fragrance and beauty is to result. Manipulation of the growth process merely stunts it. Human development is equally simple and infinitely more complex.

It was necessary for the urge for change to come from Old Zelda herself. She needed to supply the energy for the change. But much debris had to be cleared away before progress could be made and it could not be removed by others. A healing process had to take place first. This involved a genuine catharsis and an overt demonstration of belief in her worth. After that, growth was possible, but even then it promised to be slow with small steps forward and, from time to time, some backward. What could be hoped for was that after a while the tempo in the process of growth would increase and that periods of recessive movement would diminish, with longer intervals in between. Though much less ostensibly than in the case of Mrs. Long, the intervention into Old Zelda's life was also authoritative and directive, though at the same time it provided support for all apparent potentialities. The effort from the first was focused on bringing about change from within. With Mrs. Long, the emphasis, at least at first, was on changing the situation surrounding her. With the Brandons too, the immediate goal was therapeutic. It required some catharsis, but much less than in the case of Old Zelda. From the first, Mr. Brandon, Sr., and members of the family had genuine capacity for participating in planning change. When supplied with the needed information, some help in analyzing the issues and a suggestion; given freedom to take it or leave it, the family, including the grandfather and the children, could move along on their own.

The fourth factor is that the locus of a situation calling for a change varies and, therefore, necessitates differing assessments. Sometimes the need for change lies within the individual or group; sometimes within the environment. Seldom is it completely one or the other. Always the assessment of the need for change should be made in terms of where it is located. Both Ellen Merton and Mr. Brandon, Sr., needed and wanted change in their current situation. For both, some of their discomfort came from within themselves, some from their interaction with members of their families. Each family, in turn, had its own problems, and each also suffered from the impact of forces within its environment. Even without a thorough analysis of the situations, it is obvious that both Mr. Brandon, Sr., and Ellen were struggling between their desire for independence and their need for family to provide affection, companionship, and a home. Both needed a stable anchorage. But a need for change in their families was also indicated. Without change their families could not provide the environment that Mr. Brandon, Sr., and Ellen needed. Some of the difficulties consisted of struggles between family members. Some had a much larger base such as the state of transition of the family as a social institution in a small community, and the rapid changes that have taken place in the American agricultural economy. Provisions to fill the gaps created by the impact of these changes upon individuals and families have lagged behind the voids they created. For the older person these voids include a change in society's value system which had emphasized economic production and economic independence. The changes have made provisions, largely benevolent in character, that are stigmatized both in the minds of the local public and in the self-images of older people. Although they are designed to ameliorate difficulties, these types of provisions also create some.

The fifth factor in the analysis of the kind and extent of intervention indicated is that of timing. Just when or at what point should the social worker intervene? When the social worker is aware of definite needs, even though she does not necessarily interpret them accurately, the decision about timing is not too difficult. But when the needs are indefinite, or when groups of people, perhaps the whole community, are involved, the situation is more complicated. An example might be made of the development of home-care services in a town of 1,200. Mrs. Long's condition points to the need for some kind of home-health facility, but what kind? If the need for the services of a visiting nurse were verified, not only for Mrs. Long but also for others, how would the establishment of such a service affect efforts to develop other, equally necessary, programs? With the dearth of nurses, how feasible is it to concentrate first on a nursing project? With limited funds available for other home services, what services can be paid for now; what services can be financed later? On what programs is community interest currently focused? How do the persons who hold the purse strings feel? Suppose the answer is that now there is deep concern for building an adequate nursing-home. It, too, is needed. Is it better to encourage the establishment of a nursing-home and concentrate on promoting an adequate program within the institution, or should the current community interest be discouraged and home-health services emphasized? Suppose that were done, might not the action result in no action at all, now or in the foreseeable future? Would it be better to make use of the existing interest in the community and hope to expand the proposed nursing-home program to include home-services later?

Differing assessments leading to differing intervention are often difficult, and may have to be made by trial and error. Based on the information available, the social worker will make best judgment possible of the situation. However, she will continue her close observation, and if the subsequent reactions show that the decision was wrong, the assessment is modified. As far as possible, the individual, family, or group to be affected by the intervention should participate at all stages of the assessment. Social work intervention with or on behalf of older people, families, and groups should consist predominantly of the social worker's helping discover, mobilize, and build on the potential capacities of all concerned.

Like intervention in the lives of individuals, intervention in the activities of groups may be active or purposefully inactive. The intervener may be primarily concerned with ameliorating or resolving difficulties of individual members or of the whole group, or with helping free and mobilize their potential strengths. Group members may be thoroughly involved in the decision making and implementing, or they may participate little. When groups are hopelessly entangled and antagonistic, the intervener, paid or volunteer, may have to assume the responsibility for charting the course for a while. If he can work through the association leader, it will be to the good. He may be indirect and manipulative rather than direct, but the intervener's point of view prevails. Most assuredly he will want to shift to a less authoritative position as quickly as possible.

Sometimes, when a group becomes temporarily immobilized, perhaps as a result of the traumatic experience of suddenly losing a leader, or of incurring a disappointment over the outcome of efforts in behalf of a cherished goal, the intervener may become decisive but his action will have the support of what remains of the group spirit and the members' potential capacities. Difficulties may arise out of an imbalance of the group structure. The member who has effectively built up the group's morale moves away, no other member is filling his place and the group leader is confused and unable to cope with the consequent lethargy. The intervener may fill the gap. The member who customarily assumed as mundane a task as conveying the drinking water to the picnic grounds where the group met, may have become ill; no other member is a driver with a car. The intervener may step in again, and will do so with an eye out for other resources within the group that may be tapped.

If members or potential members are ill, withdrawn, or hostile, the intervener may have to make all the plans for establishing a group and may have to assume the role of leader for quite a long time. As the interaction between members develops, some role patterns will begin to evolve. Eventually, if the process continues for long enough, one or more members will invariably emerge as leaders. The intervener, at all times, will be sensitive to evidence of ability to participate and will encourage it. Many aged persons in small communities may be less likely than their metropolitan counterparts to enter into discussions, particularly about their own personal concerns and emotional conflicts. Since the elderly in rural areas and small towns have generally had less formal education than city dwellers, they may be less articulate. A good many old people are averse to airing their personal and family affairs in public. Many will have had little experience of group discussion, particularly if they have not been members of farm groups, such as those sponsored by Agricultural Extension Services, or if their church activities have not demanded their active participation.

The few associations in small communities that have been organized specifically for recreation, social welfare, and health services, are the vehicles established by society for changing the lives of people, individually and in groups. Service agencies and institutions consist, in the final analysis, of people and are for people. That agencies' buildings, material equipment, policies, and functions tend in time to take precedence over the welfare of the people they serve is characteristic of associations of all kinds, not just of social welfare organizations. Yet, if the objective is to foster necessary change, this tendency has to be kept under control. Gardner (1965) suggests as a remedy, when the associations' structure, policies, and functions become ends in themselves, that "the arts of associational renewal" be brought into play. He discusses nine rules to assure such renewal. All nine rules for renewal are as applicable to agencies in small communities as they are to the large, complex organizations that the author was considering.[2] Besides the actual or potential organizational "dry-rot" that plagues service agencies everywhere, an influence on their deterioration is the focus of social welfare agencies and institutions on decrements. Yet the need to shift gears, if battered, low estimates of self-worth are to be enhanced, seems obvious. Such changes in emphasis, although probably more clearly apparent in rural than in metropolitan areas, are difficult to initiate by agencies. Usually they are subsidiaries of national or federal, state or regional associations, so the agencies are governed by the central body's criteria of acceptable performance. "Acts of organization renewal" have to be initiated by the central agencies before the local staff can act. The standard setting, financial and educational aids of central organizations are clearly beneficial, but the almost inevitable rigid adherence to policies established in the headquarters is inhibiting, particularly for agencies in small communities. They have to proceed without the support of other health and welfare organizations in the same community and

[2] "[1] The organization must have an effective program for the recruitment and development of talent. . . . [2] It must be a hospitable environment for the individual. Organizations that have killed the spark of individuality in members will have diminished greatly their capacity for change. [3] [It] must have built-in promises for self-criticism. It must have an atmosphere in which uncomfortable questions can be asked. [4] [It must also have] fluidity of internal structure. [5] [It] must have an adequate system of internal communication. [6] [It] must have some means of combating the process by which men become prisoners of procedures. [7] [It must have] means of combating the vested interests that grow up in every human institution. [8] [It must be] interested in what is going to become and not what has been. . . . [9] An organization runs on motivation, on conviction, on morale. Men have to believe that it really makes a difference whether they do well or badly" (pp. 20–21).

with few staff members to encourage one another. The result is that the standards and policies may not always meet local needs as well as they might but continue to be administered. Even so, some rural local public welfare agencies, nursing-homes and institutions such as local Red Cross chapters and Salvation Army Corps have shown surprising abilities to act upon the needs of people individually and in groups, to emphasize their capacities, large or small, and thus helped bring about changes.

In summary, social work intervention to change conditions affecting the aged, their families, and other clusters of persons is based on differing assessments of conditions and of three broad, not mutually exclusive, categories of approaches to meet the situation. The approach recommended for most extensive use by general practitioners is designed to free potential capacities to improve the self-image and to insure and maintain optimum well-being. It seeks to maintain a high self-esteem or to strengthen a battered or under-developed one. For such an approach, creativity and empathy are particularly valuable. In an effort to release the increments of older persons and the clusters of people that they find especially significant, the social worker recognizes past and present achievements and gives unfailing, timely, enthusiastic support. Occasionally he articulates and clarifies issues, emphasizes and reemphasizes the self-determined goals to be achieved, and in other ways enables individuals, families, and groups to act. He may recognize current and visualize future needs of which the community is unaware, but he has faith that a greater use of local human potential will meet such needs. At opportune moments he may call attention to the needs. He feels competent, but does not display his expertise. Publicly he operates unobtrusively and so may feel pressure to become more directive.

When decrements in the situation are overwhelming one of two other intervention methods is indicated. When the self-esteem or relationships of an individual or group are so weak or distorted that self-direction is impossible; when other capacities for action are at a low ebb and well-being or even survival is at stake, facilitating methods of intervention are too slow. The social worker may then assume the major, if not the entire, responsibility for assessing the situation and acting. The method is characterized by direction, persuasion, maneuvers, and manipulation. The strategy that promises the best results is employed. Hence, the approach may be referred to as strategic. When applied to individuals, legal authority for action is often essential. When using this approach for individuals, families, or other clusters of persons, the social worker, with or without court sanction, with or without the cooperation from others, needs to act the expert that he is. His intervention is sure and purposeful; his skills are on full display.

After the emergency has passed, the approach may shift to one of much greater involvement of the individual or group and, in time, may become entirely facilitating. Further changes, in the individual, family, or group, or in the surrounding conditions, may indicate a different approach before potentialities can be fully released—a therapeutic or clinical approach. The social work clinician assesses the situation with the individual or group as far as possible, but he relies less on their competence to be self-directing than would the facilitator. His focus, at least at first, is on social difficulties rather than on social well-being. If the environment creates or aggravates illness, it must be changed. If the personality of the individual or the affective interaction of members in a family or group is causing the difficulties, the social worker must help toward bringing about some recognition of the difficulties and then help to find ways of relieving or resolving them. In the process, he will not only give the necessary support to self-image and feelings of self-worth, but will also define and help to clarify questions and alternatives, will offer suggestions, and will be using all the available assets and resources. At such a point these resources will be mobilized primarily to relieve or eliminate the difficulty rather than to release potential capacities. Thereafter the facilitating model may, and usually should, replace the therapeutic.

There are a number of differences in the roles of the facilitator and of the clinician. The facilitator bases his efforts primarily on his faith in the increments of the persons and groups he serves; the clinician relies heavily on their faith in his competence, which must be genuine, but may be emphasized by his donning a white coat in a clinical setting or emphasizing that a service must be requested before he can assume responsibility for a "case." In both situations there is mutual respect, but the primary focus is different.

The professional competence of the clinician is more obvious than that of the facilitator and, even though he still works *with* his patient, the clinician works *for* him to a greater extent than does the facilitator. These differences in role and status need to be very clear to the social worker as he changes his approaches. According to his assessment of the situation in the beginning and throughout the intervention, the general practitioner may use any of the three approaches or some modification of them, whether or not he is a specialist and employs one of the three specialized methods: casework, group work, or community social work. The value of delineating the approaches or models of intervention is to help the intervener see more clearly that a variety of ways may be used and how and under what conditions the primary focus should be on any one of them. An analysis may make possible a greater awareness of what is involved in a shift in the use of models.[3]

[3] The idea of developing a theory of different models of intervention was first stimulated by Morris (1963). No effort has been made to adhere to the description of the three approaches in Lippitt, Watson, and Westlog (1958), but the influence of this book will be apparent and is gratefully acknowledged.

SUMMARY

9

Elderly persons in small communities, their families and other clusters of people with whom they have affiliation show wide ranges of well-being: from the productive and contented individual to the one who is withdrawn and hostile; from the well-integrated and happy family to the family that is discouraged and unhappy; from the Senior Citizen Club that meets the needs of its members to an aggregation of old men sitting in a park who do not even constitute a group. To move toward the goal of self-other realization and greater well-being, elderly people, their families and the variety of relevant groups need to use whatever potential resources they have. The elderly person's self-concept and family and group images are vital in mobilizing potentials. To encourage the use of potential individual and group resources and to aid in the movement toward greater self-other realization, a social worker in a small community must function as a generalist, with assistance and consultation from available specialists.

Individuals and social groups are different in many ways yet have some significant common features. Of special relevance for the social work generalist is the fact that the quality of the self-image of an individual or group, and the images that others have, may significantly affect the degree of satisfaction or dissatisfaction derived from life. The feeling of self-worth in the self-image plays a particularly important role as persons, individually and as groups, proceed in the search for *being* and *becoming*.

For the elderly individual the concept of self is subject to many potential stresses and strains. Some of these he may experience in any community regardless of its size; some he may experience because of conditions in rural areas which make him particularly vulnerable. A major strain is produced by the connotations of retirement age. For many it means not that they are retiring from work but that they are incapable of it. Voluntary or involuntary retirement at the age of sixty, sixty-five, or, at the most, seventy seems to be a signal to quit work and to become inactive, regardless of one's state of health and energy. Society seems to say that when a man reaches retirement age he no longer has any capacity as a producer. In many small communities, such a verdict can play havoc with a man's self-esteem. Work has a high priority in the hierarchy of values of many elderly persons in rural and small city communities. To be considered unproductive signals for them physical decline and an increasingly poor concept of their self-worth. Men reaching retirement age usually have to change from instrumental to socioemotional roles. Since many women in thinly settled communities have devoted their adult lives almost exclusively to household duties and the well-being of their families, friends and neighbors, they have integrated their family and community responsibilities for a long time. Theirs has always been a socioemotional role. After they have adjusted to their children's moving out of the home, the change accompanying retirement age is, for them, not great. Because productive employment is more accessible in urban areas, elderly women in metropolitan areas, more so than those in small communities, go through the retirement process and experience shifts in responsibilities. Men in small communities face major changes in roles and their new tasks, if they find some, are likely to produce feelings of decreased importance.

Declining health and increasing disability may converge upon the older person at about the same time as retirement, and loss of role and status may be attributed as much to poor health as to the lack of productive employment. This occurs both in urban and in rural communities. However, the health of the elderly is likely to be poorer in small communities than in large ones. And health care tends to be easier to come by in metropolitan than in rural areas, where health services of all kinds, including specialized services, are fewer. When health services do exist, they are less available because of distances and limited commercial transportation. Another complicating factor is that in small towns and on farms many housewives, who constitute a large portion of the elderly, have never learned to drive. Even if they can drive, for some—both men and women—it is simply too expensive to own and maintain an automobile.

Further strain on the self-image might be the death of a marital partner, usually after many years of married life, and the increasing number of deaths of intimate friends and neighbors. Such losses often mean that the elderly person must give up the family home (cherished personal belongings) and live on a reduced, often inadequate, income. The financial position of older people in America is better than it was at the end of World War II, but is still less satisfactory than that of any other age group and even less satisfactory in small communities than in metropolitan areas. Social Security grants have done much to improve the lot of the old in all parts of the nation. But currently the grants for old people living on farms and coming from farms are small or nonexistent, especially for the older sectors of the sixty-five-and-over age group because their Social Security coverage has come too late to bring sizable monthly checks. Medicare is available and promises to improve the financial status of old people no matter where they live. However, the financial income of older people in small communities continues to be inadequate, and the low social position that goes with low income is likely to detract from self-esteem.

The older person views current rapid social changes from the vantage point of a longer life span than that of the middle-aged or young. Marked differences in life styles, and in values and aspirations, are often difficult to accept. Social and economic changes have come later in rural than in urban communities and are making a more pronounced impact on elderly men and women who are living in rural communities than on their urban counterparts. Religion as represented by the church in small communities tends to provide satisfactions for the older residents. Men and women of advanced years who are accustomed to attending church continue attending services quite regularly and participating in church sponsored activities, if they are physically able and have transportation. Some, especially those who cannot attend services, complain that their churches have forgotten them, that they no longer have places in the church. Some comment on the highly organized activities and seem to miss the familiar informal ways of doing things. Interest groups that are not church-sponsored and have members of all ages seem to a large proportion of old people to have few satisfying places for them. In small towns and villages peer groups are few. Professional social group work to encourage development of groups, like that in cities, is almost nonexistent. Other professional and welfare services, too, are limited.

Many old people in small communities have developed behavior patterns and ways of coping that stand them in good stead; when they retire from rearing children, farming or employment in business or industry, they find other satisfying activities. However, these activities seldom substitute entirely for any loss of status that follows retirement. Many old people remain healthy for a long time, and a surprising number of afflicted and disabled old men and women manage amazingly well to use the remnants of their potential. They display courage and strength and their self-esteem is high; they are regarded favorably by others.

Much evidence exists of family unity and solidarity. Local weekly newspapers report numerous family picnics, some of which include scores of relatives, and many "get together" meetings in homes. Young people leave the small towns and farms in large numbers. But often a child or several children live in cities nearby, and those far removed keep in touch with their parents and even their grandparents and other relatives. The self-image of the rural family and its way of life is becoming similar to that of the urban family. Modern communications, particularly television and opportunities for travel, have helped to acquaint older and younger members with new aspects of living. Old patterns of family life are breaking down, and changes in other institutions, such as the ecumenical movement of the church, are increasingly accepted by the elderly.

Few groups and organizations have planned services for and by the elderly. However, a potential reservoir of goodwill and concern exists and can be tapped in clusters of younger people and in largely church sponsored peer groups of the elderly. Groups provide opportunities for service to others and give the individual older person a feeling of worth. A collective effort may promote cohesive family units and high morale in other groups and in the community as a whole. Increasingly, local groups are subgroups of state or national associations and derive some financial support from the parent organizations. Local organizations often become satellites of larger agencies. These tend to be guided by professionals, usually in the cities, who know more about urban than rural conditions. Organization programs that involve local planning and are geared to local needs are more beneficial for the elderly than are these national programs.

There are few organized social service agencies in sparsely populated areas. The most widespread is the local public welfare agency, which, since the inception of the Social Security program in the thirties, has served the financial needs of persons sixty-five and over. However, service programs for older people have lagged behind those for others because of the prevailing attitude that if the physical needs of old people are met, not much else is possible or necessary. Yet this is a false assumption for much of the aging population. Unfortunately, the public welfare agencies that have tried to meet more than financial requirements have faced three major obstacles. The first of these is the extensive, complicated, and time consuming requirements for record keeping and reporting, many of which have grown out of increasingly detailed new laws and policies. The second obstacle is the difficult task of operating on two levels in relation to the individual and the family: the authoritative, if not authoritarian approach that is necessary when financial grants are made according to need, and the enabling approach that is essential if potential capacities are to be released. The third obstacle is the welfare worker's lack of generalized education; he has not been prepared for work with families and groups and with the community at large but has been trained primarily for the casework method or for working with one person. Even the recent emphasis on social group work has been introduced primarily as a specialized approach to complement and support casework, which is considered in many quarters to be the primary method.

Other organized welfare services in rural areas, such as those of the Red Cross and Salvation Army, are largely manned by volunteers. Their effectiveness depends on the quality of service offered locally. Community mental health clinics are being increasingly established in rural areas. The extent to which their specialized staffs can serve most effectively depends on how well they can work not only clinically with patients individually and in groups but also in other than clinical ways with many individuals and clusters of people. The Office of Economic Opportunity has developed programs for the elderly, but to date these programs have had little impact upon small communities. Multipurpose centers and other programs made available through the Older Americans Act have not covered much rural territory.

In small communities the social worker, who is necessarily a generalist without a coterie of specialists readily available, does well to focus primarily on the potential strength of the elderly, of their families and of other relevant groups. He must be more conscious of increments than of decrements. He does not ignore illness and social disorganization, and he does try whenever possible to do something about the situation. However, he begins by assessing potential capacities and works with what remains of them, rather than by focusing first on what is lost, warped or diseased. Any effort to help maintain or strengthen self-esteem is in order. This can be done only through a genuine recognition of both manifest and latent abilities and provision of opportunities and encouragement for their use. Creative and empathic activities often restore self-esteem. When ill health, disabilities and other vicissitudes of life prevent potentialities from being used, efforts to try to relieve or reduce the disabilities are in order. Frequently opportunities for using capacities could have prevented or delayed such disabilities. A commitment to the enhancement of potentialities is of prime importance.

As individuals and groups move toward or away from a state of optimum self-other realization, great variations occur in their capacities to use strengths. These varying capacities are closely associated with the self-image, particularly the image of self-worth. With affective interaction among individuals and clusters of inter-acting persons, a varying assessment of capacities is essential. The assessment is continual and determines the manner in which the social worker proceeds. In meeting varying requirements of the as-sessments the three approaches, or models, are recommended. These models are not mutually exclusive, and any one is rarely used alone for any length of time.

The model recommended for most frequent use in small communities has been described as facilitating. Designed to extend the increments of the elderly, their families, and other groups sig-nificant to them, it might also be called an extension model and its user, an extensionist. Its primary goal is to maintain and nurture a high degree of social well-being. It can be applied most produc-tively: when the situation requiring change is not of an emergency character; when the individual or group is capable of a high degree of self-direction; when interferences with the use of increments are predominantly in the environment rather than in the personality of the individual; when the achievement of a better understanding of the situation is the objective; when the goal is to release or extend the use of potentialities; and when change is to be produced by increasing growth and development.

In applying the facilitating model, the social worker must be skillful in freeing and extending potential abilities. He is sure of his professional competence. Outwardly his efforts tend to be un-obtrusive, although he displays unfailing confidence in the persons and groups with whom he works and of whom he is one. He has faith in the self-directing efforts of the aging persons and affiliated groups. Since purposeful inactivity may be interpreted as inade-quacy, his relationships with large segments of the community should be positive and he should be well known.

There are times when some change must take place before the facilitating model can be applied; then either the clinical or the strategic approach is in order. The clinical model, which might also be referred to as a healing model, is most appropriately applied: when personality disorders play a large part in the individual's in-ability to use potential abilities positively; when serious conflicts exist among individuals or groups; when biases, prejudices, or ignorance hampers development; when apathy, withdrawal, and hostility markedly interfere with a movement toward self-other realization; when the basic cause of the decrements listed above is a seriously impaired or distorted self- or group-image or greatly disturbed affective relationships.

Whether a generalist or a specialist, the social worker who applies the clinical model relies heavily on the confidence of individuals or groups. His skill should be evident. He must focus first on the decrements, to relieve discomfort and tension, but must also assess the increments and seek evidence of potential resources. As the aging person, family or group gains a capacity for self-direction, the social worker will offer support and encouragement. Eventually, the facilitating model may replace the clinical approach. In the community, the social worker applying the clinical model is recognized for his expertise. As persons in the community refer difficult situations to him for solutions, local citizen efforts in tackling them are likely to decline. With decreased involvement, public understanding and concern wane.

Suffering, distress and dangers to lives of people may become so acute or complex that very little, if any, participation by those affected is possible. Neither the facilitating nor the clinical model serves the purpose. A directive, persuasive, and even manipulative approach is applied. The strategic or directive model is needed: when an emergency exists and prompt action is indicated; when individuals or groups are temporarily stunned and immobilized because of severe illness or sudden tragedy; when rapid changes are taking place and the normal processes of keeping needs and resources in balance are too slow; and when either or both the clinical and facilitating models have been tried without success.

The role of the strategist is one of activity and authority. His touch must be sure and decisive. The public is very much aware of what he does and how he does it. His competence is on display. After an emergency has abated and the resources of the affected individual or group can again be mobilized, the clinical or facilitating model may supplant the strategic model. Changing models can cause temporary confusion, particularly when the social worker himself does not perceive the shift clearly.

Many questions are raised by two unresolved basic issues

reflected throughout this volume. The one issue relates to the loss of role of the older person as an economic producer and the changed societal conditions and values that this loss represents. The other refers to the need for relevant educational experiences for the social work generalist in rural and small city communities.

Efforts have been made to meet needs older people have as a result of their retirement from productive work. These efforts have consisted primarily of benevolences, insurances and leisure time activities. Such provisions as public assistance, Medicaid, low cost housing, reduced transportation costs, free fishing licenses and so forth are largely benevolent in character. Although such activities create conditions infinitely more desirable than hunger, poor shelter and inadequate medical care, they do not represent the important value of a fair day's pay for a fair day's work. They do not take account of the accumulated experiences of a lifetime or the wisdom of the aged to which so many glib references are made. Many old persons in small communities feel, when they accept these provisions, that they owe their existence to the heavily overtaxed and overburdened younger people, including their own children and grandchildren.

Insurance provisions like Social Security and Medicare are generally more acceptable but their costs also raise questions. Some, particularly Medicare, create problems in the complicated and difficult procedure in keeping records and making claims. Small communities have been slow to develop leisure time activities for older people. Entertainment of all kinds and participation in the arts and crafts have been encouraged. However, in most small communities there has been very little such activity except when, as an integral part of the culture, it is encouraged or it is introduced because of local leadership.

Yet many creative and service activities could be developed, and many older people have much to contribute to their local communities. Examples of such contributions range from making toys out of blocks of wood to remodeling a Senior Citizens Center or a church; from being a foster grandparent to a child to lying in bed thoroughly disabled but yet telephoning one person after another in the interest of a community cause; from locating and visiting sick, lonely and unhappy persons in town to engaging in a community survey; from mending the doorstep of a neighbor to being active in a political campaign.

In comparison with what could be mobilized, the use of potential contributions is very limited both in number and kind. In part this is because the possibilities are not recognized, either by the old person himself or by others. Lack of finances is also a limiting factor. Creative efforts and service activities cost money and many older people have none to spare. In a forward looking community ways should and could be found to reimburse expenses and also, in more instances than is now the case, to pay wages in line with service performed. For example, in sections of most small towns and cities, streets and buildings are in poor repair and unsightly, even unsanitary conditions are common. Who is better equipped to do something about the situation than the elderly man who has spent a lifetime growing things and making something out of nothing? And who would be more willing to work than the old man who always has worked and who has enjoyed it? Who should be more able to see the possibilities and values of his contribution than the planning groups and government officials who have responsibilities for the progress of the community? And if funds are available only for costs, who other than the community leaders could express appreciation appropriately for volunteer tasks? Moreover, such community beautification jobs would not take away work from the young.

Providing appropriate educational experiences for the social work generalist in small communities may be less complicated than meeting the needs of the elderly for constructive productive activity, but this issue, too, has many facets and is not easily resolved. The diversity of situations that the social work generalist encounters and the three models of intervention that seem indicated require both insight and an array of knowledge and perceptiveness that are hard to come by. Even when intellectually superior and perceptive far beyond average, he can scarcely be expected to master all that has to be known. Yet when he serves in a small community he must assume the role of a generalist, and the specialized training he has most frequently received is inappropriate. He needs to know much about working with individuals, families and groups of all kinds. And he should learn to keep in touch with the rapidly accumulating knowledge that pertains to all facets of his job. In his formal educational experience and in the agency program of staff development, carefully selected content—organized and taught in a way that makes possible a maximum learning experience for the job to be done and for continuing educational opportunities—is of prime importance.

But that requirement raises many questions. Just what kind of content should be included and how and when should it be taught? After these decisions have been made there is the task of deciding how much time, undergraduate and graduate, should and can be devoted to preparation. What kinds of knowledge and skill should be taught in the classroom, what kinds through field instruction and other means? What should be the responsibilities of agencies and schools for continuing educational experiences? How can the efforts of the student, the practicing social work generalist and the agency and school be most effectively coordinated?

These and many more are baffling questions. Current efforts are being made to find answers. Some say, "It can't be done!" But Miss Jones and other small community social workers have practiced as generalists and continue to do so without opportunities for obtaining the most useful educational preparation for their tasks. With more help from schools and agencies and better understanding of what goes into the job and how it can best be performed, small community social work will grow in effectiveness.

Both issues will raise many unanswered questions for some time to come. Some will be answered by the elderly themselves, some by the social workers who serve as generalists. Some will have to be answered by other sectors of the population. For many people, the opportunity to share in the quest for the resolution of both issues is what makes social work an exciting profession.

Bibliography

Adult Leadership, January, 1953.

AGAN, T., AND ANDERSON, E. M. "Housing the Aged in Kansas." *Bulletin 427,* Kansas State University of Agriculture and Applied Sciences, Agricultural Experiment Station, 1961.

ALLPORT, G. W. *Becoming.* New Haven, Conn.: Yale University Press, 1955.

ALLPORT, G. W. *Pattern and Growth in Personality.* New York: Holt, Rinehart, and Winston, 1961.

ALTMEYER, A. J. "The First Decade of Social Security." *Social Security Bulletin,* August 1945.

American College Dictionary. New York: Harper, 1953.

BARAN, S. The Careers of Responsible Family Members in Two Coordinated Home Care Programs for the Aged Sick. Unpublished doctoral dissertation, Brandeis University, 1969.

BAUDER, W. W. In A. L. Bertrand (Ed.), *Rural Sociology, an Analysis of Contemporary Rural Life.* New York: McGraw-Hill, 1958.

BENDIX, R., AND LIPSET, S. M. (Eds.) *Class, Status and Power.* New York: Free Press, 1953.

BENNETT, L. L. *Protective Services for the Aged: Guidelines for Professionals.* Washington, D.C.: U.S. Department of Health, Education and Welfare, 1964.

BERNSTEIN, S. "Self Determination: King or Citizen in the Realm of Values." *Social Work,* 1960, 5(1).

BERTRAND, A. L. "The Aged in a Diffused Rural Society." In D. E. Alleger (Ed.), *Social Change and Aging in the Twentieth Century.* Vol. 13, *Institute of Gerontology Series.* The Southern Conference on Gerontology. Gainesville, Fla.: University of Florida Press, 1964.

229

BIERSTEDT, R. *The Social Order: An Introduction to Sociology.* (2nd ed.) New York: McGraw-Hill, 1963.

BLAU, P. M., AND SCOTT, W. R. *Formal Organizations.* San Francisco: Chandler, 1962.

BLENKNER, M. "Social Work and Family Relationships in Later Life with Some Thoughts on Filial Maturity." In E. Shanas and G. F. Streib (Eds.), *Social Structure and the Family: Generational Relations.* Englewood Cliffs, N.J.: Prentice-Hall, 1965.

BLOEDOW, G. A. "Content of the Group Experience in the Rural Area." *Social Group Work with Older People,* report of the seminar on Social Work with Older People. New York: National Association of Social Workers, 1963.

BOOKOVER, J. J. "Aspects of Geriatric Care and Treatment: Moral, Amoral, and Immoral." In R. Kastenbaum (Ed.), *New Thoughts on Old Age.* New York: Springer, 1964.

BOWMAN, H. A. "The Family: Its Role and Function." *Proceedings of the 53rd Annual Conference, Texas Social Welfare Association,* 1963. Reprinted by the Hogg Foundation for Mental Health, University of Texas, Austin, 1964.

BRECHER, R., AND BRECHER, E. "Nursing Homes: The Many Kinds of Care." *Consumer Reports,* January 1964(a), 30–36.

BRECHER, R., AND BRECHER, E. "Nursing Homes: How to Shop for a Nursing Home." *Consumer Reports,* February 1964(b), 87–92.

BRECHER, R., AND BRECHER, E. "Nursing Homes: Costs, Charges, and Methods of Payment." *Consumer Reports,* March 1964(c), 139–142.

BRECHER, R., AND BRECHER, E. "Nursing Homes: How to Improve Them." *Consumer Reports,* April 1964(d), 194–198.

BRITTON, J. H., MATHER, W. G., AND LANSING, A. K. "Expectations for Older Persons in a Rural Community." *Rural Sociology,* 1962, 27(4).

BROTMAN, H. D. *Useful Facts,* No. 22, May 12, 1967; No. 37, May 9, 1968(a); No. 38, May 9, 1968(b); No. 42, August 9, 1968(c). Washington, D.C.: U.S., Department of Health, Education and Welfare, Administration on Aging.

BROTMAN, H. D. "Estimated Resident Population by Age Groups, Sex, Color and Residence." Washington, D.C.: U.S., Department of Health, Education and Welfare, Administration on Aging, 1968(d).

BROWN, J. *Public Relief: 1929–1930.* New York: Henry Holt, 1940.

BURGER, R. E. "Who Cares for the Aged?" *Saturday Review,* January 25, 1969.

BURGESS, E. W. "The Family as a Unity of Interacting Personalities," *The Family,* 1926, 7.

BURGESS, E. W. (Ed.) *Aging in Western Society.* Chicago: University of Chicago Press, 1960.

BURGESS, E. W., AND LOCKE, H. J. *The Family.* New York: American Book Co., 1945.

BURNS, E. M. *The American Social Security System.* Boston: Houghton Mifflin, 1949.

BURR, J. J. *Protective Services for Older People.* Washington, D.C.: U.S., Department of Health, Education and Welfare, 1964.

CARTWRIGHT, D., AND ZANDER, A. *Group Dynamics.* Evanston, Ill.: Row, Peterson, 1953.

CLARK, M. "The Anthropology of Aging: A New Area of Studies of Culture and Personality." *The Gerontologist,* 1967, *7*(1).

COOLEY, C. H. *Human Nature and the Social Order.* New York: Scribner's, 1900.

COOLEY, C. H. *Social Organization: A Study of the Larger Individual.* New York: Scribner's, 1929.

COUTU, W. *Emergent Human Behavior.* New York: Knopf, 1949.

COWLES, M. L. "Housing and Associated Problems of the Rural-Farm Aged Population in Two Wisconsin Counties." *Rural Sociology,* 1956, *21*(3 and 4).

COYLE, G. L. "Concepts Relevant to Helping the Family as a Group," *Social Casework,* 1962, *18*(7).

CUMMING, M. E., AND HENRY, W. E. *Growing Old: The Process of Disengagement.* New York: Basic Books, 1961.

CUMMING, M. E. "New Thoughts on Disengagement." In Robert Katzenbaum (Ed.), *New Thoughts on Old Age.* New York: Springer, 1964.

DE ROPP, R. S. *Man Against Aging.* New York: Grove Press, 1960.

DEUTSCH, A. *The Mentally Ill in America.* Garden City, N.Y.: Doubleday, Doran, 1937.

Directory for Leisure-Time Resources for Older Men and Women in Greater Minneapolis. Minneapolis, Minn.: Community Health and Welfare Council, 1963.

DUBOS, R. J. Address delivered to the United States National Commission for UNESCO, Tenth National Conference, Third Plenary Session, Kansas City, Mo., November 1966. Mimeograph.

DUNHAM, E. C. The Emergence of an Institution Serving Children. Unpublished master's thesis, University of Kansas, 1960.

DURKHEIM, E. *The Division of Labor in Society.* New York: Macmillan, 1933.

ELKIN, F. *The Child and Society.* New York: Random House, 1960.

ERIKSON, E. H. *Identity, Youth and Crisis.* New York: Norton, 1968.

ETZIONI, A. *The Active Society.* New York: Free Press, 1968.

FALCK, H. S. "The Use of Groups in the Practice of Social Work." *Social Casework,* 1963, *54*(2).

FERRARI, N. A. "Assessment of Individuals in Groups of Older Adults." In *Social Group Work with Older People.* N.Y.: National Association of Social Workers, 1963.

FOOTE, N. N., AND COTTRELL, L. S. *Identity and Interpersonal Competence.* Chicago: University of Chicago Press, 1957.

FULLER, W. A., WAKELEY, R. E., LUDEN, W. A., SWANSON, P., AND WILLIS, E. *Characteristics of Persons Sixty Years of Age and Older in Linn County, Iowa.* Ames, Iowa: Iowa State University of Sciences and Technology, 1963.

GARDNER, J. W. "How to Prevent Organizational Dry Rot," *Harper's,* October 1965.

GHISELIN, B. *The Creative Process.* Berkeley, Cal.: University of California Press, 1952. Republished: New American Library of World Literature, Mentor Books, 1952.

GLICK, P. C. "The Family Cycle." *American Sociological Review,* 1947, *12*(2).

GOBERLIENSKI, R. T. *The Small Group.* Chicago: University of Chicago Press, 1962.

GOFFMAN, E. *Stigma.* Englewood Cliffs, N.J.: Prentice-Hall, 1965.

GOLDFARB, A. I. "Psychodynamics and the Three-Generation Family." In E. Shanas and G. F. Streib (Eds.), *Social Structure and the Family: Generational Relations.* Englewood Cliffs, N.J.: Prentice-Hall, 1965.

GOLDSTEIN, L. "Social Growth and Development of Older People: Implications for Group Work with Older People." In *Social Group Work with Older People,* report of the seminar on Social Work with Older People. New York: National Association of Social Workers, 1963.

GROVES, E. R. *The Family and Its Social Functions.* Chicago, Philadelphia and New York: Lippincott, 1940.

HALL, D. A Study of Changes in the Service Program of a Family Agency and the Relations to Social and National Influences, from 1904 through 1955. Unpublished master's thesis, University of Kansas, 1960.

HALL, G. H. (Ed.) *The Law and the Impaired Older Person: Protection or Punishment.* Detroit, Mich.: National Council on Aging, 1966.

HALL, G. S. *Senescence: The Last Half of Life.* New York: Appleton, 1922.

HARE, A. P., BORGATTA, E. F., AND BALES, R. F. *Small Groups.* New York: Knopf, 1955.

HARRINGTON, M. *The Other America: Poverty in the United States.* Baltimore: Penguin, 1962.

HART, E. "Homemaker Services." *Public Affairs Pamphlet 371.* New York: Public Affairs Committee, 1965.

HASINGER, E. H. "Background and Community Orientation of Rural Physicians in Missouri." *Research Bulletin,* University of Missouri College of Agriculture Experiment Station Studies in Rural Health, 1963, *822*(19).

HAUSKNECHT, M. *The Joiners.* New York: Badminster Press, 1962.

HAVIGHURST, R. J., AND ALBRECHT, R. *Older People.* New York, London, Toronto: Longmans, Green, 1953.

HENRY, W. E. In P. F. Hansen (Ed.), *Age with a Future: Proceedings of the Sixth International Congress of Gerontology, Copenhagen, 1963.* Copenhagen: Munksgaard, 1964.

HINK, D. L. Interpersonal Perceptions in Selected Social Systems. Unpublished doctoral dissertation, University of Chicago, 1966.

HOCH, P. H., AND ZUBIN, J. (Eds.) *Psychopathology of Aging.* New York: Grune and Stratton, 1961.

HUTCHINSON, E. D. *How to Think Creatively.* New York and Nashville: Abingdon Press, 1949.

Iowa Commission for Senior Citizens. *Life After Sixty in Iowa.* A Report on the 1960 Survey. Des Moines, Iowa, 1960.

JAMES, W. *Principles of Psychology.* New York: Henry Holt, 1890.

Kansas General Statutes, 1875, c. 17, § 4–12.

KATZENBAUM, R., AND DURKEE, N. "Young People View Old Age" and "Elderly People View Old Age." In R. Katzenbaum (Ed.), *New Thoughts on Old Age.* New York: Springer, 1964.

KENT, D. "Aging—Facts and Fancies." *The Gerontologist,* 1965, *5*(2).

KOLB, J. H., AND BRUNNER, E. DE S. *A Study of Rural Society.* (4th ed.) Boston: Houghton Mifflin, 1952.

KREPS, J. M. *Employment, Income and Retirement Problems of the Aged.* Durham, N.C.: Duke University Press, 1963.

LEHMANN, V. "Guardianship and Protective Services for Older People." *Social Casework,* May–June 1961.

LINDEN, M. E. "Emotional Problems in Aging." *Jewish Social Service Quarterly,* Fall 1954.

LINDEN, M. E., AND COURTNEY, D. "The Human Life Cycle and Its Interruptions." *American Journal of Psychiatry,* 1953, *109*(12).

LINDESMITH, A. R., AND STRAUSS, A. L. *Social Psychology.* New York: Holt-Dryden, 1956.

LINDSTROM, D. E. "Interest Group Relations and Functions in Rural Society." *Rural Sociology,* Vol. XXVI, No. 3, September 1961, *26*(3).

LIPPITT, R., WATSON, J., AND WESTLOG, B. *The Dynamics of Planned Change.* New York: Harcourt, Brace, 1958.

LITWAK, E. "Geographic Mobility and Extended Family Cohesion." *American Sociological Review,* June 1960(b), *25.*

LITWAK, E. "Occupational Mobility and Extended Family Cohesion." *American Sociological Review,* February 1960(a), *25.*

LOEB, M. B., PINCUS, A., AND MUELLER, J. *Growing Old in Wisconsin.* Madison: University of Wisconsin School of Social Work, 1963.

LOOMIS, C. P., AND BEEGLE, J. A. *Rural Social Systems.* New York: Prentice-Hall, 1950.

LOOMIS, C. P., AND BEEGLE, J. A. *Rural Sociology: The Strategy of Change.* Englewood Cliffs, N.J.: Prentice-Hall, 1957.

LOWENTHAL, M. F., BERKMAN, P. L., and associates. *Aging and Mental Disorder in San Francisco.* San Francisco: Jossey-Bass, 1967.

MACY, D. V. Development and Change of Purpose of Mattie Rhodes Center, Kansas City, Missouri, 1895–1950. Unpublished master's thesis, University of Kansas, 1961.

MADDOX, G. L. "Activity and Morale: A Longitudinal Study of Selected Elderly Subjects." *Social Forces,* 1964, *43.*

MASLOW, A. H. *Toward a Psychology of Being.* Princeton, N.J.: Van Nostrand, 1962.

MAXWELL, J. M. "Helping Older People through Social Group Work." In *Potentials for Service through Social Group Work in Public Welfare.* Chicago: American Public Welfare Association, 1962.

MAY, R. "The Nature of Creativity." In H. H. Anderson (Ed.), *Creativity and Its Cultivation.* New York: Harper, 1959.

MC DONALD, E. L. A Study of Two Guidance Clinics in Kansas. Unpublished master's thesis, University of Kansas, 1963.

MC FARLAND, R. A. "The Psychological Aspects of Aging." In R. L. Craig (Ed.), *Problems of Aging.* New York: Marchand, 1956.

MEAD, G. H. *Mind, Self, and Society.* Edited by C. W. Morris. Chicago: University of Chicago Press, 1934.

MEAD, M. "The Contemporary American Family as an Anthropologist Sees It." *American Journal of Sociology,* 1948, *53*(6).

MONTGOMERY, J. E. *Social Characteristics of the Aged in a Small Pennsylvania Community.* College of Home Economics Publication No. 233. University Park, Pa.: Pennsylvania State University, 1965.

MORRIS, R. "Social Work Preparation for Effectiveness in Planned Change." *Council on Social Work Education, Proceedings, 1963* (New York, 1963).

MORRIS, R., LAMBERT, C., AND GUBERMAN, M. *New Roles for the Aging.* Waltham, Mass.: Brandeis University, 1963.

National Committee Against Mental Illness, Inc. *What are the Facts about Mental Illness?* Washington, D.C., 1966.

National Council on Aging. *Loaves and Fishes: A Model Community Action Program to Provide Nutritious Low Cost Meals to the Elderly.* Washington, D.C., 1965.

National Council on Aging. *The Multipurpose Center: A Model Community Action Program. VI.* Washington, D.C., n.d.

National Council on Aging. *Resources for the Aging: An Action Handbook.* (2nd ed.) Washington, D.C., 1969.

National Urban League. *Double Jeopardy.* New York and Washington, 1964.

NEUGARTEN, B. L., HAVIGHURST, R., AND TOBIN, S. "The Measurement of Life Satisfaction." *Journal of Gerontology,* 1961, *14*(2).

NEUGARTEN, B. L., and associates. *Personality in Middle and Late Life.* New York: Atherton Press, 1964.

NOSOW, S., AND FORM, W. H. (Eds.) *Man, Work and Society.* New York: Basic Books, 1962.

NYE, F. I., AND BERARDO, F. M. *Emerging Conceptual Frameworks in Family Analysis.* New York: Macmillan, 1966.

OGBURN, WILLIAM F. *Social Change.* New York: Viking Press, 1922.

OGBURN, W. F., AND TIBBITTS, C. *Recent Social Trends.* New York: McGraw-Hill, 1933.

The Older American, The President's Council on Aging. Washington, D.C.: Government Printing Office, 1963.

OLMSTED, M. S. *The Small Group.* New York: Random House, 1959.

PARSONS, T. "The Aging in American Society." *Law and Contemporary Problems,* Duke University School of Law, 1962, 27.

PARSONS, T. "Revised Analytical Approach to the Theory of Social

Stratification." In R. Bendix and S. M. Lipset (Eds.), *Class, Status and Power.* New York: Free Press, 1953.

PATTERSON, S. L., WYLIE, M. L., AND TWENTE, E. E. *Mobilization of Aging Resources for Community Service.* Terminal report, Public Health Service Grant No. MH 14888 (previously known as No. MH 01472), National Institute of Health. Lawrence, Kan.: University of Kansas, 1968.

PEERBOOM, P. "Major Trends in Health, Education, and Welfare." In *Trends* (1966–67 Ed.), Washington, D.C.: U.S. Government Printing Office, 1968.

Pennsylvania State University, College of Agriculture. Agricultural Experiment Station Bulletins, No. 574, February 1954a; No. 582, August 1954b.

PIHLBLAD, C. T., AND ROSENCRANZ, H. A. *The Health of Older People in the Small Town: An Interim Report.* Columbia, Missouri: University of Missouri, Department of Sociology, 1967.

POLLOCK, E. S., LOCKE, B., AND KRAMER, M. "Trends in Hospitalization and Patterns of Care of the Aged Mentally Ill." In *Psychopathology of Aging,* P. H. Hock and J. Zubin (Eds.). New York: Grune and Stratton, 1961.

RAY, F. Introduction to *Social Work with Groups: Selected Papers,* National Association of Social Workers. New York, 1958.

RICHMOND, M. E. *What Is Social Case Work?* New York: Russell Sage Foundation, 1922.

ROGERS, E. M. *Social Change in Rural Society.* New York: Appleton-Century-Crofts, 1960.

ROSE, A. M. Foreword to *Social Group Work with Older People,* report of the seminar on Social Work with Older People. New York: National Association of Social Workers, 1963.

ROSE, A. M. "Social Growth and Development of Older People: Social and Cultural Factors." In *Social Group Work with Older People.* N.Y.: National Association of Social Workers, 1963.

ROSE, A. M. (Ed.) *Human Behavior and Social Processes.* Boston: Houghton Mifflin, 1962.

ROSEN, B. M., ANDERSON, T. E., AND BAHN, A. K. "Psychiatric Services for the Aged: A Nationwide Survey of Patterns of Utilization." Paper presented at the 4th annual meeting of the American Orthopsychiatric Association, March 1967. Washington, D.C. Mimeographed.

ROSOW, I. *Social Integration of the Aged.* New York: Free Press, 1967.

RUTHMEYER, R. *Wyoming Aging Study*. Laramie, Wy.: University of Wyoming, 1964.

SALTZ, R. *Foster-grandparents and Institutionalized Young Children, Two Years of a Foster-grandparent Program*. Detroit, Mich.: Merrill-Palmer Institute, 1968.

SANNES, P. "Philosophy of Public Welfare Toward the Aging." Paper presented at In-Service Training Program, University of North Dakota and The North Dakota Mental Health Association, July 1963. Grand Forks, N.D.

SHANAS, E. *Family Relationships of Older People*. New York: Health Information Foundation, 1961.

SHANAS, E. *The Health of Older People: A Social Survey*. Cambridge: Harvard University Press, 1962.

SHANAS, E., AND STREIB, G. F. (Eds.) *Social Structure and the Generational Relations*. Englewood Cliffs, N.J.: Prentice-Hall, 1965.

SLOCUM, W. L. *Agricultural Sociology*. New York: Harper, 1962.

SOROKIN, P. A., ZIMMERMAN, C. C., AND GALPIN, C. J. *A Systematic Source Book in Rural Sociology*, Vol. 3. Minneapolis: University of Minnesota Press, 1932.

STEIN, M. I., AND HEINZE, S. J. *Creativity and the Individual*. New York: Free Press, 1960.

STONE, G. P. "Appearance and the Self." In A. M. Rose (Ed.), *Human Behavior and Social Processes*. Boston: Houghton Mifflin, 1962.

STRAUSS, A. L. (Ed.) *The Social Psychology of George Herbert Mead*. Chicago: University of Chicago Press, 1956.

SWENSON, P. "Adequacy in Old Age, the Role of Nutrition." *Journal of Home Economics*, November, December, 1964. Quoted by National Council on Aging. *Loaves and Fishes: A Model Community Program to Provide Nutritious Low Cost Meals to the Elderly*. Washington, D.C., 1965.

TAYLOR, T. C., ENSMINGER, D., LONGMORE, T. W., DUCOFF, L. J., RAPER, A. F., HAGOOD, M. J., MC KAIN, W. C., JR., AND SCHULER, E. A. *Rural Life in the United States*. New York: Knopf, 1949.

THUMIN, F. J., AND BOERNKE, C. "Ability Scores as Related to Age among Female Job Applicants." *Journal of Gerontology*, 1966, 21(3).

TRIER, T. R. "Characteristics of Mentally Ill Aged: A Comparison of Patients with Psychogenic Disorders and Patients with Organic Brain Syndromes." *Journal of Gerontology*, 1966, 21(3).

TWENTE, E. E. "Aging, Strength and Creativity." *Social Work, 10*(3).

U.S., Bureau of the Census. *Age by Race, Nationality and Sex.* Washington, D.C.: Department of Commerce, 1960.

U.S., Bureau of the Census. *Current Population Reports,* Series P-60, No. 37. Washington, D.C.: Department of Commerce.

U.S., Bureau of the Census. *Statistical Abstract of the United States: 1968.* (89th ed.) Washington, D.C.: Department of Commerce, 1968.

U.S., Bureau of the Census. *Statistical Abstract of the United States: 1969.* (90th ed.) Washington, D.C.: Department of Commerce, 1969.

U.S., Congress, Senate, Special Committee on Aging, *Developments on Aging, 1968.* Report pursuant to S. Res. 223. Washington, D.C.: U.S. Government Printing Office, 1969(a).

U.S., Congress, Senate, Special Committee on Aging, *Fact Sheet,* 1969(b). Mimeograph.

U.S., Department of Agriculture, Economic Research Service. *Recent Population Trends in the United States, with Emphasis on Rural Areas.* Washington, D.C., 1963.

U.S., Department of Health, Education and Welfare. *Foster Family Care for the Aged.* Washington, D.C., 1965.

U.S., Department of Health, Education, and Welfare, Administration on Aging, Washington, D.C.: "Three Years of Progress Under the Older Americans Act." *Aging,* 1969b, *171.* "Resources for Elderly Included in 1968 Housing Act." *Aging,* 1969c, *172.* "New Definition of Protective Services for Aged is Proposed." *Aging,* 1969a, *171.*

U.S., Department of Health, Education, and Welfare, Bureau of Vital Statistics. *Annual Summary for the United States, Births, Deaths, Marriages and Divorces.* Washington, D.C., 1967.

Vital Statistics. Washington, D.C.: U.S., Department of Health, Education, and Welfare, 1967.

WASSER, E. "Responsibility, Self-Determination, and Authority in Casework Protection of Older Persons." *Social Casework,* May–June, 1961.

WEBER, R. E. "Definition, Case Identification, and Sample Characteristics of Older Persons." In *A Crucial Issue in Social Work Practice: Protective Services for Older People.* New York: National Council on the Aging, 1965.

WEISS, V. M. "Multiple Client Interviewing: An Aid in Diagnosis," *Social Casework,* 1962, *43*(3).

WILBER, G. L., AND MAITLAND, S. T. "A Study of Rural Residents." Bulletin 652. Mississippi State University, Agricultural Experiment Station, 1963.

WILKENING, E. A. "Some Perspectives on Change in Rural Societies." *Rural Sociology*, 1964, 29(1).

WILLIAMS, R. M. *American Society: A Sociological Interpretation*. New York: Knopf, 1951.

WYLIE, M. L. Explorations of a Proposed Community Organization Program for the Aging. Unpublished master's thesis, University of Kansas, 1963.

YINGER, J. M. *Toward a Field Theory of Behavior*. New York: McGraw-Hill, 1965.

YOUMANS, E. G. *Aging Patterns in a Rural and Urban Area of Kentucky*. Lexington, Kentucky: University of Kentucky, Agricultural Experiment Station, 1963.

YOUMANS, E. G. *Health Problems of Older Persons in Selected Rural and Urban Areas in Kentucky*. Lexington, Ky.: University of Kentucky, Agricultural Experiment Station (1963).

Index